PRAISE FOR *INTRODUCTION TO PEOPLE ANALYTICS*

"Khan and Millner provide an excellent roadmap for the HR function to be more data-oriented and analytical. They provide multiple concrete examples of what HR professionals need to do to become more strategic by adopting a commercial mindset that is rooted in the business and in people analytics. A must-read for anyone who wants to improve their engagement and impact with the business."
Alec Levenson, Senior Research Scientist, Center for Effective Organizations, Marshall School of Business, University of Southern California

"Resources are dispensable. People are not. I congratulate the authors on structuring a new view of people and analytics in organizations… a pleasing step ahead of the human resources school. The content is well-balanced with graphics and illustrations and this work will be high-value reading for practising managers and scholars of business."
Javaid Ahmed, Senior Fellow, Strategy and Market Innovation, Institute of Business Management, Pakistan

"Understanding the world of data analytics can be daunting for any HR practitioner. However, this book is invaluable in explaining the purpose of data, how to interpret and analyse it and how to pragmatically apply it effectively within your business. *Introduction to People Analytics* is a must-read for any HRBP who wants to get to grips with understanding the commercial mindset and how data can drive the practitioner of the future."
Lisa Bailey, HR Business Partner, Aston Villa Football Club

"Data analytics often creates a scary and incomprehensible image in the minds of HR people with non-statistical backgrounds. However, Khan and Millner have presented concepts and examples in such a simple and practical manner that people at any organizational or academic level can comprehend the fundamentals of people analytics and its application for making effective people decisions within an organization. I am sure that this book will become part of every HR course in academia – it is a must-read for all HR professionals."

Sohail Rizvi, CEO, Institute of Knowledge and Leadership, University of Management and Technology, Dubai Knowledge Park, Dubai, UAE

"The number of times I have attended HR conferences and panel events, discussing the topic area of HR data and how it has been transformational for a business...

I'm sure I speak for a huge number of frustrated SME HR directors who sit in the audience of such events and think to themselves: 'But it's all big-company related, it just isn't relevant to me and my organization'. Sure we can do the basics with HR data but we don't have the systems to do it for us and the insight rarely tells a compelling narrative to evidence our recommendations.

So forgive my surprise at coming across this book: A fresh look at the topic area that shows how data can be transformational in driving strategic people decisions in organizations of any size. With a whole variety of case studies that bring to life how data and the insight it provides are relevant for us too – and simple, practical stage-by-stage advice on how to build a compelling evidence-based approach. This is a game-changing contribution to the data discussion."

James Madeley, HR Director, Portland

"Khan and Millner's *Introduction to People Analytics* has refined a new perspective in exploiting organizational data as a tool for performance improvement. The authors have taken a very creative and inspiring look at the current context of HR and the emerging trend of data analytics. With clarity, insight and a strong practical orientation from thought-provoking case studies, this is not only a book for HR practitioners but also an ideal book for any manager."

Danny Soetanto, Associate Professor, Entrepreneurship and Strategy, Lancaster University Management School

"As an experienced practitioner and early pioneer of evolving the HR 'personnel' function into a leading edge, data-driven and technically advanced, thought-leading solution provider, I found *Introduction to People Analytics* absolutely captures the full scope of thinking needed to comprehend the complex systems and human psychology integration that organizations need to embrace today. Millner and Khan do a brilliant job, providing big picture context, useful infographics, and theoretical and

tactical thought leadership examples in every chapter. This is the most fully comprehensive and pragmatic literature on the subject that I've read, which I'm certain will bring every HR practitioner's thinking, knowing and doing to the level of a true Chief People Officer, ready to tackle the tectonic shifts required for building highly responsive, adaptive and agile organizations to compete at blinding speed."
Jeff Wellstead, VP of People, ONI

"This book is a power station to start on the journey of people analytics. It clearly shows that when all other functions in an organization are experiencing disruption, making use of AI, using Big Data to grow their businesses, and using Agile technologies, there is no reason for HR not to gear up. After reading *Introduction to People Analytics*, I believe that any HR professional will have many ideas on where to start on this journey, irrespective of the type of business they work in. The case studies in the book show that many organizations have used the power of people analytics to contribute to the success of their organization. From simple data such as salaries to complex data points like facial expressions, the book explains how it is possible to use data to solve complex problems and issues in an organization. *Introduction to People Analytics* provides a roadmap for HR transformation."
Aqsa Asim, Training Manager, National Institute of Banking and Finance, Pakistan

"There seems to be a disconnect between most commentators and practitioners. For commentators it's all about data and analytics but for practitioners it's all about delivering value to their business. Khan and Millner have built a bridge between the two showing how a pragmatic use of data can help HR practitioners ensure what they are doing is based on a proper analysis of the problem and therefore guarantee that their solutions will add value to the business."
Nick Holley, Director of CRF Learning, Corporate Research Forum

"Khan and Millner have managed a nearly impossible task, seamlessly merging HR domain knowledge with practical models from the growing fields of data analytics/science and human capital reporting. This is an essential title for analytics professionals moving into HR and for HR professionals who want to harness the power of analytics for their organization. The quality and clarity of the text and the rich organizational case studies will have me reaching for this book again and again."
Laurence Hopkins, Head of Research, UCEA

"In recent years, people analytics has become one of the important corner-stones of impactful HR. Nadeem Khan and Dave Millner have written a great introduction to this area, which adds value for HR and business students as well as for experienced professionals who want a thorough and practical introduction. This book is a great addition to the growing people analytics library."
Tom Haak, Director, HR Trend Institute

"Despite the title, the book goes a fair way beyond just 'how to do numbers in HR'. In essence, it is a thought-provoking and clear narrative that can serve as an excellent starting point for any Strategic HR Manager to think about what the changes in the modern world mean for their function and their business as a whole, and, perhaps more importantly, how to future-proof them – all based on solid evidence from analytics. The book will be of interest both to HR Managers, or Strategic Managers in general, and consultants working in the area."
Dr Pavel Bogolyubov, Programme Director, MA HR and Consulting, Organization, Work and Technology, Lancaster University Management School

"*Introduction to People Analytics* provides an important and detailed insight of how a data and technology-driven HR function is critical to the success of any organization. It focuses on the practical aspect of people analytics, using clear frameworks, project methodologies, risk analysis, evolution paths and, critically, how to deliver exceptional actionable business insights critical for a rapidly changing world!

The book offers lots of real-life case studies that demonstrate the power of data and people analytics in driving organizational insights. This will be of interest to any people analytics practitioner to help them define, in practical terms, how to deliver critical and transformational insights.

It also demonstrates how to apply people analytics to show the 'path ahead' rather than just the 'rear view mirror', helping organizations to make better talent decisions – exactly what a strategic HR function of any organization must be able to deliver."
Hani Nabeel, Chief Behavioural Scientist, iPsychTec

"A compelling and deep insight into the world of people analytics and the importance of using data sensibly in overcoming HR challenges. What I appreciate most is that this book talks about the importance of HR using the language of business and being more commercially oriented, because at the end of the day we are all – HR too – here to grow our business. This book will enable HR practitioners to use the power of data to bring credibility and respect to what they contribute in the boardroom, really earning them a seat at the table."

Nida Nasir, GM Human Resources, KFC Pakistan

"This is truly 'a practical guide to data-driven HR' but yet much, much more – this book provides a roadmap and guide to creating a modern people management function within any organization. The concepts are clearly explained and illustrated with case studies and practical models. I particularly liked the model of the HR Service Station versus the HR Power Station... which would you rather be running? This book is for business people who work in HR and the learnings within it will take you to the top of your game, allowing you to be the best while managing a constantly changing environment. Just buy it!"

Gordon A Headley BSc, CEng, MBA, FCIPD; VP HR, Vision RT Ltd

"A very well-researched book that builds a compelling case for using data in HR. It provides a practical guide that enables HR practitioners to move from integrated talent practices to business impact driven HR, and change roles from respected facilitators to trusted advisers valued at the C-Suite level. Khan and Millner provide an easy to follow roadmap for this change, supported by practical tools for each step, and with guidance from business leaders across industries to support their approach. This is a useful personal transformation guidebook for all HR practitioners globally. This content should be made part of senior leadership programmes!"

Ayesha Chowdhry, Senior HR Practitioner, and Member, Board of Governors, Pakistan Society for Training and Development

"An interesting insight on how HR can play a pivotal role in the coming years as digitalization shapes organizations. Pressure is building on organizations as the attitude of customers and employees changes. Thus timely forecasting is the need of the hour, and without having a clear understanding of data and people analytics it is going to get critically difficult for an organization to compete and succeed. This book lays out a futuristic perspective, showing where we are, where we are heading and how best we can be proactive in the way we face the imminent challenges. *Introduction to People Analytics* is an extremely interesting book for professionals keen to equip themselves fully with information on analytics and its growing need and importance."

Shakeel Mapara, Head of HR and OD, Sanofi-aventis Pakistan limited

"Corporate learning and development will be a competitive advantage enabler in the digitalized world of tomorrow. This requires L&D to transform its classical approach and continuously align its strategy to ever-faster changing business requirements. People/learning analytics provides exactly those insights needed to enable L&D to turn into a competitive advantage enabler. *Introduction to People Analytics* gives a very pragmatic, step-by-step approach that demystifies analytics for anyone curious to explore how people analytics can support achieving business goals faster."

Patrick Veenhoff, Director, Area9 Lyceum, and Founder, oncorporatelearning.com

"A very insightful and compelling guide to how HR professionals can unlock and drive the true value of HR in any organization through people-related data analytics."

Anas Ahmed, Vice President HR and Corporate Comms, Venture Dive

"A must-read primer for anyone considering having some deeper understanding on how to collect, analyse and make use of data for taking key HR decisions for any business. Read this book and learn from one of the best works."

Ali Khurram Pasha, Director Human Resources, Habib University, Pakistan

"Whether you are feeling a need for change of your HR service provision, a different direction, or just want to explore the art of the possible for HR, this book will really make you stop and think. If you are unsure as to what the difference is between data and analytics and whether analytics can add value to your HR service then this book is for you. Or, if you don't have a great deal of time and you want to dip in and out of the latest thinking around HR, check out the 'key takeaways'."

Rebecca Bishop, Group HR Director, The LTE Group

"Khan and Millner make a compelling case for executing far-reaching changes in organizational drivers, especially the people function. These are driven by rapid shifts in the digital world, driving the people function and the Chief People Officer (CPO) to measurably transform their roles. The authors' research strongly points towards the requirement that the CPO must be proactively engaged with the CEO and the CFO in building and executing plans for effective operating, business and strategic results. Alignment between the people strategy and the business is vital to ensure its greatest impact. *Introduction to People Analytics* develops an overarching focus on emerging expectations of the people function, driven by digital shifts, automation and skills gaps. A must-read for business leaders and HR practitioners!"

Aamir Niazi, Chairman of the Board, HRSG; Chairman, PMEA Governing Board, and Chairperson, Women Entrepreneurs Network

.

Introduction to
People Analytics

A practical guide to data-driven HR

Nadeem Khan
Dave Millner

KoganPage

First published in Great Britain and the United States in 2020 by Kogan Page Limited

2nd Floor, 45 Gee Street
London
EC1V 3RS
United Kingdom
www.koganpage.com

122 W 27th St, 10th Floor
New York, NY 10001
USA

4737/23 Ansari Road
Daryaganj
New Delhi 110002
India

Kogan Page books are printed on paper from sustainable forests.

Hardback   978 1 78966 181 1
Paperback   978 1 78966 180 4
eBook   978 1 78966 182 8

British Library Cataloguing-in-Publication Data

A CIP record for this book is available from the British Library.

Library of Congress Cataloging-in-Publication Data

Cataloging-in-Publication Data is available. Library of Congress Control Number: 2020000248

Typeset by Hong Kong FIVE Workshop, Hong Kong
Print production managed by Jellyfish
Printed and bound by CPI Group (UK) Ltd, Croydon CR0 4YY

*For Mikaail, Jibrael, Zaena, Urwah, Mahad and Mohib
– reflect on your day not just by the 'harvest you reap',
but also by the 'seeds you sow'*

*For Chris, Lee, Jacob, Hayden, James and Mel – wisdom, they say,
comes with age and experience. Remember, you have one life,
but many choices, so keep choosing wisely*

CONTENTS

ABOUT THE AUTHORS

Nadeem Khan is a business author, keynote speaker, futurist, leadership coach and consultant in organizational strategy, digital transformation and the future of work. Over the past decade, he has advised and worked with many of the world's best-known organizations, including Coca-Cola, Goeth Institut, Avery Dennison, PARCO and Avari International Hotels, on improving business performance through their people.

Born in Pakistan and brought up in the UK, Nadeem received his initial education in Scotland. After returning to Pakistan, he received his MBA from the Institute of Business Management, qualified as an academic to kick start his career in academia and subsequently ventured into organizational development consulting. Nadeem was later awarded a scholarship by the Department of Leadership & Management at Lancaster University to take up a master's programme in Human Resources & Consulting. At Lancaster, Nadeem's research interests were focused on understanding the importance of human capital analytics to improve organizational performance, which culminated in a distinction.

Nadeem resides in England with his family and has since been part of several globally recognized initiatives that are revolutionizing HR, people management and the future of work.

A fellow of the Chartered Institute of Personnel and Development (CIPD) and advance level 7 postgraduate diploma holder in human resource development, Nadeem is a regular contributor to *People Management* magazine, the UK Domain and LinkedIn. He is an instructor and trainer for AIHR Academy, MBL Seminars and the North & Western Lancashire Chamber of Commerce. Nadeem also dedicates his time as a mentor to Lancaster University's career mentoring programme. With the ambition to transform HR, Nadeem turned down his offer for a PhD and took up the baton to contribute towards the global HR community by joining hands with Dave to create this book and lead HR into the future. Currently, he is the managing director at Optimizhr Ltd – a data and people analytics solution provider offering services that amplify and align organizational strategy with capability towards business optimization.

Dave Millner is widely recognized through his social media profile (@HRCurator) as one of the leading global influencers on "all things" relating to the future of HR, the application of workforce analytics in the workplace and organizational effectiveness strategies. His main areas of expertise and specialism are organizational development and design, employee engagement and experience strategies, workforce frameworks, executive coaching and HR and digital transformation programmes, all underpinned by data.

Dave was born and educated in the UK, and joined NatWest where he originally operated in their retail and corporate businesses. He obtained the Chartered Institute of Bankers (ACIB) qualification and moved into a corporate risk assessment role for a number of years. As part of his development programme at NatWest, he joined their full-time assessment and development team for two years as a facilitator and trainer, focusing on identifying high potential employees through, at the time, innovative assessment and development centres. He then joined a Think Tank team focused on changing the role of personnel to HR, and acted as a senior consultant for some 10 years focusing on people frameworks, assessment and selection, leadership development and changing the role of HR across the business.

He became a member of the Chartered Institute of Personnel and Development (CIPD), and had by this stage completed a Psychology degree at the Open University. He is now a Chartered Occupational Psychologist (CPsychol).

Dave left NatWest/Royal Bank of Scotland in 2000 to join PSL (a psychometric development consultancy) where he was their Consulting Director focusing on assessment and development-based solutions for organizations across the UK and Europe. Kenexa acquired that business in 2006 where he was the Consulting Director (EMEA) in the assessment practice, but evolved his role to deal with large corporate clients, where the focus was on capability shifts and organizational transformation. This included intensive work projects across the Middle East region between 2008 and 2013.

In 2013 Kenexa was acquired by IBM and Dave's role evolved into running some of their large global engagement projects across the globe and acting as an evangelist for the role of HR. This involved the promotion of technology, analytics and data in the transformation of the HR function, as the challenges of the digital world of work become more and more relevant to all organizations. As part of that, he became a regular presenter at conferences promoting the future of HR, the role of technology and the need for analytics and new techniques so that HR can demonstrate tangible business value in the ever-changing world we now face.

In 2018, he left IBM so that he could focus on his passions, namely HR transformation, analytics and the vital role that HR can provide to organizations, and has been supporting HR functions to become more commercially-focused so that they can provide a transformational work-force experience to their employees. He is an associate with the Corporate Research Forum (CRF), Hult Ashridge Business School and the Centre for Effective Organizations at University of Southern California, and an adviser to iPsychTec.

This has all culminated in the partnership with Nadeem to write this book – we hope you enjoy it.

www.hrcurator.com

FOREWORD

We are amidst a new, a fourth, industrial revolution, that is going to bring unprecedented change to the world of business. Organizations are being disrupted by transformative technologies such as artificial intelligence, robotic process automation, smart machines, extended reality, blockchains, and more. Many of these technologies are potent enough to cause disruption on their own but as they are all coming at once, and reinforcing each other, they are forcing organizations to fundamentally rethink how they operate.

One of the most valuable business assets of this Fourth Industrial Revolution is going to be data and our ability to extract value from that data. In our increasingly digitized world, the volumes of data are exploding and organizations that are able to harness that data will outsmart and outperform their competition. Data has become the lifeblood of modern businesses, and the most successful organizations of the future will use data in all parts of their business, including (or maybe especially) in the people function.

The Fourth Industrial Revolution is also going to have a major impact on the world of work, the jobs people will do in the future and the skills that will be required to thrive. In this context, the people function has to be a strong strategic business partner that helps to shape the organization in terms of people, structures and culture while simultaneously transforming itself to become more data-driven and digitally enabled. This is a double whammy that HR and people teams have to cope with.

The people function has to help the organization upskill its digital and data competencies, reinvent jobs, reimagine organizational structures and help create data-driven cultures. At the same time it has to reimagine its own function as data and digitization are transforming processes such as recruitment, onboarding, learning and performance management, to name a few.

Business leaders will be expecting HR and people teams to be a key agent of change and a power function that enables evidence-based decision-making and provides the business with valuable analyses and insights. HR leaders will need to ensure they collect the right data and establish the skills, technology and culture to turn that data into insights. In my experience, HR teams are often lagging behind other functions, such as marketing or finance, in terms of their data literacy. Increasing data literacy among HR professionals will be a major differentiator between those HR teams that will thrive in the future and those that will be seen merely as cost centres that provide mandatory services, which of course make them vulnerable to being shut down or outsourced.

This is where this book comes in. Nadeem Khan and Dave Millner provide a powerful blueprint to establish a people function that is able to leverage data effectively. They provide the reader with intelligent approaches, practical models and plenty of real-life case studies, as well as insights from key thought leaders that give an extremely practical guide to data-driven HR.

I agree with Nadeem and Dave on the important point that data and analytics have to be aligned with key business goals. In practice, I see too much data analysis and reporting taking place because HR teams have the data, rather than analysis that is based on true strategic information needs.

In this book you will learn that it is vital to align your business strategy with your people strategy, and your people strategy with your people analytics strategy. This will help you move from reporting and analysing the past, something I see too often in HR teams, to analytics that are informing the future and providing critical insights that help get organizations ready for the Fourth Industrial Revolution.

Bernard Marr, futurist and bestselling author of
Data-Driven HR: How to use analytics and metrics to drive performance,
Data Strategy: How to profit from a world of big data,
analytics and the Internet of Things and
The Intelligence Revolution: Transforming your business with AI

PREFACE

It was Amsterdam, November 2018, and a thought-provoking people and workforce analytics conference had ended. There is always that moment when people catch their breath, having been driven for the past two days by the uninterrupted timetable of sessions, workshops and networking. At that moment, Nadeem Khan, a researcher and organizational development specialist, and Dave Millner, a seasoned occupational psychologist, met and immediately recognized that there was a meeting of minds when it came to the topic of people analytics. Both of us see HR, or as we like to call it the people function, as being critical to success for organizations, especially when we view all the workplace challenges that need to be addressed.

Technology implementation is increasingly relentless, against a backdrop of connecting with a workforce which is more varied in terms of expectations, capability and aspirations than ever before. Every business however large or small is consumed with mountains of data and other support functions. Recently, marketing has proactively used data and analytics to reposition themselves as a strategic partner to the executive team. Across HR, the advent of people analytics has started with large and medium-sized corporates seeing the opportunity that data can bring in terms of new or different insights.

Against that backdrop, we decided to write a book that is aimed at the HR, HR business partner and learning and development practitioner across the globe. Our book is not full of complex equations and terminology that only an advanced statistician would understand, as our aim is to take you, the practitioner, on a journey that will encourage you to adopt more of a commercial mindset allied to a willingness to use data, which will enable you to see people and business issues in a different light. From the feedback we've received, data scientists and analytics experts will also find some learnings in terms of understanding the context and challenges that HR have to operate within – as you will see, numerical expertise can't do without HR and vice versa. So, what does this book unfold?

The topic of people analytics is heating up. Not a day goes by without more articles about the subject and various conferences promoting the "sexy" side of analytics, with stunning visualizations and complex stories of how analytics has saved various organizations significant amounts of money.

There remains a place for these, as they are something to be aspired to, but the whole, and we mean the whole, HR function needs to be thinking in this way for the perception of the function to realistically change.

The topic of people analytics is confusing. Although data scientists, analytics experts and psychologists will be needed to undertake more complex predicative type of analysis, as it requires expertise and experience to be able to interrogate the data; a large proportion of these insights can be understood using mathematics.

What we do want to ensure is that the HR function talks about their interventions by using the language of the business, which is always commercially-orientated, rather than the HR focus that we have become too familiar with. As we continue to upskill leaders and managers about their workforce responsibilities, we have to ensure that we make it relevant and understandable for them – the challenge is that their numerical capabilities may well be superior to those in our functions.

The topic of people analytics is future-orientated. The future of work has been talked about for the past five years, with stories about all jobs being replaced by robots and automated processes. Automation is here and it will impact on the job landscape, but the key point is that with automation comes data, and so for us to ignore this new source of data is foolhardy. Digital technologies can provide new sources of people insight, new ways of collaborating across an organization and help with resolving challenges and issues that had not been considered before.

The purpose of our book, first of all, is to clarify the concept of people analytics and secondly to show how its application can be used to improve organizational efficiency. We hope to demonstrate how organizations across the globe are using people analytics and moving towards the establishment of a people function that forms the premise/cornerstone of our research.

We have structured the book into four sections, using where possible case studies, learning scenarios and examples from other organizations and vendors.

Part One: Context for change outlines the challenges facing the HR function of today and some of the changes that the function has made thus far, but, more importantly, the changes to establish a people function. We help you explore the opportunities that exist to align the function with the business objectives of the organization, making the connections across the business that will help ensure that the right decisions are made going forward and ensuring that value is truly sought across the people practices, all underpinned by a more data-based approach.

Part Two: Making the shift to a data-based approach looks at the crucial commercial mindset that is needed to make that change. We explore how this will impact on the people function and practitioners of the future, and focus on how to start the journey of thinking about issues in a more numerically-oriented way.

Part Three: People analytics delivering value is about outlining a framework about how organizations can undertake their analytics journey. This is not a prescriptive way that determines how everyone should develop this expertise, but it enables us to share case studies and examples that will help you understand some of the key principles that are necessary to make a successful transition to being more data-driven. We also share what the cultural implications are of making such a shift and outline a framework to help you take forward these types of projects, whether you are working with an analytics expert or not.

Part Four: Looking to the future has two lenses through which we glance forward. From an individual perspective, we share a proven process and methodology that will take you through how to become more data-driven in your role, from reviewing your business key performance indicators to how to consider implementing change. Finally, we end by looking to the future, and how the people function of the future will evolve with people analytics at the heart of it, driving new ways of working and different data-based outcomes.

We remain optimistic and excited about the future of HR as we act as a catalyst for business change, behavioural and cultural shifts, all underpinned by evidence and data-based insights. After all, people remain a real competitive advantage, and even with an increasingly automated agenda that will still remain true.

We couldn't have completed this book without the help, support and valuable insights shared by analytics and HR experts, various vendors and academic organizations who share the same vision as us regarding the current and future importance of the function – thank you so much!

Enjoy the data journey – the credibility and capability of our function relies on us making this change today.

ACKNOWLEDGEMENTS

To say this book is written by Nadeem Khan and Dave Millner overstates the case. Without the significant contributions made by other people practitioners, this book would certainly not exist! We would like to thank all the experts, practitioners and academics who agreed to be interviewed for our book. The insights gained from them have been invaluable, and determined the direction of our research.

We are especially grateful to Dirk Jonker, CEO of Crunchr and John Pensom, CEO of PeopleInsight who shared insights and gave access to their research, which helped lay the foundations for Chapters 6 and 9 respectively. Also to the Corporate Research Forum who have been instrumental in sharing their research, which we have referred to across a variety of chapters.

We would like to thank the team at Kogan Page for enabling us to deliver the notion of writing a book and making it into a reality. Finally, we thank in anticipation our readers who will apply, critique, and build on these insights, ideas and concepts.

PART ONE

Context for change

1

Redefining HR

The context for change

The world is full of data, and it is impacting on all our lives. It predicts what we would like to buy based on our previous buying habits, it tells us how our cars are performing on a minute-by-minute basis and it tracks our well-being at work through various applications.

Businesses have been exploring the world of Big Data for ten years, to shape their strategies in response to fierce global competition, demanding customer expectations and relentless operational challenges in terms of efficiency, effectiveness and productivity. As Bernard Marr[1] believes, "Those companies that view data as a strategic asset are the ones that will survive and thrive". But what about HR in this area?

Look at Credit Suisse, for example. They measured the return on investment (ROI) of people analytics in their organization, and found that one single percentage point of attrition was worth between $75 million and $100 million in savings for the business.[2]

Over the past five decades, HR has dealt with an influx of increasingly complex business challenges, all of which have created the demand and desire for more of a data-driven profession than we see today. There are outliers, such as Credit Suisse, who are embedding analytics and data-driven approaches into the heart of their HR function – but this tends to be the domain of large corporates, and is not seen across every HR department. Our belief is that smaller organizations have the agility and capacity to more easily obtain the data that drives a change in emphasis. It's the mindset that is missing and the desire to deal with those numbers; we didn't join HR to deal with numbers all day, did we? The challenge for HR practitioners – and we mean in the broadest sense practitioners in HR, learning and development (L&D) and other teams within the current HR function – is to focus on the data. After all, words without numbers are just opinions!

This chapter will cover:

- **HR and the new world of work**: This is about the key digital themes and trends that are impacting upon a lot of organizations today. We'll introduce the Three Ds model as a means of summarizing the complexity of the world in which we are now operating.
- **The shift of HR into a people function**: This will look back at the progress that HR has made to date, and consider the next shift that is required; namely, a people function to deal with the challenges of today and proactively reposition the old HR function of the past.
- **Tomorrow's people function**: The key challenge for the people function of the future is to change its mindset so that it focuses not just on numbers but on the complex business demands that inevitably revolve around generating income and growth rather than just focusing on cost reductions (after all, how many more costs are there left to be reduced?).

HR and the new world of work: the Three Ds

These days it's a challenge to keep up with the fast pace of the workplace, with technology and changing demographics creating rapid shifts. Businesses and employees are expected to embrace constant new innovations like never before, and there are bound to be even more changes on the horizon as we transition into the agile workplace of the future, with technological advances permeating all aspects of the workplace. Not a day goes by without further challenges, insights and reports becoming available about the impact of automation, change and the way in which work will change.

Figure 1.1 highlights the recurring themes that have emerged from these numerous reports, and summarizes the major themes that have to be considered if you and your organization want to be "futureproof".

The digital world of work

The key elements of the digital world of work are driven by the continually-changing disruptors that are impacting on all organizations, such as the constantly changing markets and external forces, the increasing shift to contingency workers and the clamour for automation.

Let's explore some of these mega trends, as they will all impact upon the future HR function, its practitioners and the changing demands that will be made on the function.

FIGURE 1.1   Digital world of work mega-trends

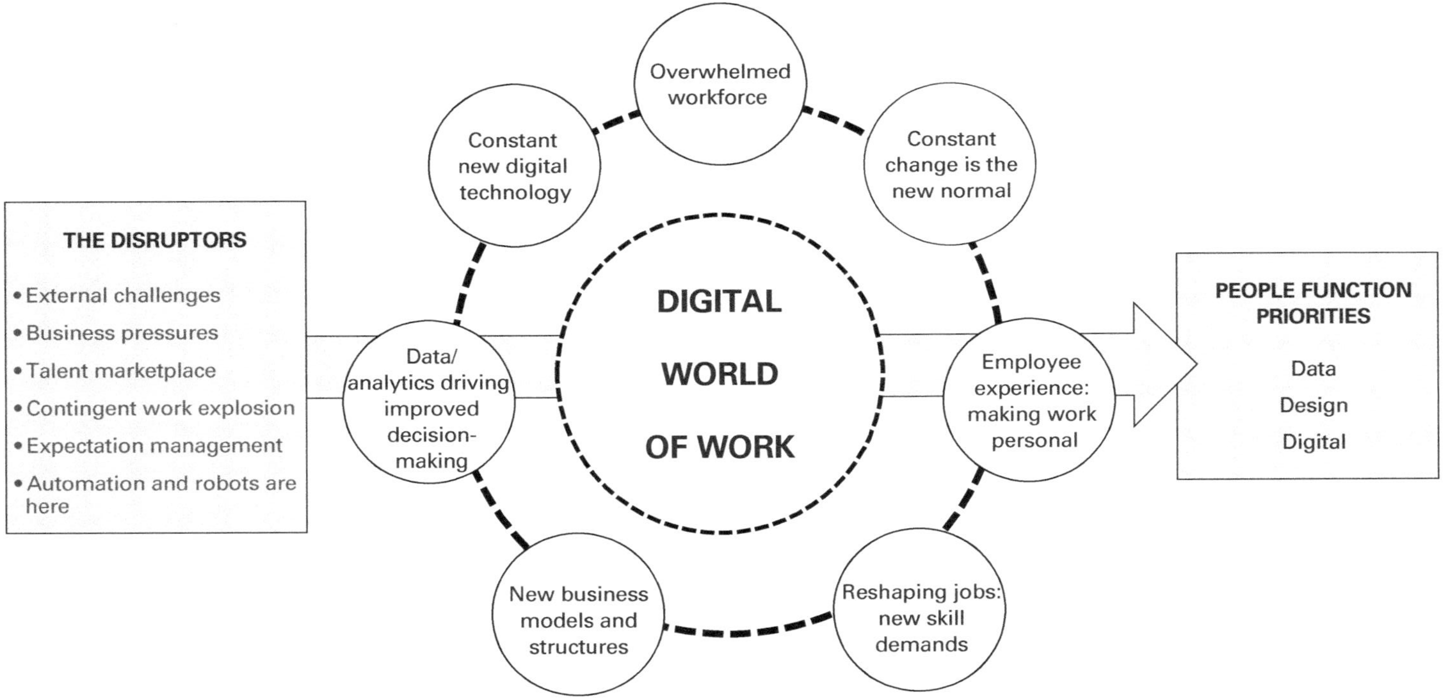

PEOPLE FUNCTION PRIORITIES

Data
Design
Digital

Constant change is the new normal

Employee experience: making work personal

Overwhelmed workforce

Reshaping jobs: new skill demands

DIGITAL
WORLD
OF WORK

Constant new digital technology

New business models and structures

Data/analytics driving improved decision-making

THE DISRUPTORS

• External challenges
• Business pressures
• Talent marketplace
• Contingent work explosion
• Expectation management
• Automation and robots are here

THE OVERWHELMED WORKFORCE

There is pressure across all levels of the workforce, with expectations of employees increasing all the time. Simultaneously, supervisors, managers and leaders are having to manage across more complex relationships than ever before, with increasing automation and ongoing change. The key challenges revolve around:

- **Execution**: a desire to achieve "more with less" driven by the challenging cost agenda that is understandably a feature of most organizations.
- **Employee expectations**: there is an increasing need to learn new processes, skills and practices as automation increases. But there are challenges with this, such as having the time to learn and grow vs the increasing demands for rapid delivery and task/process completion. For example, as work-based "apps" change overnight, will we have sufficient time to learn, and unlearn, what is required?
- **Manager priorities**: their challenge is finding the right balance between operational task/process completion vs the increasing desire for the "human touch", which is so vital when creating an environment that employees want to work in.
- **Leader "bandwidth"**: they have a clear execution focus driven by demanding multiple stakeholders and expectations. However, their role in terms of breadth and depth of issues is becoming increasingly complex, ranging from culture to project sponsorship to inspiring the workforce with clear motivational messages.
- **Wellbeing**: all of these challenges are adding to the wellbeing agenda which is becoming more of a workforce issue than ever before, with stress and ill-health becoming operational challenges that need to be facilitated.

Whatever the challenge may be in this area, the workforce data that can be collected is vital to understanding how the workforce is really feeling. It's best to find out before they walk out of the door!

CONSTANT CHANGE IS THE NEW NORMAL

This has been talked about for many years, but is now very clearly becoming a reality. Some of the common challenges are:

- **Resilience to change**: for years resistance to change has been the challenge, but the fact is that change affects everyone in the workplace – from new automation-based learning, through to process changes and refinements.

It's about building up resilience to change within the workplace, as resistance is now futile; it's going to occur whatever happens, so start embracing it!

- **Change programmes**: large-scale programmes still exist in organizations, but the key difference is that these are now a series of smaller pilots and projects that inform the bigger picture. That means high workforce involvement[3] to obtain buy-in, and real-time insights that not only help with the quality of the solution that is being developed, but also build a real connection with the workforce through that involvement.

IBM's reimagined performance management process is an example of the impact of high workforce involvement in the positioning and implementation of change.[4] The change process revolved around determining the strategic change required, and deciding where to start. This was followed up by obtaining the workforce's buy-in to support the transformation effort, in this case through crowdsourcing design ideas across the whole organization and promoting the benefits of change to senior management by demonstrating possible data-based workforce improvements.

Subsequently, the design and implementation of the revised process through numerous iterations and feedback loops was undertaken, all driven by employees being continuously involved in the design process. More and more change is being accompanied with data and insights from the workforce to ensure that the change is right first time around; after all, organizations that have been through numerous reorganizations and change initiatives obviously didn't get it right the first time around!

EMPLOYEE EXPERIENCE: MAKING WORK PERSONAL

The "battle for the hearts and minds of employees" is becoming more important than ever before, especially as different generations are now operating in the workplace. What we do know is that everyone in your business is trying to contribute, but if we insist on using the stereotypes that are played out in the media about Gen Z, Millennials, and so on, managers are not going to be able to manage people effectively. As we all know, when it comes to leading and engaging people, you never really know how someone responds best until you've worked with them for a while and entered into a meaningful dialogue with them.

That's why the employee experience is so important, as there are different expectations across the workforce, and employees are no longer as patient or accepting of certain organizational practices as they have been in the past. Additionally, in an increasingly automated world, how can organizations use that technology to make the experience at work both positive and personal for each employee?

There are many different definitions of "employee experience" – the simple one that resonates with us is that it refers to "the perceptions and feelings of the employees towards their job experience at work".[5] Research undertaken by IBM Workforce Institute highlighted five dimensions that captured the key elements of the employee experience:

1 belonging: feeling part of a team, group or organization;

2 purpose: understanding why one's work matters;

3 achievement: a sense of accomplishment in the work that is done;

4 happiness: the pleasant feeling arising in and around work;

5 vigour: the presence of energy, enthusiasm and excitement at work.

Links are being made between automation and the employee experience, to provide personalized solutions and information for the workforce in a cost-effective and sustainable way. The scope of this revolves around the complete employee lifecycle, as Figure 1.2 summarizes, with automation driving innovation and approaches that are designed to make the experience at work more individualized and future-focused.

As Figure 1.2 outlines, some of the rapidly developing technology applications will focus on not only an improved experience, but improved efficiencies across the HR practices. In the area of recruitment, we are already seeing chatbots assist in the screening process, with automated analytical based processes helping to match candidates. Blockchain is being used for CV verification purposes, and video-based interviewing is being utilized to not only speed up the process but bring more rigour to the interviewing process. Gamification-based techniques are increasingly being utilized to bring both assessment rigour and an improved candidate experience.

Once recruited, onboarding through virtual reality-based work and job previews are being used by some organizations, all supported by automated onboarding activity so that any new employee is effective and "up and running" from Day One. L&D will be significantly impacted, with a more personalized approach that includes again gamification and virtual reality for learning, nudges that trigger timely self-development support and technology that outlines possible career pathways, promotion matching and automated artificial intelligence (AI)-based coaching.

FIGURE 1.2   Automation and the employee experience

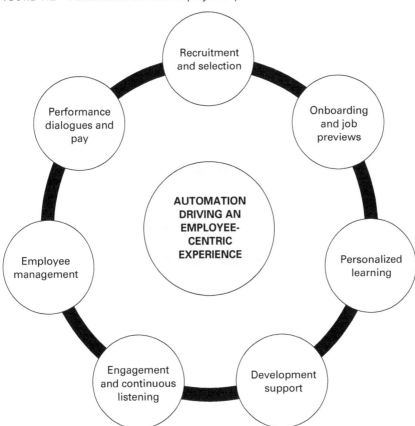

Across the rest of the employee lifecycle, complex AI and machine learning technology-based techniques formulate diagnosis and remedial insights into engagement-based feedback, productivity and workflow management support, performance dialogue and rewards-based tracking and recommendations, all driven by data and analytical predictions that can save organizations significant amounts of time and money.

The strength of this whole approach is that with the data that these methods generates, comes insights and evidence to back up why something should be done; it's about making better informed quality decisions based on the evidence that the new technology systems can provide.

RESHAPING JOBS: NEW SKILL DEMANDS

Whilst the employee experience focuses on the emotional aspect and impact of organizational change, the business-led automation debate means that

FIGURE 1.3 Reshaping jobs in an automated and disruptive world

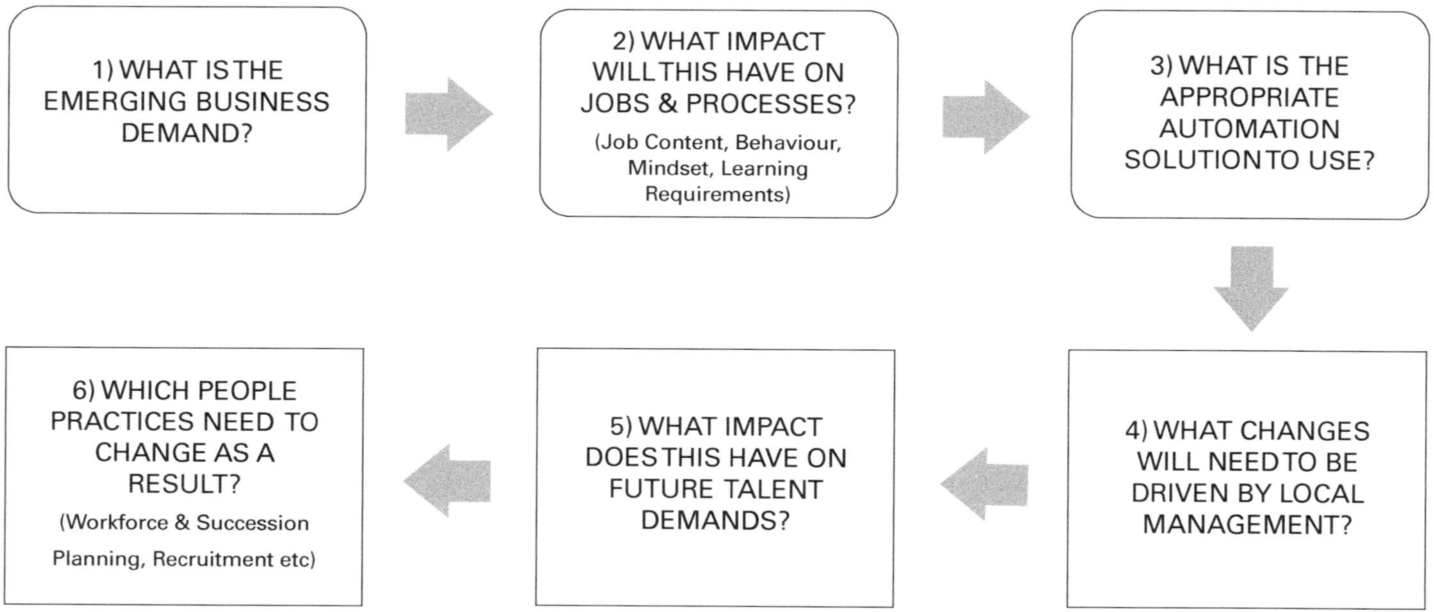

3) WHAT IS THE APPROPRIATE AUTOMATION SOLUTION TO USE?

4) WHAT CHANGES WILL NEED TO BE DRIVEN BY LOCAL MANAGEMENT?

2) WHAT IMPACT WILL THIS HAVE ON JOBS & PROCESSES?

(Job Content, Behaviour, Mindset, Learning Requirements)

5) WHAT IMPACT DOES THIS HAVE ON FUTURE TALENT DEMANDS?

1) WHAT IS THE EMERGING BUSINESS DEMAND?

6) WHICH PEOPLE PRACTICES NEED TO CHANGE AS A RESULT?

(Workforce & Succession Planning, Recruitment etc)

there is a clear need to determine an approach that optimizes the combination of human and automated work. Figure 1.3 outlines a process and some of the key considerations and questions to consider.

Ravin Jesuthasan and John Boudreau suggest that this automation review process follows two major steps; namely, deconstructing the work and evaluating the return on improved performance (ROIP), and optimizing human and automated work by considering the types of available automation, and whether automation will replace, augment or reinvent the human worker.[6]

According to the broader media, it would appear that the threat of jobs being replaced wholesale is a global phenomenon. Our perspective is that the extent of this change is being overstated. Certainly, repetitive tasks and processes, rather than jobs will be replaced by automated processes and new technologies. However, jobs will need to be redesigned, merged, changed and in some cases will disappear – but new jobs will also emerge as processes and practices are redefined and changed.

Whatever emerges, the three major dimensions of work (see Figure 1.4) will remain in place, as they have done for many years:

- **The work**: What work is being completed? This will range from totally automated processes and practices to increasing machine-based work, partially automated practices and the existing "human-led" domain knowledge-based work that is required (although the ability to automate this is being increasingly explored).

- **The workplace**: Where is the work being completed? With increasing technology advancements becoming available, the need for a defined static workplace is being reshaped, with different working methods and work locations being redefined in terms of where and when work is being completed.

- **The workforce**: Who does the work? This will be full-time and part-time employees of the organization, with freelancers, gig workers and managed services/contractors providing support in line with business requirements. The management and facilitation of this different "total workforce" will mean many new ways of operating for leaders, managers and employees alike.

FIGURE 1.4   The dimensions of work

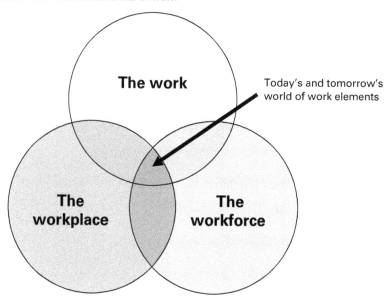

Changes in the work, the workforce, and the workplace are deeply intercon-nected. Changes in one area can have important consequences, for both employees and employers, that have not needed to be considered before. After all, what the future of work ultimately looks like isn't a foregone con-clusion, as everyone tries to define what it means for their organization, their employees and the way that talent is developed. If only there was one solution that fitted every organization's needs!

The flow of data and the insights they can bring will enable organizations to anticipate what needs to be done, to redefine strategies and ensure that the workforce is "set up for future success". Data is the fuel that will bring these challenges to life and identify opportunities for the HR function to be a clear part of the strategic future.

NEW BUSINESS MODELS AND STRUCTURES

For many years organizations have been seeking that "golden bullet" that will transform their operating model and structure from an efficiency and/or profitability standpoint. Organizational structure issues revolve around the fact that the structures in place today were originally designed for an environment of stability, predictability, and control – which are not the fea-tures that drive digital or business transformations.

The demands of today's, and tomorrow's, organizational structure re-volve around the need for fluidity, speed and responsiveness. New innova-tive ideas need to be created and implemented quickly so as to maximize competitive advantage. With technology that is quicker than ever before, an organization's workforce can sometimes be seen to not respond as quickly or as positively as desired. The structures of organizations must focus on tomorrow's demands as much as today's, otherwise competitive advantage could be lost.

This brings a whole new set of organizational design-based problems, that range from the operating model of the organization through to provid-ing the right technologies for the workforce and workplace that is being created. The role of data in the organizational design process will be vital to ensure that the facts and insights that data provide hold as much credence as the "well informed opinions" that are always shared at the time of organizational redesign. Ask yourself the question: "Why have there been so many restructures?", and the answer will be: "Because we didn't get it right the first time!"

DATA AND ANALYTICS DRIVING NEW DECISION-MAKING

We are promoting the "added value" that using data and analytics can bring to any HR function, whatever their size and priorities. The essence of this is that every organization, whether a competitive business, government or not-for-profit organization, is a data business. We have more data than we can cope with, and the challenge is to identify a breadth and depth of quality data that will inform and drive improvements across an organization, whether those are efficiency- or profit-based.

The power of data is that it can provide insights that will make the cus-tomer or employee experience better than ever before. Both of these aspects are of course critical to organizational success.[7] It's a culture change process, not merely the development of capabilities to undertake data-based analy-sis. The end result is that data and insights are being produced to help inform management so that they can make better informed decisions than ever before. This is not about taking their accountability and responsibility for decision-making away.

This whole process is a journey. Charlotte Allen, global head of work-force insights and analytics and chief of staff of HR at AstraZeneca, believes: "HR will not be replaced by data analytics, but HR who do not use data and analytics will be replaced by those who do".

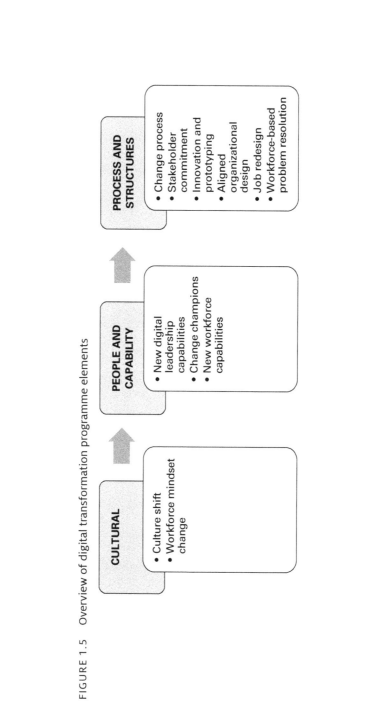

FIGURE 1.5 Overview of digital transformation programme elements

CULTURAL

- Culture shift
- Workforce mindset change

PEOPLE AND CAPABILITY

- New digital leadership capabilities
- Change champions
- New workforce capabilities

PROCESS AND STRUCTURES

- Change process
- Stakeholder commitment
- Innovation and prototyping
- Aligned organizational design
- Job redesign
- Workforce-based problem resolution

CONSTANT NEW DIGITAL TECHNOLOGY

The process of digital transformation will look different for every organization, but in general terms it is the integration of digital technology into all areas of an organization that results in fundamental changes to how that organization operates, and how it delivers value to its customers. This whole process is again about a cultural change, and will mean moving away from longstanding business processes to relatively new practices that may still require some "fine-tuning".

The velocity of technological change is immense, but digital transformation is not just about technology; it's more about the people and a new way of working that:

- is an integral part of corporate strategy;
- starts with a change in mindset in terms of how to operate at work using technology;
- enables a better customer and employee experience;
- embraces all the technologies that employees use to get their work done;
- enables the organization and its employees to deliver more efficiently and with more value than ever before.

The process of digital transformation and the implementation of the technology that drives it has been around ever since the World Wide Web was invented in 1989. The issue is that the complexity and relentlessness of the technological solutions being developed today is at a level never before seen. Consequently, the process of implementing true organizational-wide technological change is quite complex.

We have outlined some of the key characteristics and areas that need to be addressed in Figure 1.5.

There are many aspects to consider when aligning the workforce and business challenges so that digital transformation programmes can provide the necessary data that will be required to measure success and progress, such as:

- involving the business at the outset in the process of what data is required moving forward;
- starting with the business objectives that need to be measured – not the technology itself (that's merely the enabler);

- assessing the current state of the organization in terms of data, technology, workforce capability and so on;

- envisioning the desired future state in terms of culture, technology, structure, workforce and leadership capability, and the data that will be required to help understand the success, or otherwise, of the changes that have been implemented;

- undertaking a gap analysis in terms of capabilities to design, build, implement and sustain the desired changes to the workplace by obtaining the required data so that insights can be obtained;

- focusing on today and tomorrow when designing the data and analytics-based solutions required;

- understanding which analytics and data sources will be required to ensure that the measurement of the process improvements can be clearly and easily understood;

- building the data and analytics solution into your "business-as-usual" activity.

The critical point is that the digital future of work is about constant change; it's not another one-off transformation project that will be delivered, creating a "new normal". That means those employees that will be more successful are those that:

- embrace constant change as being a part of their daily job;

- adopt a more flexible and agile approach to their work;

- constantly learn as their jobs and performance expectations continue to change;

- accept increased accountability in their jobs, as technology provides greater flexibility and speed to perform and deliver, probably with less management and process checking than before.

The Three Ds

These complex trends and factors conspire to create a very clear agenda for the future HR function moving forward – the Three Ds, as summarized in Figure 1.6. Mike Haffenden, owner and partner of Strategic Dimensions and managing director of the Corporate Research Forum, believes: "HR is there to support the business, so you can't talk about the future of HR unless you talk about the future of business".

FIGURE 1.6   The people function priorities – the Three Ds

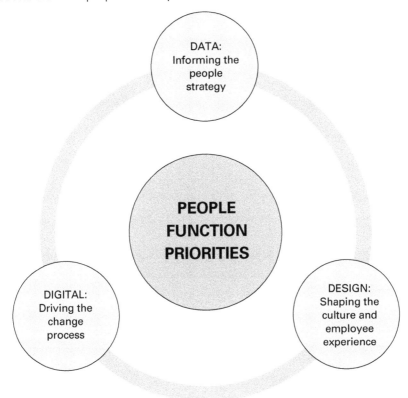

These three elements are interconnected and reliant upon each other to ensure that they drive better outcomes from each aspect.

DATA
This is crucial to be able to understand:

- the success of various people practices in terms of "adding value" to the organization at a business and/or strategic level;

- the opportunities for improvement and enhancement across both the people practices and the employee experience, which is a crucial imperative for the future workforce;

- the ability to demonstrate alignment between the people/workforce strategy and the business strategies and commercial demands that are being made of the HR function.

DESIGN

This will become a critical area for the HR function to focus on, in terms of:

- shaping the design of the new organization of the future;
- designing the new and reshaped jobs that automation will demand;
- identifying the new behavioural and technical capabilities and requirements that the new world of work will make of the workforce, its managers and its leaders.

DIGITAL

This is not just about supporting organizational change that drives new transformation-based initiatives; it is also about the digital HR change initiatives that are starting to become more commonplace in HR functions across the globe.

Digital HR is about process optimization, in which social, mobile, analytics and cloud-based technologies are leveraged to make the HR function more efficient. However, the application of new technologies is not what makes the function digital. It's also about culture alignment, talent practices, structures, and processes to balance efficiency and innovation opportunities, all focused on ensuring that there is an ability to provide a clear sustainable measurable impact on the organization as it continuously transforms.

The shift of HR into a people function

The HR function has been known by many names, with some organizations referring to it as "talent", "human capital", "human resources", "workforce" and most recently "people". Most recently, experts have argued that the function needs to be split into two parts: an HR function and a strategic HR function.[8, 9] The HR function is responsible for supporting the workforce on their day-to-day administrative tasks such as recruitment, onboarding, compensation and benefits, whereas the strategic aspect looks at how people-based insights can improve organizational performance.

More recently, HR function improvements have been achieved through the introduction of new technological advancements such as AI, chatbots, cloud-based HR systems and machine learning. Technology has the ability to make a huge impact on the transactional and operational activities of HR such as recruiting, onboarding, training, leadership development, performance management, compensation and benefits, rewards and recognition.

Some organizations are there already, but some are still considering it given the scale, scope and expense that may be incurred.

The theory is that this should provide more time for HR to deal with the larger organizational challenges, and achieve that strategic position that they strive for. Nevertheless, we still find HR professionals facing problems with operational challenges when it comes to embedding and aligning these technologies with business strategy and demonstrating the value of their practices to business leaders. These challenges can include:

- expensive, time-consuming IT support and continual system add-ons;
- disparate clunky platforms that aren't really that scalable;
- the speed of changing compliance issues and their impact on technology features;
- inadequate data or not easily accessible data;
- management of multiple vendors;
- cybersecurity challenges in terms of data storage and secure access.

These are not the type of issues that HR practitioners anticipated dealing with when they originally joined the function.

Changing the function: hasn't this already happened?

There has been a significant amount of change in HR functions across the globe, particularly over the past ten years. Changing the behaviour and approach of the HR practitioner has been a critical part of that process, although there is still much work to be done – especially when it comes to the commercial use and application of people data which forms the bedrock of the analytics approach.

As outlined in Figure 1.7, change has occurred; the challenge is whether the function is making the business impact that it needs to. Progress has been made when you consider the operational personnel function that previously existed, but the shift from being an integrated talent practices function to a business-driven one is more difficult.

HR still seems to be regarded as an overhead that is downsized when times get tough either through a reduction in its budgets or by reducing its own headcount, if only to increase the employee to HR ratio (which remains one of the most meaningless metrics ever devised; all it has ever told us is that there are less HR people available to talk to!). Other elements have been streamlined with technology or focused outsourcing, but with the

FIGURE 1.7   The evolution of HR

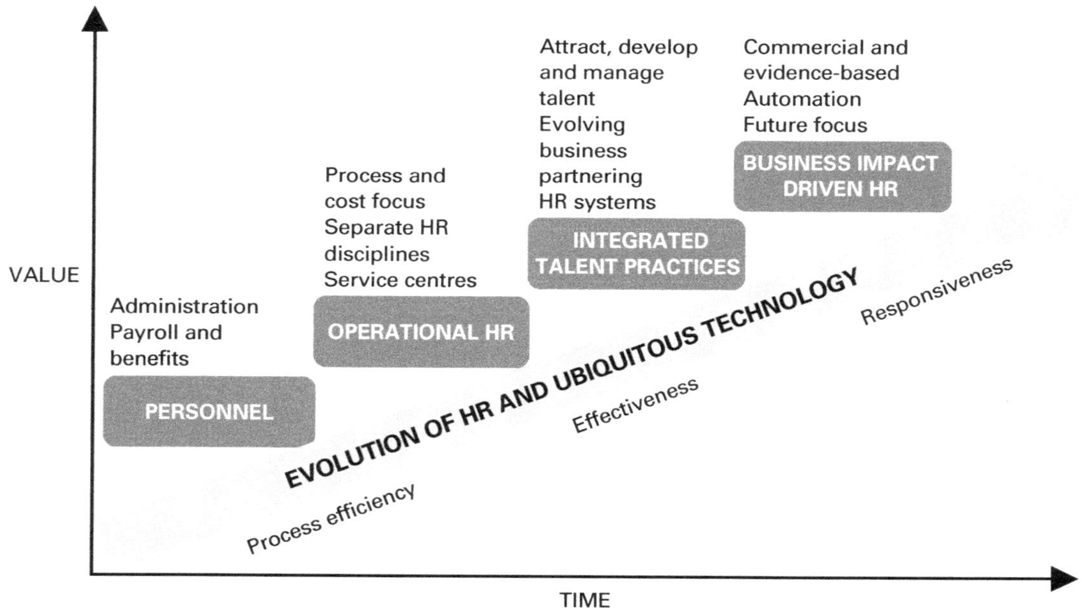

VALUE

PERSONNEL

Administration
Payroll and
benefits

OPERATIONAL HR

Process and
cost focus
Separate HR
disciplines
Service centres

INTEGRATED
TALENT PRACTICES

Attract, develop
and manage
talent
Evolving
business
partnering
HR systems

BUSINESS IMPACT
DRIVEN HR

Commercial and
evidence-based
Automation
Future focus

EVOLUTION OF HR AND UBIQUITOUS TECHNOLOGY

Process efficiency

Effectiveness

Responsiveness

TIME

world changing at an increasing rate, HR must respond to these changes with more than its traditional "do more with less" approach. It needs to revamp everything it does.

It needs to improve its impact and credibility if it is to be seen as a corporate function that can influence top management regarding the importance of the people agenda. The key is whether the benefits are being seen to make a difference in the organization's eyes and that of the top team. HR can't use an old map to find a new route; here are some thoughts about further changes that could make the journey for HR faster and more transformational. It's all about changing the old perceptions that exist about our function.

PROACTIVE AND RESPONSIVE

There is still a strong reactive aspect being seen. Instead of developing solutions in response to a demonstrated need, it is crucial that to meet the future needs of the business and to lead organizational change, HR must not wait for others to lead – but must instigate research, innovation teams and scenario-based plans that place HR on the "front foot".

Where HR functions have adopted this approach, in companies such as Unilever, ABN AMRO and Schneider Electric, the impact on their perceived credibility is significant and they are still to this day proactively pushing the boundaries.

MEASURING VALUE

All head office and corporate support functions continue to come under ever-increasing pressure to demonstrate their value, and HR functions must respond by becoming more financially-orientated and accountable. By aiming to become more data-, metrics- and analytics-orientated, every HR initiative or solution needs to be assessed on a "zero cost" basis, which assumes you add no value unless you can prove otherwise.

The clamour for metrics is not about measuring everything that HR does, but focusing precious resources on those solutions that produce a higher return. For example, why aren't all administrative processes placed into operational centres with other business processes? Just because they are people-based, that doesn't mean that they need to be retained under the control of HR. Eventually whether it is in twelve months or three to five years, the world of chatbots will have developed to such a point that technology will have overtaken the human approach to basic HR information and transactions.

ADDING VALUE

The real challenge for HR has always been the ability to truly demonstrate added value and a real tangible competitive advantage for an organization. Measurement is critical, but it's about measuring those key elements that "add critical value and return" to the organization. This can mean anything from demonstrating ROI through to assessing and creating predictive analytics that truly show the business impact that HR can make, based on existing data.

Some organizations may explore the true value for money that organizations derive from its people, in terms of an employee's collective capability and the costs associated with that individual.

EFFECTIVE PEOPLE PRACTICES

HR has considerable thought leadership expertise, and needs to educate managers more on the tools that will:

- ensure that top performers are retained;
- improve their ability to motivate, develop and challenge their staff;
- provide the most predictive recruitment methods that identify top performers;
- identify the most effective development interventions;
- identify the benefits packages that increase the performance of the best people;
- prove which people management practices have the most impact on performance.

This all needs to be underpinned by clarity about who truly owns the people agenda and the respective roles that local management and HR have to play in that. The "unsaid conversation" seems to be an issue in some organizations.

BEING STRATEGIC

HR has been striving to be strategic for some time, but is this really attainable? Being "strategic" means producing results that impact upon critical business objectives, and so if you want to take credit for some strategic result, you must first assume some degree of ownership or accountability over that strategic area. That's the business challenge you face when using data and analytics to show your value. Numbers can go up and go down, but using data is the way to show why something has happened, rather than focusing on the immediate impact on the HR function of those reductions. That's the commercial world that every business manager faces each day.

Many people equate being strategic with having some degree of formal authority or control, but there is really no automatic connection between the two. Strategic individuals seldom have as much power as they would like. For example, in most organizations the Chief Financial Officer (CFO) takes responsibility for all financial actions, but, in fact, has little direct power over how the budget and finances are spent. Most of the CFO's power comes from educating and influencing others, not from any formal authority to change direction, make product/service decisions, or even manage execution in a particular way. CFOs take responsibility for the financial matters that they have determined to be important to the success of the organization, even though in most cases, they do not have total control or power over the situation.

HR cannot use this "lack of control" excuse if it expects to be considered a strategic/commercial function. Taking responsibility for things you don't completely own or control is what leadership entails. If you accept that HR is responsible for the "output" or results of the people management practices, not just the operation of the systems, then you must advise, cajole, educate and somehow influence managers and employees throughout the organization so that they can attain the highest level of productivity.

LEADERSHIP FOCUS

HR must allow managers to make and own their informed people decisions, with HR shifting from the process implementer role, which still exists in a whole range of organizations, to that of a facilitator or internal trusted adviser who will provide clear thought leadership on effective people practices. This is not just about changing the name of the HR role to that of business partner – it is about changing the way that HR operates and behaves, driven by a far more commercial mindset.

HR CAPABILITY

It may be unfair to make generalizations – but a lot of HR practitioners are strong in relationship-building, but lack the commercial nous that is critical to build that important credibility with clients. The "new" HR practitioner needs to develop their capability in business and finance, and have a solid technology appreciation as well as being someone who can balance the risks that are sometimes required to resolve business challenges.

Above all, HR practitioners must have an informed view about the business world that they are operating in. Remember, everyone appears to be an HR or people expert until it gets difficult – so why shouldn't we have a view about marketing, operations and so on? It also demonstrates and builds credibility.

As we can see, HR as a professional discipline is definitely on the right path. But what do executives think about the progress that has been made? Here is an insight from Greg Ridder, a highly experienced global executive.

THOUGHT LEADERSHIP INSIGHT
View from the boardroom

Greg Ridder, chairman of Kogan.com and various global executive boardroom roles based in Australia

Greg Ridder has held various global executive roles over the past 20 years, including CFO, CEO, company president, and more recently chairman and boardroom roles as his current portfolio has expanded. His experience in global and Asia Pacific-based organizations enables him to share his thoughts about the importance of being commercial and data-orientated in today's increasingly fast-changing world.

Today's commercial context and expectations of senior leaders

There are some things that never go away: hard numbers, metrics, they're always there. I'm yet to find companies that don't have a Profit & Loss account (P&L), balance sheet, cash flow statements, etc. These are pretty fundamental the world over, so those things become inescapable, and typical metrics reporting and scorecards tend to be mostly "lag" indicators. We need more qualitative assessments and lead indicators, which we all know are much harder to get.

Almost every organization has a strategic agenda, and it is vital that we can quantify the progress, or lack of it, that is being made. Often this shifts to issues of commercial context, so we need those conversation starters that move us to what's causing things to happen, what's in our control, what's within our influence, what's directly in our market context, and so on.

Once we've got that strategic context, it's all about what you are doing and how you are trying to move down that pathway, or motorway. But there are always speed humps, there are detours, there are roadworks; there are all sorts of things that take us through performance deviations from time to time. The critical response is: how do we calibrate, how do we reorient ourselves to account for those, and how do we move on?

This means that executive leaders must have the capacity to risk-calibrate, provide insight, anticipate scenarios and create options. Those sorts of things tell me that they grasp the circumstances and that they also have an awareness that there are many routes to the same destination. Additionally, within the executive team you also want them to be capable in their own individual functional expertise to strongly run with any revised plans of action. Some executives are broader than others, but you are looking for that context interpretation expertise; not necessarily that they have the answer to all things but that they understand the commercial context they are operating in, and know how to find and apply the information and answers that are relevant.

When talking about leadership, I often use the example of an arrow. Once it's set on its journey, it goes to where it has been pointed. The CEO and leadership group are at the arrowhead, and they have more intimate knowledge of what they are targeting and visibility of where they are going. However, they often forget that their organization is further back at the shaft and feather end of the arrow. Wherever that arrowhead goes, the shaft and feathers are going to be pulled along with it – so purposefully determining how you provide the same view of the objective to your workforce is very important, or you risk them being disconnected from the objective.

Expectations of HR leaders

20 years ago, the focus of HR would be on soft-skill requirements, recruitment demands and informing executives about engagement, and a few simple metrics about staff turnover. The issue was that people were not used to being measured and being evidence-based.

Certain organizations which are really people-heavy, such as quick service restaurants, fast food chains and so on have had to be more dynamic in their approach. I was talking to a Chief People Officer who had been charged with finding "X" number of people from Australia for regional management roles in China. Their rollout plan was something like one store every twenty-six hours in China, and every store essentially needed one hundred people to do the different shifts! Not only did they need to find them, but they also needed to train them in the ways of the organization.

That person was the right hand man to the CEO because the first-to-market in that sector would make all the difference and that meant having a large, trained and structured workforce at the ready.

Whether your organization is as dynamic as the retail sector is irrelevant, because HR practitioners need to know the business imperative both today and tomorrow. If they don't grasp that strategic agenda, then they are not able to impact both. It's about:

- How do we get outstanding performance today?
- How are we shaping the organization for the future? Not all organizations are on growth dynamics – some of them are being disrupted, and for them it might be about how you reshape the organization and redeploy resources in a technological disruptive world.

Constant awareness of strategic intent and anticipating the future needs of the business will make HR leaders valuable as they will be keeping their eye on the external environment, especially anticipating those industry dynamics, regulatory changes, and the rapidly-developing technological shifts. They don't have to be the strategic planning expert, but they have to know about the external shifts and the possible impact upon the workforce and skills required moving forward.

There is another aspect that really grabs me, and let's call it cultural acuity; the ability to see, feel and influence actions and behaviours. These are the things that build brand and contribute to the internal synergy of the workforce, and HR practitioners have to be strong enough to call out those who threaten to compromise it. There are real "value destroyers" lurking out there in this world, and we need to make sure that we are aware of those. I don't believe any organization can ignore externalities anymore and say that's outside our four walls.

I work in a number of businesses, either as the chairman or on the board. One in particular lives in the data world; it's a substantial online retailer. We would argue in that business that we are statisticians and analysts masquerading as retailers, because we don't back judgement and "this feels good" or "trust me". We use algorithms that draw from what is happening in the world, and then say: if it's happening in the world, we can apply elements of that to our business. For example, we would argue that we sell "already in demand products", because the data is telling us there is a demand out there, so we source products that fit that profile.

Everyone in that organization is very comfortable about dealing in really objective data-orientated ways. That means that the conversations are actually quite different and much more interrogative in terms of looking to validate and test the veracity of where things are at. The culture in that organization is particularly strong around data and analytics, and they expect it everywhere in the organization. In a number of other organizations that I work with at boardroom level, there is no such approach and it is very "soft". Inevitably there is no real HR presence in the strategic conversations.

HR, data and expectations

Anecdotally, the very best HR practitioners I have ever worked with have gone on to be CEOs themselves. They had the commercial imperative and understood how to shift an organization and its workforce when the business demanded it.

Today, data and analytics are important to back up our judgement with evidence. The key HR question has got to be "have we got the evidence?" We have performance metrics available to us on so many fronts in terms of tracking data, efficiency, conversion rates, business development pipeline, new product development and success rates, so why should HR be any different in our pursuit of business improvement?

It's important to find both real measures and relative performance measures so that we can strive for improvement all the time. There is a whole range of others we would see; engagement, net promoter score (NPS), customer satisfaction, skills trained for and demonstrated etc – so that they can all be measured at certain points in time and longitudinally so collectively we can track whether there is deterioration or improvement.

The role in HR is a tough one, but my pleas to the HR community would be:

- **Think strategically**: Know the strategic agenda of the organization. Understand the big picture, because then you can influence the smaller parts of that picture. If you don't, you are always just going to be reactive to the activity and points of view of others. I expect leaders to be proactive, as I want them to move the agenda forward all the time. I want to give them a long runway to show their skills, exhibit their craft and question and challenge the business.

- **Partner with confidence**: HR have to have enough confidence to act and to make things happen. At the most senior level, I expect the HR practitioner to be a partner with the CEO. It's not a one-to-one partnership, because the CFO is going to have a similar sort of relationship, but they have to at least be a recognized peer of the C suite. If they are seen as an adjunct, they won't have the credibility and therefore the respect of their peer group to be a valued contributor on everything, not just when it leans into the HR world.

- **Be insightful**: HR practitioners need to be proficient across a wide range of roles. They have got to be insightful, forward-thinking and proactive, and the role of data and analytics is key to building that credibility which is so important for anyone who is operating with or in the boardroom.

- **Embrace measurement**: Be prepared to be measured yourself, to measure the performance of others and to measure your contribution to the strategic delivery; that's where the importance of data is a crucial element.

Greg's views revolve around an increased commercial perspective allied to a more proactive stance, all underpinned by the data and evidence that is available. Greg doesn't treat HR any differently from other functions in terms of expectations, credibility and capability, and so the need for change can't be ignored.

Some significant changes have already been made, but some would argue that HR needs to grow holistically into a more strategic function altogether. We can see that HR could also split itself into two subsets, like Finance has from Accounting, and Marketing from Sales. Both Finance and Marketing are strategic functions of the latter. We believe this divide is worth exploring so that HR becomes the commercial partner that it aspires to be. To do that, more radical change is required as we have many years of fixed perceptions about us as a function that need to be reversed, and behavioural change by us, allied to more tangible business outcomes, are the fundamental levers for that change!

There is work to do. Mike Haffenden, owner and partner of Strategic Dimensions and managing director of the Corporate Research Forum, believes: "The world has changed, and yet I'm not sure that HR has".

Tomorrow's people function

We would like to focus our attention on the strategic function of HR; we would call that the people function. It's important for us to understand the scope of each of these terms: "talent", "human capital", "human resources", "workforce" and "people". In the wider business world, these terms have often been used interchangeably; however, when they are interpreted they are very different. To express HR's desire to become a more strategic function, each of these terminologies has been used to define the function in terms of what it seeks to achieve for a business.

Below we have sought to synthesize why it is important to adopt the name "people" for the strategic wing of HR.

"Talent"

Chambers *et al*'s 1998 article, 'The war for talent'[10] initiated the use of the word "talent" as a function for HR. Most of the research around managing talent assumes that organizations need to effectively attract, motivate, develop and retain high-potential and high-performance incumbents.[11]

Nevertheless, given the importance of diversity, the unique skillset each individual brings to the table and their combined importance to the overall culture of an organization, "talent" tends not to reflect the focus that tomorrow's digital world now demands.

"Human capital"

Finance has always had a strong influence on business, and so we see a lot of organizations using the term "human capital" or "human capital resources".

Most of the research that we use today has been derived from industrial organizational psychology; however over the years the term "human capital" has been controversial, as this concept suggests that people are a form of capital that are owned and controlled by an organization. Hence, this term is perceived to treat people as though they were machines.[12]

"HR" and "workforce"

"HR" is a good descriptor, as it covers the management of human resources and its interface with other business units. Similarly, the expression "workforce" encompasses the entire group of workers, not just full-time employees, and allows for the future inclusion of robots that will potentially replace current jobs within an organization.

However, both terms express a "looking-in" agenda for the function that has disqualified it from moving towards a cross-functional approach and developing a true people strategy that aligns to the business strategy. It's argued that for HR to be able to input into the business strategy it must enable a "looking out" approach that entails not only understanding the business, its operations and finance, but also customer-centricity.[13]

"People", the new frontier

Evidence shows that HR departments are producing more data than ever before.[14] With data everywhere, it is now possible for us to gather information from not only inside, but also outside the organization and see how it impacts organizational performance and culture. We therefore believe that "people" is the clearest way to express how the function should perform the strategic affairs of HR. As the scope of the term is almost limitless, the people function can aim to encompass synthesizing insights from the activities related to HR, the entire workforce, business operations and the customer.

Whilst we suggest using "people" as the name of the function, there will be organizational, cultural or local issues that may mean that other names are utilized. With increasing technological capability evolving in a lot of organizations, the people function has for the first time the opportunity to really link together all people-related activities within and outside the organization, improving the decision-making process and therefore the performance of the organization. That's why people data and the process of analytics is so crucial to the development of the function. Now more than ever, leaders and practitioners within the people function need to not only have this important skillset and expertise, but also a vision for this function that clearly aligns with the overarching business strategy.

Is HR fit for purpose?

A couple of years ago, experts argued in a provocative series of articles why HR is set to fail the Big Data challenge.[15] They argued that HR practitioners – we'll call them people practitioners – lacked sufficient knowledge and understanding of analytics, as well as suffering from IT solution limitations, which meant they failed to justify the value of HR data for the organization. There is now a huge momentum in organizations trying to create a case for data-driven HR, with expert practitioners focusing on the evolving role of the Chief HR Officer (CHRO).[16]

Whilst the CHRO is the focal point for domain knowledge and workforce-based insights, every executive needs to have a very clear people focus whatever their interest. Research has shown that organizations want their HR to contribute strategically, but they are perplexed about HR's role in the business and believe that this is mainly due to the lack of analytical skills that are holding HR back. As human capital is considered one of the most expensive assets on the balance sheet, sometimes amounting to more than 70 per cent of a company's expenditure, executives are always concerned with how human capital adds measurable value to the business.

Emergence of a new leader: the Chief People Officer

Time and again, CHROs have been criticized for their inability to provide a holistic view of the value created by the workforce, understand data and analytics, and contribute to the business strategy. In short, CHROs have not proven to be the business partner CEOs require, thus, CEOs are naturally more inclined to reach out to the CFO for this type of support.

To embrace change, the role of CHRO must be reimagined as Chief People Officer (CPO). The CPO will have cross-functional business experience and a clear understanding of business challenges and opportunities across various sectors, allied to being data-savvy. Their priority activities should include:

- being a business partner to the executive team who truly owns the critical people asset;
- embedding people analytics into day-to-day processes to drive better decision-making and improve organizational performance;
- predicting the fit between workforce capability and future jobs;
- forecasting and diagnosing issues relevant to cultural alignment, engagement and people development;
- prescribing actions and recommendations to improve organizational agility that unlocks or creates value, by looking at business issues through the people lens using technological solutions;
- owning a people-centric culture that is underpinned by data.

With this in mind, the "Golden Triangle" is a clear basis to increase the significance and impact of the people function by maximizing its relationship with the CEO and the CFO. See Figure 1.8.[17]

Armed with increasing amounts of technologically-derived data and insights from across the organization, the CPO will be able to provide recommendations that reflect not just the workforce and people side of the business, but incorporate it as a part of ongoing strategic imperatives. This would enable the CPO to be a real driver of a people strategy that is aligned to business strategy, and ultimately operate as a true strategic partner to the whole organization.

FIGURE 1.8   The Golden Triangle

Role of the people function

At a primary level, HR reduces human capital risk by not only hiring, training, retaining, motivating and engaging, but also aligning the entire workforce to the overall business strategy. For the majority of HR functions it is a difficult endeavour to show how the workforce truly contributes to overall business performance. With the operational tasks that represent the core functionality of HR being automated by technology, the people function can contribute to measure the value that these intangibles create.

The key tasks of the people function need to include:

- measurement, reporting and analysing of the intangible value of the business;
- development of a people/workforce strategy, in some cases termed Strategic Workforce Planning;
- alignment of the workforce strategy to business strategy, underpinned by a data-driven people-centric culture, all of which will drive an employee experience that retains talented employees at the organization.

An important aspect of the new team that will encompass the people function will include key competencies such as good data analysing skills, storytelling, business acumen, visualization, organizational psychology, accounting, finance and change management.[18]

CEOs globally find human capital amongst their top challenges, yet they undervalue their CHRO and HR function. Much of this has to do with the credibility and capability of the function; nevertheless, with the introduction of the people function and a new leadership agenda, this can change.

Selling the people function to top management

This shift won't happen through the behaviour of the CPO alone. In 2005, Fast Company published an article entitled 'Why We Hate HR'.[19] It is harsh in terms of the view of the HR function, but there are elements, that unfortunately, are still relevant today! Changing perceptions of the HR function is a challenge, but, as we know, people's perceptions are their reality.

CPOs and their leadership team are well aware of the importance of being "strategic" and getting an opportunity to influence the top management on people issues. New infrastructures and approaches need to be supported by changes in working practices. Rather than just working harder, agreeing to unreasonable requests and focusing on delivering operational changes, what is needed is the demonstration of key business outcomes that will get the attention of the CEO and their top management team. That means that people practitioners will need to provide clear business and functional thought leadership and (amongst many qualities) be able to:

- credibly talk about and influence others about people issues with a commercial and business mindset, not just a people perspective;
- see issues from a wider business perspective;
- work collaboratively and effectively with different teams and work groups to make changes happen;
- bring a focused business insight to people-based issues;
- deliver what they say they will deliver, and on time;
- proactively provide business and thought leadership on organizational and people-based issues at both an operational and a strategic level.

The underlying theme is that the people function must be able to converse in a more commercial way, and that is the reason why people data and analytics has been such a hot topic over the past few years. If the people function wants to be strategic, that means they will be impacting on what the CEO is measured by and what they care about. CEOs and their top team are impressed by people that understand what they are focused on – which tends to be profitability, revenue growth, customer attraction/retention, shareholder value and performance forecasts.

This excludes the major people function challenge, and that is the people. They will be one of the organization's largest fixed costs but also one of the key differentiators between you and your competitors. If the people function can identify what is important to the top team, it can then develop a plan to market or sell its capability to help resolve and support the achievement of those key business drivers. This will need to include the use of performance metrics, data, ROI models and studies, all aligned in terms of value, bottom-line savings and improved efficiencies.

CEOs and their top team need to be shown how you can help them achieve their business goals, and that's why demonstrating value through data is so crucial: hence the need to identify linkages between the commercial side of the organization and the people data. Nearly everything the top teams does is strategically driven and focused on a numerical outcome.

Don't aim to just satisfy them, but to inspire them and show them what their people can achieve. Many HR functions have been historically cut, downsized or outsourced because they fail to provide quantifiable proof of their value in a language that CEOs and the top team understand – that is, financial and commercial performance.

The people function as a profit centre

With the ongoing global economic uncertainties that the people function has faced over the past five years or so, it's not surprising that the function has tended to focus on process efficiency, which has meant ongoing trade-offs between quality and cost. When cost containment efforts start, the results can be fairly significant, but as time passes and efforts continue, the value of the savings starts to diminish. Today, cost containment efforts relating to people are likely to be a small proportion of the overall corporate budget, so the savings are likely to be minimal – when the focus should be on growth, which has far fewer limitations.

Every Head Office function has to focus on "adding tangible value", and should ultimately aspire to become a profit centre in their own right. Their focus is likely to change over the next few years,[20] where strategy creation and evolution, fluidity, technology and new operating models will be a core feature of the demands that are made on all Head Office functions.

Against this backdrop, analytics can support the people function in demonstrating the economic value of its programmes and practices. Figure 1.9 looks at the future of the profession, and shows how the people function of the future needs to have:

FIGURE 1.9   Demonstrating the economic value of the people function

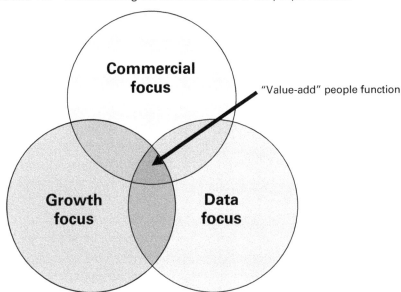

- A commercial focus: which activities will impact on the business effectiveness of the organization (costs, efficiency, productivity)?
- A data focus: how can the people function prove the financial benefits and "added value" of their interventions?
- A growth focus: which activities can tangibly impact on the "bottom line" of the organization (increased income and growth streams, key business measures for governmental and not-for-profit organizations)?

Data and analytical processes will help to answer these crucial questions. This means that there needs to be an ongoing drive to demonstrate the business impact of everything that the people function does. This might be a direct correlation between its activities and improved business outcomes such as sales or process efficiency, or the link between a particular people process, such as recruitment for example, and its impact on productivity, sales revenue or profit.

The impact of an analytics approach is that instead of focusing on the justification of their existence, the focus can now be on reflecting back to the organization (using their business language, not our "HR speak") the tangible impact that our people-based programmes can provide to an organization. That mindset means that we can now think about being a profit centre, not a cost centre, because we are "on the front foot" and talking about growth, profitability and productivity, not about process efficiency and the HR-to-employee ratio.

The shift to a profit centre mentality starts with the people function focusing on those aspects that the CEO and their top team get measured by, and focusing on providing data-based insights and more importantly growth-related data based on our interventions and programmes. Collaborating with the finance function means that their business data and numerical expertise can also be utilized to build tangible business insights that "raise the bar" for both functions' performance levels, for example, income targets, not process completion targets. It's important to think in terms of business outcomes at all times, not just focus on people-related outcomes that focus on growth/income and cost savings where feasible.

Analytics shifts expectations of the function and its internal clients. We need to be thinking: 'What's next?' The ultimate outcome of an analytics approach is not that the people function is more numerate, but that the function is known to be a commercially-orientated profit centre in its own right and no longer just a cost centre. That is the opportunity that exists for our profession – we can and must do it, especially as the disruption that is all around us reiterates that people are the true challenge of today's world![21]

KEY TAKEAWAYS FROM THIS CHAPTER

1   The future digital world of work will bring a range of new challenges to the people function, none of which have an "easy fix". The people function needs to proactively be involved in defining and shaping the solutions to these challenges.

2   The business will not wait for the people function to get involved; they may well perceive that they are better informed in the areas of Data, Design and Digital (the Three Ds). This is HR's opportunity to shine!

3   Technology is changing the world that we all operate in; the rapid and relentless level of change means that HR has to embrace new technological methodologies more than ever. Business leaders and employees are now expecting the sort of technology experience that they have as a consumer.

4   Past changes to HR have made a difference, but it is now critical for HR to focus on a business impact-based approach that is centred around being

more commercially-focused, more data- and evidence-based, and more analytical in its approach.

5 HR has put too much emphasis on trying to be strategic, when a more impactful commercial focus is what business leaders and executives see as more important in terms of bringing added value to an organization.

6 Changing behaviour across the whole HR function is the key to changing historical perceptions of it. Boardrooms need a clear and well-defined people focus more than ever before, and that's why HR has to shift to more of a proactive people function.

7 The role of tomorrow's people function is measurement, proactive analysis and the development of robust people strategies that are clearly aligned with rapidly-changing business demands.

8 The role of the CPO is key, not only as a role model and figurehead of the function, but as a crucial member of the executive team. The valuable connection that the "Golden Triangle" brings in terms of people focus, business data and strategic ownership is vital to drive the new expectations that will move the function from its operational talent focus to one of business impact.

9 The people function needs to focus on income and growth as much as cost management. The opportunity to make huge cost savings may have probably gone, whereas the opportunity to find new income streams and new ways of improving productivity, for example, are far more impactful on the organization. The creation of the people function as a profit centre can only be achieved with data and analytics.

10 With the people function using data and analytics, this can provide broader and more business-orientated insights than have been demonstrated before.

References

1 Marr, B (2017) *Data Strategy: How to profit from a world of big data, analytics and the Internet of Things*, Kogan Page, London

2 Baillie, I (2018) What is the Business Value of People Analytics? *myHRfuture* [Online] www.myhrfuture.com/blog/2018/11/2/what-is-the-business-value-of-people-analytics (archived at https://perma.cc/P2VC-USXY)

3   Zafar, Dr F, Butt, A and Afzal, B (2014) Strategic Management: Managing Change by Employee Involvement, *International Journal of Sciences: Basic and Applied Research (IJSBAR)*, **13** (1), pp 205–17

4   Kiron, D and Spindel, B (2019) Rebooting Work for a Digital Era, *MIT Sloan Management Review*, [Online] https://sloanreview.mit.edu/case-study/rebooting-work-for-a-digital-era/ (archived at https://perma.cc/EU6D-NLDP)

5   IBM Smarter Workforce Institute (2016) The Employee Experience Index, *IBM* [Online] www.ibm.com/downloads/cas/JDMXPMBM (archived at https://perma.cc/6DB9-XAVR)

6   Jesuthasan, R and Boudreau, J (2018) *Reinventing Jobs: A 4-step approach for applying automation to work*, Harvard Business Review Press, Brighton, MA

7   Morgan, B (2018) The un-ignorable link between employee experience and customer experience, *Forbes* [Online] www.forbes.com/sites/blakemorgan/2018/02/23/the-un-ignorable-link-between-employee-experience-and-customer-experience/#60502f9448dc (archived at https://perma.cc/384F-ER42)

8   CIPD (2015) Changing HR Operating Models, *CIPD* [Online] www.cipd.co.uk/Images/changing-operating-models_tcm18-10976.pdf (archived at https://perma.cc/Z8NK-VEZT)

9   Charan, R (2014) It's time to split HR, *Harvard Business Review*, **92** (7), pp 33–34

10 Chambers, E *et al* (1998) The war for talent, *McKinsey Quarterly*, **3**, pp 44–57

11 Lewis, R E and Heckman, R J (2006) Talent management: a critical review, *Human Resource Management Review*, **16** (2), pp 139–154

12 Wright, P M and McMahan, G C (2011) Exploring human capital: putting 'human' back into strategic human resource management, *Human Resource Management Journal*, **21** (2), pp 93–104

13 Michie, J *et al* (2016) *Do We Need HR? Repositioning people management for success*, Palgrave Macmillan, London

14 Guenole, N, Ferrar, J and Feinzig, S (2017) *The Power of People: Learn how successful organizations use workforce analytics to improve business performance*, Cisco Press, Pearson Education, Inc, USA

15 Angrave, D *et al* (2016) HR and analytics: why HR is set to fail the big data challenge, *Human Resource Management Journal*, **26** (1), pp 1–11

16 Charan, R, Barton, D and Carey, D (2015) People before strategy: a new role for the CHRO, *Harvard Business Review* [Online] https://hbr.org/2015/07/people-before-strategy-a-new-role-for-the-chro (archived at https://perma.cc/Z9PJ-QXS9)

17 Hesketh, A and Hird, M (2009) The golden triangle: how relationships between leaders can leverage more value from people, *Lancaster University Management School* [Online] https://pdfs.semanticscholar.org/1c0c/b4ca509de78a470962ca8854283e0a621bb1.pdf (archived at https://perma.cc/CU5Q-MAAZ)

18 Green, D (2017) The best practices to excel at people analytics, *Journal of Organizational Effectiveness: People and Performance*, **4** (2), pp 137–144

19 Fast Company Staff (2005) Why We Hate HR, *Fast Company* [Online] www.fastcompany.com/53319/why-we-hate-hr (archived at https://perma.cc/BY5N-HCUL)

20 Caglar, D, Couto, V and Trantham, M (2019) HQ 20: The next-generation corporate center, *Strategy + Business* [Online] www.strategy-business.com/article/HQ-2.0-The-Next-Generation-Corporate-Center?gko=3c886 (archived at https://perma.cc/Y9H3-8A5V)

21 Kane, G C *et al* (2019) *The Technology Fallacy: How people are the real key to digital transformation*, MIT Press, MA

2

The age of data and people analytics

We've talked about the context for change with continuing globalization of markets, the technology disruptions that are occurring, and the shifting demographics and changes that have impacted on every organization, whether they are small or large. This is the VUCAR (Volatile, Uncertain, Complex, Ambiguous and Responsive) world of today; we have added an 'R' in VUCA as it's pointless looking at all these challenges unless the organization makes tangible and quick responses to those disruptors.

Those organizations that respond in the quickest and most effective way will have the competitive advantage, albeit for a short period of time. It is a chaotic "new normal" that promises exciting changes for the people functions of tomorrow, but only if they can embrace and utilize the power of data and operate in an agile and strategic way. The age of measurement is here, and we have to be a part of it.

This chapter will cover:

- **Measuring business value**: This looks at what business value embraces, both the tangible and intangible aspects of a business, and how HR decides what to measure and how. We look at the sources of people data and how this is necessitating a shift from reporting to analytics.

- **Data and people analytics in HR**: We look at the changing business demands that are impacting on the way that data runs our lives, and how other industries and functions have made the change to using data. We introduce the principles and scope of analytics in HR.

Measuring business value

As professions mature, they tend to define more consistent standards and metrics that enable professionals to gauge progress and impact. We have learnt to measure everything tangible such as time, weight and space all the way to measuring business value in terms of money and assets, depicted through the financials of a business. Standards such as the Generally Accepted Accounting Principles (GAAP) for finance are established, but stakeholders have realized the fact that gauging long-term business value is more complex than viewing these narrow financials.

This paradox led us to realize that business value is a combination of both tangibles and intangibles (financials and people value). Today, businesses value these intangibles with their own unique metrics and measures that make it difficult to benchmark business performance across an industry. This has brought forward the need to develop standards around measuring these intangibles – and who better to take responsibility for measuring, reporting and analysing the value of these intangibles than the people function?

The 80/20 switch

Over the past three decades, the drivers of value creation for a business have shifted dramatically, from the tangible (machinery, buildings, land and inventory) to intangibles such as people, goodwill and brand recognition. Previously, 80 per cent of this business value could be accounted for on the balance sheet and we knew what to measure – but this ratio has flipped, and now 80 per cent of the business value is off the balance sheet and depicted through the intangibles.[1] This change has encouraged business leaders to actively look for measures to enable them to maximize the effectiveness of these intangibles and how they link to business outcomes.

So, what exactly are these intangibles? A fundamental source is human and consumer value. Experts have categorized human value into human capital deployment, organizational culture and employee wellbeing. Consumer value includes innovation, consumer trust and consumer health,[2] whereas talent has been broadly categorized as human capital, social, reputational (political) and intellectual (business model) capital.[3]

Our view about this intangibles debate can be seen in Figure 2.1. Whilst intangibles can be seen to be a bit of an academic debate, there are some core elements that are common, and this is an important source of people data.

FIGURE 2.1   Measuring intangible value

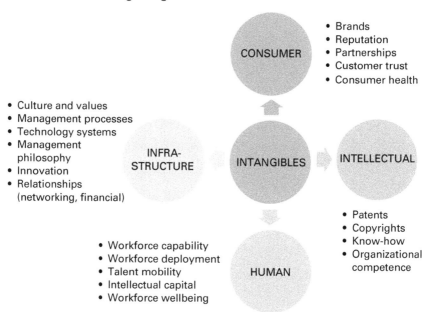

- Culture and values
- Management processes
- Technology systems
- Management philosophy
- Innovation
- Relationships (networking, financial)

CONSUMER
- Brands
- Reputation
- Partnerships
- Customer trust
- Consumer health

INFRA-STRUCTURE

INTANGIBLES

INTELLECTUAL
- Patents
- Copyrights
- Know-how
- Organizational competence

- Workforce capability
- Workforce deployment
- Talent mobility
- Intellectual capital
- Workforce wellbeing

HUMAN

MEASURING THE RETURN ON PEOPLE – IT'S ABOUT INTANGIBLE VALUE

Almost two decades ago, a UK government task force was established to produce a report that would highlight how organizations are measuring human capital. However, this failed to materialize. Human capital measurement refers to the way in which organizations gauge the value created by their people, policies and practices. Some measures may be highly important for one organization, but irrelevant to another.[4] What's more, organizations have their own subjective measures when it comes to more technical metrics such as employee engagement.[5] In addition, too much time is spent mining, cleaning and analysing this data, let alone ensuring the data quality from the orthodox Human Resource Information Systems (HRIS) that HR uses.[6] All this makes it difficult to compare the value of one organization to another.

Businesses still do not have a common way to manage, measure and report on the value of the people dimension of their business. The primary concern is that the cluster of metrics and measures available to capture employee value lack credibility across the rest of the business, as they capture value in terms of cost rather than investment.[7]

The irony is that organizations, large or small, tend to consider their workforce as a cost first and an investment second. These are hidden in the cost of goods sold, and cannot be solely depicted on the balance sheet, and because we are still grappling with human capital standards and measures, we are unable to provide real evidence of the value that people create for a business. The heart of this issue revolves around the following facts:

- HR has traditionally never been a decision science profession;
- human capital measurement comes from accounting, and HR's focus historically has been on cost;
- HR has been mostly asked to measure the workforce through cost and process.

The evolution of HR measurement has revolved around cost – some analytical approaches such as utility analysis, this being a quantitative method that estimates the actual value of benefits generated by an intervention based on the improvement it produces in worker productivity, and then through HR scorecards and metrics.

The old methods of measurement have not been totally discarded, and have been supplemented with new techniques, hence creating a rather complex set of solutions.[8]

HOW HUMAN CAPITAL ADDS VALUE TO ORGANIZATIONS – ISO 30414

The workforce of a company is often one of its largest costs, and measuring the true return on investment in people (RoP) has been challenging. There have been several initiatives to measure and analyse the workforce, but they differ between businesses and countries, making it a challenge to accurately benchmark and be globally relevant. There is no stipulation to report human capital; in accounting there are set standards that are published each year under the International Financial Reporting Standard (IFRS), which prescribes how to account for everything in a business. For HR to establish standards around human capital has been a long drawn-out exercise despite experts highlighting the need for smarter reporting to go beyond financials and provide insights around the long-term value creation of an organization.[9]

One of the recent efforts to "knit" all the value that is created by intangibles of a business has been the introduction of ISO 30414 in human resource management.[10] This looks to synthesize the standards that measure and report on key human capital areas. The report provides many relevant key metrics that are recognized internationally, and is applicable for all types and sizes of organizations. It provides guidance on areas such as culture, recruitment and turnover, productivity, health and safety and leadership.

Organizations are actively aware of the value that human capital brings to the business and are now being encouraged to report on areas of their workforce that will allow organizations to not only measure, monitor, track and understand how well people are being managed and developed, but also allow a more data-driven decision-making approach across all the people practices. By providing many relevant key metrics that are recognized globally, this initiative can be an important first step towards creating a consensus on how businesses really create value through intangibles and how to measure that value in ways that are useful to businesses and investors alike.

Measuring human capital initiates a data-driven approach to identifying effective people management practices, which, if done correctly, can only support the demand for people analytics.

Types of people data

We've talked a lot about people data but what types of data are there in HR to collect? Our research suggests that people data can be categorized into three different levels of sophistication: basic, intermediate and higher.[11]

BASIC LEVEL

This includes the use of existing data to communicate essential information such as absence, accidents, turnover and so on. Reporting this data enables organizations to identify measures towards efficiency and effectiveness, and tackle issues such as absenteeism or improvements in diversity. These basic measures can be divided into hard measures, such as number of training days, and soft measures, such as employee satisfaction.

HR frequently collects these measures so they can report the operational performance of the function itself; however, they are not commonly integrated with the wider business strategy.

INTERMEDIATE LEVEL

This involves designing data collection for specific workforce needs. They tend to be collected in an ad-hoc manner, and are used in a descriptive format to show workforce value to the business, which can lack strategic foresight for the business.

This data can be categorized into five broad categories, such as performance data (eg absence analysis, costing, workforce and organizational performance), demographic data (eg gender, equal opportunity analysis), recruitment and retention data (eg turnover analysis, people costs, sourcing data), training and development data (eg evaluation), and opinion data (eg employee engagement).

HIGHER LEVEL

This includes the collection of both quantitative (financial) data and qualitative (motivations, feelings and opinions research) data by identifying key performance indicators (KPIs) in relation to business strategy and integrating all the collected people data back into the business model. The resulting data is used to advise on strategic choices and further communicate intangible value to a range of audiences through a range of analytical processes.

Outcomes at this level are used to identify drivers for the business, enabling better informed decisions internally and reporting externally on progress in relation to strategy.

WHO IS RESPONSIBLE FOR UNDERSTANDING PEOPLE VALUE?

Experts agree that good-quality people information presented to the board attracts the same degree of interest as financial information.[12] When compared to, say, finance and marketing, HR tends to be unable to link it to business outcomes, and that is where the challenges exist. One of the drawbacks of HR's measures not aligning with organizational objectives is that it highlights how HR does not have an analytical mindset or numerical orientation.

Even then, just reporting numbers without analysing and predicting outcomes will have no real impact. For the HR function to be taken seriously, it should provide not only the predictive analysis, but also the best course of action for the people side of the business, prescription.

From reporting to analytics

There is a misconception that by only reporting human capital, you will then be able to identify and drive forward actionable insights. Research shows that HR spends too much focus on basic reporting tasks such as data mining and data management, to the detriment of analysing this data.

Reporting is about highlighting the current workforce composition and past trends of key HR metrics, through dashboards that may include KPIs for important workforce data. Analytics aims to examine the root cause of a workforce issue, and provides knowledge to mitigate any possible associated risks. Reporting focuses on the past whereas analytics focuses on the future with insights that can influence decision-making.[13] See Figure 2.2.

FIGURE 2.2   Shifting from reporting to analytical insights

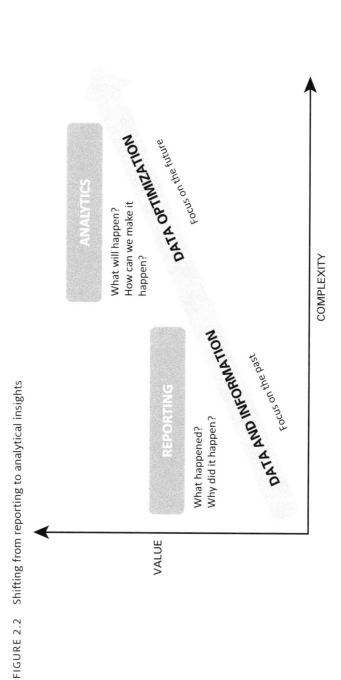

The current HR technology systems are discrete from the business data and tend to disable HR from linking this data with business performance data; this is improving, though. These systems can hinder HR's ability to provide value through providing insights, but we envisage that HR measures and reports this data, with the people function later undertaking diagnosis and analysis.

The people function's role is to focus on linking this data with other business data sources such as marketing, finance, sales and operations. All the collected data can then be linked back through a broader system that gauges the relationship between people, business strategy and performance.

Today in the digital age, everyone is talking about Big Data and analytics and how using them can lead organizations towards productivity and performance gains; and so we move towards the evolution of Big Data and people analytics. Ed Houghton, head of research and people analytics at CIPD, reinforces this stance when he says: "The people analytics dimension and what we do with the data is going to be far more useful to the C-Suite than HR analytics, which tends to be more operational and mainly for the management of the HR operations".

Data and people analytics in HR

The world has witnessed four industrial revolutions to date, all of which stemmed from major technological breakthroughs:

- **Industry 1.0**: the introduction of the steam engine and mechanical machines in the 18th century;

- **Industry 2.0**: the introduction of electric power in the 19th century;

- **Industry 3.0**: the development of computer desktops and the internet in the 20th century;

- **Industry 4.0** (**today**): the interconnectedness of machines, ubiquitous technologies and systems for optimal performance.

Today's businesses are going through a digital evolution and transformation that is happening at great speed. Industry 4.0 is about the adoption of artificial intelligence (AI), automation and machine learning, all of which has, and will, create opportunities to significantly redefine work as we know it. New relationships will emerge across a range of business sectors, such as managers managing interactive machines and machines interactively guiding humans. Manufacturing has gone through some of those changes already, for example in the car industry, but the scope and breadth of change will be immense.

At a consumer level 5G has arrived already and 6G is already being scoped out in parts of the world.[14] The speed of technological change will not stop, and the world of work will continue to evolve and change. However, Industry 5.0[15] is already being talked about, in terms of robots truly making humans work better and faster, and taking that relationship and interaction between people and machines to another level so that real efficiencies and productivity can be materialized out of new methodologies. The term "cobots" is being used, to reiterate the collaborative nature of people in robotic technology.

Each industrial revolution has impacted on the evolution of organizations. Consider the sporting world, for example, where data is now a powerful tool that is a part of every professional sports coaching team toolkit, monitoring everything from diet to distances covered, number of tackles made, number of passes, conversions and so on.

Michael Lewis's Moneyball story[16] identified the power of data and how it could provide a competitive edge. Bill Gerrard, an expert sports scientist reflects on the power of that story.

THOUGHT LEADERSHIP INSIGHT
The Moneyball story

Jeremy Snape, founder and managing director of Sporting Edge, in conversation with Bill Gerrard, professor of business and sports analytics at Leeds University and data analyst at Az Alkmaar Football Club

Bill's principal research focus is sports analytics and the statistical analysis of performance data within an evidence-based coaching regime in both individual and team sports, to support decisions on talent identification, player recruitment and development, training priorities, injury management, team selection and tactics. Bill has worked with a number of elite sports teams around the world. He has also worked with Billy Beane, the General Manager of the Oakland Athletics in Major League Baseball, whose application of sports analytics has been the subject of the Hollywood film and best-selling book, *Moneyball*.

Jeremy Snape, CEO of high-performance consultancy Sporting Edge, interviewed Bill Gerrard about his insights into the world of analytics in sport and how analytics can help create more of a level playing field in the sporting world. Bill's thoughts were as follows:

"The Moneyball story is in essence what I call a case study of a 'David Strategy'. It's an organization that had restricted resources with a small budget, yet it had to compete against financial giants such as the New York Yankees who, at the time the book was written – 2001 and 2002 – were spending three to four times more on players' salaries than the Oakland Athletics. They wanted to be able to compete and chase glory, but they wanted to do it on a sustainable basis and they found the 'David Strategy' that worked for them.

"Their solution was to use data analytics as an input into their recruitment process, so they went out specifically to try and identify talent that was affordable, and importantly talent that the statistics suggested was undervalued, so they could get more for their dollar. Ultimately, as the line in the film says it so well 'the objective is to buy wins, not players', and that is what they did. They went out and used statistics and the available data, and recognized that other teams were allowing conventional judgement and non-analytics-based decisions to dominate their recruitment strategies.

"Oakland were incredibly successful at using data to drive their decision-making. In the 2001 and 2002 seasons they had the second and third lowest salaries, and in both the 2001 and 2002 seasons they had the second-best regular season win percentage. Indeed, in one season, out of hundred and sixty-two games scheduled, they lost one game more than the Yankees did, who had spent about one hundred million dollars more than them.

"It's an incredible case study, but it's one that shows you can use data to try and level the playing field. It doesn't matter whether it's in sports or business – it's using your available resource as efficiently and as effectively as you can, using brains to make up for lack of brawn when you don't have the resource."

Courtesy of SportingEdge: www.sportingedge.com (archived at https://perma.cc/JAX4-SUXZ)

The Moneyball story was so successful because there was a leader, in this instance Billy Beane, who took a risk to use data analytics to help him run his business. It was a combination of the analytics and the conviction of the leader who believed that he could change his organization's fortunes through the insights that the data provided.

From sports to marketing, the power of data has already been embraced, whereas HR has been slower to respond to this revolution. Marketing's change of focus to embrace data has already moved the function to a far more strategic level than ever before. Michael Lieberman has been in marketing analytics for many years, and sees the shift and opportunities that data can bring to HR as significant; so much so that he is now working in both functional areas. His reflections below outline the opportunities and challenges that he sees.

THOUGHT LEADERSHIP INSIGHT
The journey – marketing-based analytics for talent management

Michael D Lieberman, founder and president of Multivariate Solutions,
a research consulting firm

How people analytics helps human resource management
As marketing analytics has revolutionized the field of marketing, and predictive analytics has maximized effective micro-target marketing, people analytics is changing HR. It enables the HR function to:

- make better decisions using data;
- create a business case for HR interventions;
- test the effectiveness of these interventions;
- measure and improve the employee experience;
- quantify employee engagement;
- optimize organizational development.

Today, the majority of HR functions focus on reporting employee data. This doesn't suffice in today's data-driven economy. Analytics are crucial for HR professionals to analyse the vast amount of organizational data to gain tangible insights and drive acquisitions, optimize leadership communication, measure employee effectiveness and make crucial decisions based on data-driven evidence.

Insights into marketing based analytics
Analytics has provided marketing intelligence, and analytical tools can support our clients' growth, efficiency and risk management objectives. Data-driven insights, no matter what industry, begin with the journey's end. One must have an implied analytic path to begin to use analytical tools to make that journey. Start with the end in mind.

Whether we are seeking branding insights, customer choice modelling, seeking the optimal price for a product or service or evaluating employee engagement, keep an eye on the prize. Envision the three to five bullet points the analyst must deliver to the C-Suite, whether they are the CMO, the CEO, or the CHRO. These will be the only output they will read. This "method" mentality will lead organizations to adopt more efficient analytical practices, build a culture of data-driven decisions, and lead the HR industry as a whole to adopt analytical methods into their everyday operations.

All analytics need human eyes

In HR, AI and machine learning are beginning their ascent to the top of the analytics hot topics. However powerful, though, these techniques still need human eyes to analyse and deliver the action plan. Moreover, these techniques do not always outperform older, tested methods that have been in use in HR for a long time, such as the Caliper Profile for sales recruitment or Belbin Team Types to assist team development.

Training for the future people analytics professional

My first piece of advice to any HR practitioner entering the analytics field is to learn basic statistics; the equivalent of an *Introduction to Statistics* college class. I do not necessarily advise the HR analyst to become a professional statistician, but I would expect them to understand that correlation does not indicate causation.

The HR analyst must be able to read a regression analysis (a powerful statistical method that allows you to examine the relationship between two or more variables) output, a time series regression, or the odds-ratio percentage chance of an employee leaving the firm. They must understand what a measure of collaboration means, and basic predictive analytics.

What should they do/not do

The analytics role is only one part of the HR practitioner's role. There are only a finite number of data analyses that can be properly employed in the people analytics space, and these form the core of most day-to-day analytics output. I highly recommend that the people analytics professional becomes familiar with some of the most common techniques used in people analytics, such as metrics, employee churn analytics and so on.

I advise organizations to move away from the classic performance reviews. With modern data capture techniques, it is possible to analyse performance more comprehensively, with less focus on specific parts of a job that might cause employees to alter their behaviour. These sorts of techniques remove some of the "gut feel" workings in a large organization, as it lessens the weight of the opinion of a single manager of an employee's performance and, thus, leads to a feeling of job wellbeing and, usually, improved performance.

Observations: making the change from marketing analytics to the people analytics space

It is important to remember that people are people. Unlike a product, where the analyst's goal is to maximize sales, value, or efficiency of distribution, people analytics works to both enrich and enhance the professional lives of employees as well as making their respective enterprises more efficient, and thus more profitable. Everybody wins.

As outlined, the techniques exist. Understand what the goal of your function is, and then be familiar with the necessary techniques. Do not depend too highly on platforms as the magic bullet to solve all of your HR needs. These can be effective tools, but only as effective as the HR practitioner who is using them. Platforms are a means to an end, not the end in themselves.

www.mvsolution.com (archived at https://perma.cc/2MHM-CM6L)

Michael is reiterating that exploring data is about unlocking business value. Why would HR not want to do that if the function is to progress and move to another level?

People data and analytics

Organizations that have adopted advanced people analytics capabilities experience on average a 25 per cent increase in productivity, alongside a huge rise in recruitment efficiency and a reduction in attrition rates.[17] The CIPD also confirms that, according to their research, using people data leads to improved business performance. People analytics not only helps organizations understand the changing workplace, but also provides insight to drive customer behaviour and engagement and can lead to improved business outcomes. Nevertheless, it is important to understand that a crucial barrier to attaining people analytics excellence and momentum is the absence of a people analytics strategy of any kind, let alone a coherent one that aligns to the business strategy.

What we propose is that the people function should develop a well-thought-out strategy that focuses on what really matters to the overall business, and which should ultimately align with employee actions, behaviours and the culture of the organization. This ensures people analytics can not only enable the business to measure and track progress in relation to the business strategy, but also assist the people function to manage the overall people strategy by prescribing future actions to the board and ultimately reach its strategic business objectives.

There are three terms that are used interchangeably when describing data:

- HR data;
- workforce data;
- people data.

However, they are not necessarily the same.[18] HR data captures and measures the functioning of the HR team and tends to be self-reflective in terms of HR's operational performance. Workforce data encompasses HR, the complete workforce and the increasing automation data sources. People data encompasses HR, the entire workforce data and customer/business insights.

True people analytics encompasses HR, the entire workforce data, and operational and customer-based insights. People analytics should measure and analyse this information and pull it together to improve decision-making and business performance, essentially providing strategic insights for the organization. See Figure 2.3 (adapted from CIPD).[19]

SMART HR 4.0 AND THE PEOPLE FUNCTION

Traditionally HR is responsible for managing all aspects of an employee's lifecycle, from recruitment to retirement or exit. Although the rapid growth of technology and digitalization have enabled HR processes to become more automated, HR is still viewed by many organizations as only playing an operational role. Whilst technology was seen as being the enabler that would cement HR's role in the boardroom, it has led to holding it back due to HR being caught up in the day-to-day operational tasks that are required by some technology infrastructures.

Therefore, our proposition of splitting up the department and letting the people function take the role of people strategy emerges again. Experts have also argued for the concept of Smart Human Resources 4.0 (SHR 4.0) which has emerged as part of the overall Industry 4.0, characterized by digital technologies such as the Internet of Things (IoT), Big Data, analytics, and AI that are powered by increasingly fast networks.[20]

FIGURE 2.3   The scope of data

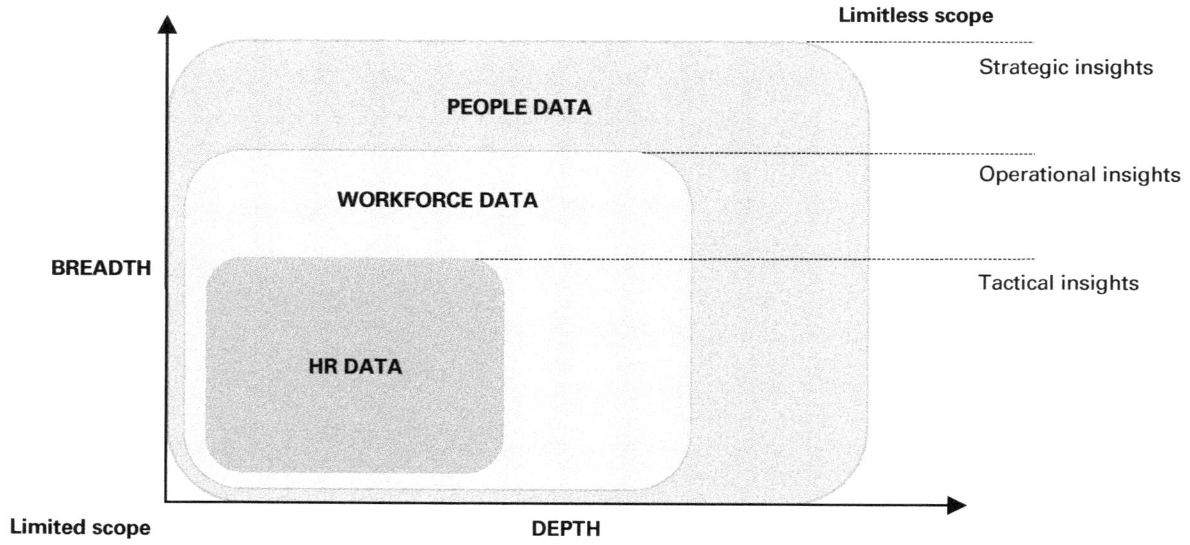

Adapted from CIPD (see note 19 for full reference)

We believe it has the potential to unlock the true functionality of the people function. Nevertheless, HR and its practitioners need to embrace data and numbers more than ever before!

The explosion of data – data becomes big

Today, everything we do creates data and leaves a digital footprint behind us. From our mobile phones to our credit cards, each item in our lives can be precisely tracked back to us. Big data is everywhere with every digital process, system, sensor and mobile device transmitting it.

There are many different categorizations of Big Data but from a simplicity perspective we have focused on IBM's four Vs of Big Data:

- volume (massive amounts of it);
- velocity (speed);
- variety (range);
- veracity (accuracy).

IBM further acknowledges the fact that much of this data is received in an unstructured form.[21] Big data is "the ability to harness information in novel ways to produce useful insights or goods and services of significant value". The above definition translates Big Data as a form of analytics, as it seeks to draw out intelligence from data and translate it into business advantage.[22]

The data we now create is relentless. From simple sensors to smartphones and wearables, the IoT encompasses everything connected to the internet and refers to the ability of these devices to communicate and learn from each other.[23] The total installed base of IoT connected devices is projected to amount to 75.44 billion worldwide by 2025, a five-fold increase over a ten-year period.[24]

By 2025, the data gathered by such devices in the digital universe is expected to reach 175 zettabytes;[25] one zettabyte being equal to one billion terabytes. To put this into perspective, at the end of 2013, we had generated only 4.4 zettabytes of data, and this has grown exponentially since then. Up to 90 per cent of this data will be unstructured and gathered from the IoT. Other non-traditional sources, often termed "dark data",[26] will also become a feature; this is data that is acquired through various computer network operations but not used in any manner to derive insights or for decision-making.

In the broadest sense, analysing most of this untapped data is now possible, and this can assist businesses not only to predict their customers' buying patterns and behaviour, but also assist them in understanding their workforces' needs, motivations and challenges.

Big Data is being exponentially added to by this additional unstructured data, and to extract insights from this complex data, Big Data projects rely on cutting-edge analytics involving data science and machine learning. The veracity of this information is enhanced via computers running sophisticated algorithms that shift through the noise created by Big Data's massive volume, variety and velocity. In the age of technology, gathering insight from this data is a competitive advantage many are grappling with.[27]

Technology and the transformation of the people function

The integration of technology into the core working of the HR function is becoming a crucial challenge for every organization; corporates are looking for that integrated and aligned global system that brings together data and practices in a unified way, whereas small organizations are looking to adopt perhaps their first HR system that will help provide basic automated solutions for their workforce. Wherever your organization is placed on the technology journey, HR technology is the key enabler for new process design that will bring a whole new experience to the workforce across the whole employee lifecycle. Technology drives the Three Es across HR: efficiency, effectiveness and engagement in the people function.

Accordingly, HR and L&D practitioners need to be prepared for the future technological workplace, and that means adopting more of a "customer experience mindset" approach to improving the perception of the solutions that are being offered by the function. That means solutions that need to be user-friendly, engaging, simple and easy to adapt. Using new technology platforms, people practitioners need to bring people and processes together like never before. That will mean that technology-driven change management will become a core capability that needs to be mastered, developed and strengthened by teams, who are capable of leveraging the latest technology that deliver personalized online experiences.

Consequently, HR and L&D practitioners have to develop their own digital literacy and also improve the digital savviness of the workforce to cope with the evolving demands and expectations that will be made of them. Building on this, HR functions can then use analytics to predict and assess everything across the whole employee lifecycle, all driven by the breadth and depth of the data that their technology platforms provide.

THE FUTURE OF AUTOMATION IS HERE

Technology can free HR from the routine and mundane processes such as payroll, responding to employee questions and scheduling recruitment interviews. From there, quality time can be spent on those practices and processes such as organizational design, succession and workforce planning, that are more "value-add" and strategic in terms of shaping the workforce of tomorrow.

Artificial intelligence has the ability to reduce the workload and take the guesswork out of a number of key people practices, such as recruitment.[28] With AI as a part of the process, significant volumes of résumés, CVs and automated application forms can be analysed using key data sources, helping to identify potentially successful candidates. This frees up much of the recruitment team's time, and enables them to focus on interacting with the workforce.

Many organizations are now using 'pulse' surveys to measure how involved their workforce is within the business. Where previously such surveys were conducted by HR and took weeks, sometimes months, to analyse, today they can be facilitated through AI, and the results can be provided to managers and their teams in "real time". AI has the power to create insights from people data both inside and outside the organization, such as Glassdoor, a website where current and former employees can anonymously review their perception of their current/previous organizational experience.

LEARNING AND TECHNOLOGY

Technology has revolutionized learning and development, but there is still much to be done. The future of learning driven by AI technology will embrace:

- Micro-learning that is mobile-first, innovative, well designed, relevant, and on-demand to meet the needs of the workforce.

- Personalized learning driven by the learner's needs that includes nudges, tips, e-learning and so on when the learner wants to learn.

- "Push to pull" learning that is on-demand, with multiple format channels of videos, resources, etc.

- Work to learn, as employees will have to take a lattice approach to learning, namely learn, unlearn, relearn, repeat.

- Decentralization of knowledge and learning, so that information will be open to all, allowing organizations to unlock the speed of knowledge sharing across the business. Knowledge will no longer be power.

- Automated learning as the new normal, as humans will be taught by machines. AI will offer data-driven suggestions to improve worker performance and deliver information when the learner needs it most.

Where previously employees had to attend training events, they can utilize new learning methods to learn "on the go". Digital platforms and online learning solutions are now more tailored to individuals' needs and work demands than ever before. AI will take learning to another level so that workforce capability can be assessed, and then drive personalized recommendations based on individuals' roles, interests and demands.

This leads us to analytics being used in learning, as each employee's progress can be tracked via their own organizational identification number. This can range from the time taken to view the video to the time taken to answer a question; such data can provide insights that were never previously available and help to augment workforce development. There is still more to come though. Josh Bersin's advice is: "Employees (your customers) will not use a fragmented, complicated experience to learn. Completion rates and satisfaction is driven by the elegance and simplicity of the complete learning experience."[29]

In the future, AI will become a priority support tool for most HR functions, especially if talent challenges and the need to demonstrate the value of the people function continues. The big question is whether AI technology will be used in a positive way to assist the whole workforce, or whether it will simply be used to further reduce costs and total headcount numbers.

There's a way to go, HR!

Digital transformation is happening faster than ever before, and the adoption of AI is inevitable. Ultimately, reducing the burden of basic HR tasks will enable HR to become a "tech and touch" profession, technology with a real human touch. Jobs are being redefined due to automation, and we are now looking at ways of how to make work a better place for our people. Technology has allowed us to tap into information that can show us an employee's engagement and productivity level, enabling us to see how this can be improved by making better performance and evidence-based decisions.

Organizations have an abundance of people data, and many know that they need to use that information for improved performance and productivity. Whilst technology is improving all the time, global productivity remains weak, despite the increasing levels of employment being seen globally. The increasing number of jobs that are being created continue to be in relatively low productivity, low-wage jobs.[30]

Whilst most organizations use people data for tactical reporting and core dashboards, much of the data can go relatively unused, leading to missed opportunities to leverage it as a critical enabler of business success. The imperative to boost productivity with informed and insightful people decisions has never been stronger.

Interest in people analytics has been growing on the back of this technology revolution, and HR functions have the ability to generate more people-based data than ever before. Those who are able to leverage that data proactively will be more successful in terms of demonstrating the business value of the function. This means CEOs are now looking to their CPOs/CHROs and their function to lead culture change, manage people strategy and optimize business performance.

FIGURE 2.4   The people practitioner: the impact and relationship connection

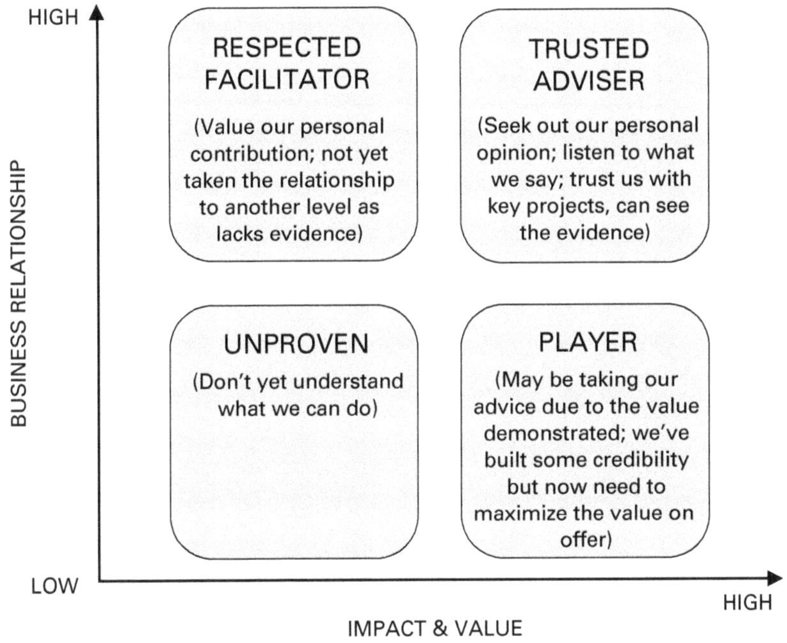

The people practitioner's role as an adviser to the business is crucial, and the focus on data and evidence are crucial to fulfilling the business relationship (see Figure 2.4). The people function has the opportunity to understand, harness and leverage the best insights from using people analytics as a part of their strategic toolkit.[31] This change will not only solidify their status as a business partner, but also guarantee their position as a strategic trusted adviser to the business, through both relationships and evidence of the value that can be demonstrated.

KEY TAKEAWAYS FROM THIS CHAPTER

1 HR has to understand the benefits of what it can do with 'people data' and what it will be able to do with a more data-based business focus. Data reporting in HR has helped, but there are many insights that are not being considered because of a lack of analytical approaches to business challenges.

2 Other sectors and business functions have made the shift to a more data-centric approach. Whilst change can be concerning at times, the focus should be on opportunity, not threat.

3 Data is not going to disappear, and the need for HR to embrace data and what it can prove and tell us will also not disappear. Data is here to stay, and it's a matter of when the shift is made by HR, not if.

4 The explosion of data and technology means that organizations need to make themselves more employee-focused than ever before. People are at the heart of this new approach, with new tools and automated processes being the focus for that change.

5 Technology is a game-changer in terms of how it can change people practices and provide a new experience for the workforce, improving accessibility to information and services that can change the historic perception of the function.

6 The role of a trusted adviser can be reaffirmed through a more evidential data-based approach to people and business problems and challenges.

References

1 Hesketh, A (2014) Managing the value of your talent: a new framework for human capital measurement, *CIPD* [Online] https://www.cipd.co.uk/Images/managing-the-value-of-your-talent-a-new-framework-for-human-capital-measurement_2014_tcm18-9266.pdf (archived at https://perma.cc/GG8U-ZB6P)

2 Blasio, F *et al* (2018) Embankment Project for Inclusive Capitalism, *Coalition for Inclusive Capitalism* [Online] www.epic-value.com/static/epic-report-web-df894ad112b70406d9896c39f853deec.pdf (archived at https://perma.cc/J334-QRNA)

3 Sparrow, P, Cooper, C and Hird, M (2015) *Do We Need HR? Repositioning people management for success*, Palgrave Macmillan, London

4 Robinson, D (2009) Human capital measurement: an approach that works, *Strategic HR Review*, **8** (6), pp 5–11

5 Wright, P M and McMahan, G C (2011) Exploring human capital: putting 'human' back into strategic human resource management, *Human Resource Management Journal*, **21** (2), pp 93–104

6 Bondarouk, T V and Ruel, H J M (2009) Electronic human resource management: challenges in the digital era, *International Journal of Human Resource Management*, **20** (3), pp 505–14

7 Bassi, L, Creelman, D and Lambert, A (2015) Advancing the HR profession: consistent standards in reporting sustainable human capital outcomes, *People and Strategy*, **38** (4), p 71

8 Levenson, A and Fink, A (2017) Human capital analytics: too much data and analysis, not enough models and business insights, *Journal of Organizational Effectiveness: People and Performance*, **4** (2), pp 159–70

9 Bassi, L, Creelman, D and Lambert, A (2015) Advancing the HR profession: consistent standards in reporting sustainable human capital outcomes, *People and Strategy*, **38** (4), p 71

10 ISO (2019) New ISO international standard for human capital reporting, *ISO* [Online] www.iso.org/news/ref2357.html (archived at https://perma.cc/4V7X-T9ML)

11 Torrington, D *et al* (2011) *Human Resource Management*, Pearson, Harlow

12 Robinson, D (2009) Human capital measurement: an approach that works, *Strategic HR Review*, **8** (6), pp 5–11

13 Hill, S and Houghton, E (2018) Getting started with people analytics: a practitioners' guide, *CIPD* [Online] https://www.cipd.co.uk/Images/peope-analytics-guide_tcm18-51569.pdf (archived at https://perma.cc/U5UD-DY4E)

14 University of Oulu (2018) University of Oulu To Begin Ground-breaking 6G Research as Part of Academy of Finland's Flagship Programme, *University of Oulu* [Online] www.oulu.fi/cwc/node/52107 (archived at https://perma.cc/U9MK-D7DB)

15 Universal Robots (2018) Welcome to Industry 5.0: The "Human Touch" Revolution Is Now Under Way, *Universal Robots* [Online] https://info.universal-robots.com/hubfs/Enablers/White%20papers/Welcome%20to%20Industry%205.0_Esben%20%C3%98stergaard.pdf (archived at https://perma.cc/SBA3-SETL)

16 Lewis, M (2004) *Moneyball: The art of winning an unfair game*, W W Norton & Company, New York

17 McKinsey (n d) People Analytics, *McKinsey* [Online] www.mckinsey.com/solutions/orgsolutions/overview/people-analytics (archived at https://perma.cc/A5LV-CWFQ)

18 Khan, N (2019) When it comes to people analytics, terminology matters, *People Management* [Online] www.peoplemanagement.co.uk/voices/comment/people-analytics-terminology-matters (archived at https://perma.cc/K3VP-5LHM)

19 Hill, S and Houghton, E (2018) Getting started with people analytics: a practitioners' guide, *CIPD* [Online] https://www.cipd.co.uk/Images/peope-analytics-guide_tcm18-51569.pdf (archived at https://perma.cc/U5UD-DY4E)

20 Sivathanu, B and Pillai, R (2018) Smart HR 40 – How Industry 40 is Disrupting HR, *Human Resource Management International Digest*, **26** (4), pp 7–11

21 IBM (n d) Big Data Analytics, *IBM* [Online] https://www.ibm.com/analytics/hadoop/big-data-analytics (archived at https://perma.cc/TBK9-PDPK)

22 Mayer-Schönberger, V and Cukier, K (2013) *Big Data: A revolution that will transform how we live, work, and think*, Houghton Mifflin Harcourt, Boston, MA

23 Burgess, M (2018) What is the Internet of Things? *WIRED* [Online] www.wired.co.uk/article/internet-of-things-what-is-explained-iot (archived at https://perma.cc/S3KT-GQCG)

24 Statista (2016) Internet of Things (IoT) connected devices installed base worldwide from 2015 to 2025, *Statista* [Online] www.statista.com/statistics/471264/iot-number-of-connected-devices-worldwide/ (archived at https://perma.cc/K85F-6ART)

25 Patrizio, A (2018) IDC: Expect 175 zettabytes of data worldwide by 2025, *Network World* [Online] www.networkworld.com/article/3325397/idc-expect-175-zettabytes-of-data-worldwide-by-2025.html (archived at https://perma.cc/MGD4-BKG3)

26 Kambies, T *et al* (2017) Dark analytics: illuminating opportunities hidden within unstructured data, *Deloitte* [Online] www2.deloitte.com/insights/us/en/focus/tech-trends/2017/dark-data-analyzing-unstructured-data.html (archived at https://perma.cc/AHS2-4BT7)

27 George, G, Haas, MR and Pentland, A, 2014 Big Data and Management, *Academy of Management Journal*, **57** (2), pp 321–26

28 Guenole, N and Feinzig, S (2018) The Business Case for AI in HR, *IBM* [Online] https://www.ibm.com/downloads/cas/AGKXJX6M (archived at https://perma.cc/VY46-K6JQ)

29 Bersin, J (2019) Learning technology evolves: integrated platforms are arriving, *JoshBersin.com* [Online] https://joshbersin.com/2019/06/learning-technology-evolves-integrated-platforms-are-arriving/ (archived at https://perma.cc/3UY7-83R9)

30 OECD (2019) Low productivity jobs continue to drive employment growth, *OECD* [Online] www.oecd.org/industry/low-productivity-jobs-continue-to-drive-employment-growth.htm (archived at https://perma.cc/UB7B-4BRU)

31 Adams, L (2019) *The HR Change Toolkit*, Practical Inspiration Publishing, London

PART TWO

Making the shift to a data-based approach

3

The commercial HR mindset

Internationally recognized HR thought leader Dr John Sullivan believes that HR has to change its ways. He believes that between 60 and 80 per cent of the average organization's costs is down to people, and yet a lot of HR functions neither understand business nor are able to outline the commercial return from that expense.

We outline what being commercial actually means in the context of an HR/people role, and, more importantly, how you as a people practitioner can develop your capability in this area, as it underpins everything that is needed if you are developing more of a data-driven approach.

This chapter will cover:

- **The need for a strong commercial orientation**: The mindset shift now required is underpinned by a more commercial outlook. We'll describe what being more commercial looks like, as it's the key to all data- and analytics-based activity.

- **Developing your commercial orientation**: This includes a self-assessment framework to assess your own commercial capabilities, which we know are so important to underpinning everything that is involved with data and analytics.

The need for a strong commercial orientation

HR has created this commercial challenge for itself by adopting the Ulrich Model, which requires the identification and development of HR business partners (HRBPs). Within that role comes the responsibility for being much more than just an HR or people expert, and hence the need for commercial/business acumen, has become an issue for the function to address. David

Creelman, CEO of Creelman Research, believes that commercial HR needs to have a positive impact upon the business.

The increasing demand for data- and analytics-based activities has raised the expectation for HR to be more commercial, or just business-smart. Unfortunately, the general feedback is that HR has not stepped up in this area. Korn Ferry's 2017 survey of Chief Human Resource Officers (CHROs) showed that as the function becomes more strategic and high-profile, practitioners needed to step up their game when it comes to business insights and achieving results.[1] When asked which skills or capabilities are most lacking when searching for HR talent for their own teams, the top answer given was commercial/business acumen (41 per cent), followed by the ability to turn strategy into action (28 per cent).

What is commercial orientation?

"Commercial orientation" is the set of skills that enables individuals, departments, functions and teams to deliver excellent performance for an organization, function or business unit so that revenue or sales, profitability and/or cash generation can increase. The impact of achieving this is to increase value, which ultimately will impact on an organization's shareholders or stakeholders.

Over the course of our research into analytics and the impact on the people function, a large number of senior executives reiterated that analytics alone cannot shift the people function to where it wants to be. They see it as a clear differentiating tool that will provide clearer and broader insights into what is happening in the workforce, and the organization as a whole.

The fundamental requirement before embarking on any analytics journey is to ensure that all the HR practitioners understand the importance of having a commercially-orientated mindset. The excellent Corporate Research Forum report *Developing Commercial Acumen for the HR Function*[2] outlined the following qualities that differentiate strong commercially-orientated executives:

- commercial acumen – an orientation or lens through which executives approach problems and situations; the ability to analyse a situation and work out what needs to be done;
- foresight – the ability to anticipate market and competitor trends to see the "big picture" as well as the detail;

FIGURE 3.1   What is commercial orientation?

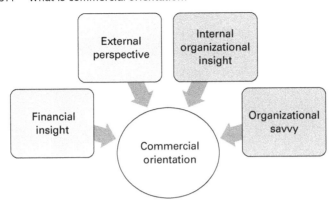

- putting the business first and the function within which you work second;
- a constant emphasis on continuous improvement;
- a firmness of purpose, resilience and follow-through once decisions have been made;
- the ability to persuade others that the proposed actions are "right".

Our research from interviewing a range of HR and commercial business leaders is that there are four themes that underpin commercial orientation. See Figure 3.1.

FINANCIAL INSIGHT

This is about having a comprehensive appreciation of what drives profitability and cash flow in your business, by understanding cash management and the various elements of the organization's balance sheet. This must be backed up with an understanding of current/future financial stability requirements including past/future challenges and what impact people-based costs will have upon income, productivity and so on. Additionally, there needs to be a clear view of and opinion about the whole range of risks that can impact on the organization's ability to achieve its desired performance levels.

This is not about becoming a financial accountant, but about really understanding the organization's costs, profit margins and income streams, and applying this knowledge in your daily interactions with business leaders. This is fundamental to the mindset shift that is required when applying some of the principles associated with data and analytics that will be explored throughout this book.

EXTERNAL PERSPECTIVE

This means having a clear understanding of the external environment, the activities of your competitors and the sector in which your organization is based (the issues, opportunities, risks, legal changes that may occur and so on) that are happening or are expected to happen externally. It will require an understanding of the rationale behind your competitors' strategies, and may include some form of "best practices" evaluation or even some short-term benchmarking. It's important to know the similarities and differences between your own organization and your competitors/peers.

Try to work with other functions in your organization and obtain their insights on competitors and the marketplace. These will be invaluable when you are trying to forecast the implications of implementing any type of change in your organization.

INTERNAL ORGANIZATIONAL INSIGHT

This is about understanding the organization you work for (eg critical inter-dependencies across functions, business strategy, the culture, desired out-comes, KPIs and so on). That will drive a clear appreciation of top management's strategic agenda.

Additionally, you need to truly understand your organization's products, services and solutions, as well as understanding your external customers (how do they buy solutions, what is the desired customer experience, etc). This area is about investigating and diagnosing business issues based on a knowledge of the broader organizational agenda.

ORGANIZATIONAL SAVVY

This is about knowing how things get done in your organization and being mindful of its written and unwritten rules. You should understand how power and influence works across your organization. You will need to build your network so that you become more of a known quantity to senior management, and can access information and people when required. It will also help you understand the politics that exist across the organization.

One key issue for HR has been the need to challenge the business when necessary, and this can only happen successfully when you are mindful of the organizational dynamics and the level of diplomacy that may be required to execute any change or process.

LEARNING SCENARIO
Being commercial

The business request

I was briefing an HR Director and one of their HRBPs on an employee engagement session that I was running for their executive team. The meeting was interrupted by the VP of Business Development, who had an urgent request that he wanted to discuss. I offered to leave, but that wasn't deemed necessary.

The VP went on to request that 1,100 sales people in the organization urgently needed some sales training; he suggested two days' training minimum. The rationale was that sales results were not growing as required, and their asset turnover ratio (which I knew from previous sales forces I had worked with was net sales/revenues as a percentage of total assets) was weak. The VP had put aside a $1.1m investment for the programme.

The HRD and HRBP asked some questions about the state of the actual sales results to budget, and the reason behind the degree of urgency. The VP was under immense pressure to deliver the budget for that year. The final question asked by HR was: "When do you want it delivered?", "Within the next six weeks," was the answer – which wasn't challenged!

After the VP left the room, the HR Director asked me what I thought. My observations were as follows:

1 What was the usual asset turnover ratio for their sector? The HR team wasn't clear about what this ratio was, or indeed their organization's performance in their sector.

2 How much incremental revenue was the VP prepared to commit to over the next two years to create an acceptable return on investment for the training programme?

3 How was sales effectiveness actually measured in their organization?

4 How much was going to be invested in this programme? The figure of $1.1m quoted by the VP was incorrect. Based on the sales figures, the daily average salesperson revenue per day was $6,000. Therefore, training 1,100 salespeople over two days = 2,200 days × $6,000 = $13.2m of missed sales opportunities. The investment for this training was therefore $1.1m + $13.2m = $14.3m (a bit different).

My overall observations were that the request was not fully thought through, that something didn't seem right about the request, and that the evidence for the training requirement seemed circumstantial and weak.

The outcome

The HR Director spoke to Finance, and investigated the sales force performance figures in more detail. They revealed inconsistencies that didn't suggest a broad sales capability issue. The asset turnover ratio for the organization was 32 per cent higher than its largest competitor! Further conversations were held with the VP, and a diagnosis of training needs was quickly instigated as a pilot to ascertain what, if any, were the issues here.

The underlying problem wasn't the sales force, but the sales managers and the way they were being managed to achieve their results. As a result, a different solution was implemented.

The commercial orientation learnings

1   The HR Director and HRBP didn't understand the metrics that were used to measure sales forces (weak financial insight).

2   They forgot that time is money; a fact that most organizations ignore and write off, when this is a crucial basic tool that can drive all sorts of different valuable cost-based insights (weak financial insight).

3   They had no appreciation of their sector's performance in the sales environment (weak external perspective).

4   They didn't ask the relevant commercial questions to truly understand the underlying business issues (weak internal organizational insight).

5   They committed to delivering the requested solution, without sufficient diagnosis or challenge (misdirected organizational savvy).

www.hrcurator.com (archived at https://perma.cc/WPA4-ANNL)

Relationship development

Understanding the different types of relationships that you as an HR practitioner will have to develop will ensure that your commercial credibility is developed and maintained, especially once you start to use data and analytics more with your clients.

The Four As model (see Figure 3.2) can remind you of the different "players" across the organization:

FIGURE 3.2   The relationship model – the Four As

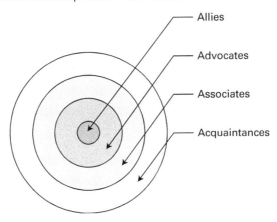

- **Allies:** You are aiming for all of your clients and connections to become your allies or receptive to your work, your ideas, insights and way of working.

- **Advocates:** Ideally you would like clients and colleagues to be advocates of you and your capability in the world of HR so that your reputation is reinforced by them across the organization.

- **Associates:** Your associates are your colleagues in the HR community, and it is crucial that you build effective working relationships across the function, especially as you learn about how to apply data and analytics in the new world of HR. Breaking down the silos across the people function is crucial to overall success to ensure that a consistent message is being communicated, whether it is coming from talent acquisition, learning and development (L&D), or elsewhere.

- **Acquaintances:** Your wider acquaintances are important, especially if they have the skills and capabilities that you may need them to help you develop, such as analytical skills, data interpretation, numbers-based calculations, and so on.

Commercial orientation in government and not-for-profit (NFP) sectors

Looking outside the commercial business world, it is also relevant to talk about commerciality in the way that HR operates; the focus here is more on value creation. A trend over the past decade has been to seek ways of introducing commercial methods into government and NFP organizations, all aimed at providing greater "value for money".

In government and NFP organizations, there is an aspect that is different from commercial businesses. Commercial organizations are looking to broadly meet the needs of two sets of stakeholders, customers and shareholders, whereas government and NFP are explicitly answerable to a much wider variety of stakeholders, and operate in an environment where the marketplace is highly disjointed.

The principles and awareness required to be more commercially-orientated remain as important irrespective of where your organization operates. The critical element is that building this capability will ensure that you as an HR practitioner will be able to share a view about any business or organizational issue, rather than being just people-centric – that is a critical differentiator in building your credibility.

What about being strategic?

For years the people function has sought to be "strategic" – but is that achievable? After all, who in any organization is strategic every day? Our preference would be for the people function to focus on being commercial, as that's a 365-day-a-year challenge, and has immediate impact on business outcomes.

Once that can be demonstrated, then guess what – as if by magic, you then seem to be regarded as being strategic! That's the reason why people analytics is so important, if we are to be taken seriously as a function that can make an impact on the bottom line.

Demonstrating commercial orientation

As can be seen, it's crucial to the future of the profession that the people function talks commerciality in everything it does; the focus is more on value creation and hence the increasing demand for numerical/evidence-based insight. That means that some key aspects of how the function behaves need to be demonstrated to the business – the Six Cs (see Figure 3.3):

1 **Curiosity**: It's vital that HR practitioners are constantly curious about the business in which they are employed. The people function needs to be able to give a comprehensive synopsis of the business environment within which the organization operates, and be able to focus on those aspects that drive competitive advantage. A comprehensive understanding of the business and its challenges will also enable appropriate prioritization when it comes to determining where best to invest in the people function.

2 **Credibility:** Every HR practitioner needs to be financially-literate; this drives true business credibility in the eyes of senior executives and leaders. That means being able to interpret financial statements, financial terminology and the financial indicators that drive organizational outcomes. The key is to be known as a colleague who can "add value" whatever subject is being talked about and whatever decision is being made.

3 **Confidence:** The shift to a more data- and evidence-based outcome approach requires confidence across the people function to make it happen; after all, not every number or analysis project will reveal an insight. However, the people function does need to demonstrate that it is "on top of the numbers". This means being very conversant with the KPIs or "people metrics" that are used to determine the success or failure of a section, team and department. Measuring performance against KPIs, especially in the form of ratios, provides the evidence to highlight strengths and weaknesses. This requires the confidence to not only interpret the data but also to challenge and question the business about the observations identified.

4 **Courage:** The people function needs to be continually focusing on generating, evaluating and then implementing new and better ways of working, especially with the increasing demand for automation. This means having the courage and bravery to identify performance improvement opportunities and different ways of doing things – not just within the people function.

5 **Connected:** Being collaborative is important in bringing together different functions, ideas and leaders. This is where interpersonal skills – influencing, presenting, negotiating, leading, facilitating – are as important as the "hard" skills around finance and numeracy. Indeed, one of the hallmarks of commerciality is a firmness of purpose, a tough-mindedness to make things happen, to seize the initiative and to take difficult decisions when needed. The head needs to rule the heart in telling colleagues and direct reports what they need to hear, not what they want to hear.

6 **Capability:** Continuous development of capabilities is becoming more important across the whole workforce, and the HR practitioner is no exception. Apart from improving financial understanding, there are several other important topics such as having a good grasp of business strategy and how it is formed, being conversant with operational effectiveness techniques, knowing what process improvement is about and keeping up to date with the continual technological advancements that change almost on a daily basis. High performers never stop learning![3]

FIGURE 3.3   The commercial HR practitioner – the Six Cs

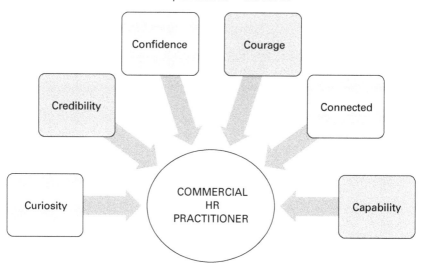

Developing your commercial orientation

Your commercial orientation capabilities

As we have discussed, commerciality is crucial to the future of the profession and underpins the data and analytics-based approach that is being advocated here. Courtesy, again, of Corporate Research Forum, Table 3.1 provides a self-assessment checklist that will enable you to assess the extent to which you have the commercial mindset required to act effectively in a people practitioner role.

TABLE 3.1   Commercial orientation self-assessment

Commercial orientation self-assessment	DISAGREE								AGREE	
	1	2	3	4	5	6	7	8	9	10
FINANCIAL INSIGHT										
1 I know what income statements, cash flow statements and balance sheets are all about.										
2 I know the meaning of important financial terms such as cash flow, earnings, EBITDA, equity, net present value (NPV), operating profit and working capital.										

TABLE 3.1   *continued*

	Commercial orientation self-assessment	DISAGREE									AGREE
		1	2	3	4	5	6	7	8	9	10
3	I have a working knowledge of the financial performance indicators that my business concentrates on; for example, days sales outstanding, operating margin, return on capital employed and total shareholder return.										
4	I immerse myself in the figures so I really know what is going on in my business/ function.										
5	I make an active contribution when our business and financial performance is being reviewed.										
6	I have prepared budgets and financial forecasts.										
7	I'm able to prepare a business case for a longer-term project (for example, recruiting additional staff for a new activity) using, if necessary, project appraisal measures like net present value (NPV) and the internal rate of return (IRR).										
8	If my business unit/business is a quoted company (one with a stock market listing), I watch the trends in our share price and read analyst reports to gain a more informed view of our performance and prospects.										
9	I can comment on the strengths and weaknesses in our latest set of financial results.										
10	I have attended formal training/learning programmes relating to financial skills.										
	EXTERNAL PERSPECTIVE										
11	I read the business press regularly to keep up to date with the latest news and developments.										
12	I am curious. I devote time to learning about business by reading journals like the *Harvard Business Review*, doing research and networking.										

TABLE 3.1   *continued*

	Commercial orientation self-assessment	DISAGREE									AGREE
		1	2	3	4	5	6	7	8	9	10
13	I am very familiar with the competitive environment within which my business operates including the political, economic, social, technological, legal and environmental trends which affect our activities.										
14	I can comment on the strengths and weaknesses of our competitors and the ways in which we achieve competitive advantage.										
15	I am clear about the ways in which the business I work for makes money.										
16	I am able to discuss our latest financial results and to assess the impact of a competitor's new product launch.										
17	I read the most important parts of our Annual Report (such as the Chief Executive's Review) to gain a greater insight into our commercial objectives and business strategy.										
18	I am aware of our competitors' strategies and approaches to drive their success.										
19	I can clearly differentiate between my organization's business and people strategies and those of our strongest competitors.										
20	I have a clear view of how to capitalize on our competitors' weaknesses when it comes to people strategies and tactics.										
	INTERNAL ORGANIZATIONAL INSIGHT										
21	I have a good working knowledge of the core products and services my business markets and sells.										
22	I fully understand what other functions do in my business and how they fit together.										
23	I have been fully involved in implementing a strategy for a business unit (an activity with full profit and loss accountability).										
24	I have lots of ideas about the ways in which my business and/or function can make more money and operate more efficiently.										

TABLE 3.1   *continued*

Commercial orientation self-assessment	DISAGREE							AGREE		
	1	2	3	4	5	6	7	8	9	10
25 I have a good working knowledge of the business plan for my business or function.										
26 I'm an active strategic thinker, with views and insights about the strategy that my business or function is or is not following.										
27 I am very familiar with important process improvement techniques such as lean thinking, six sigma, process mapping, cause-and-effect diagrams, flowcharting and design thinking.										
28 I have a working knowledge of important project management tools such as critical path analysis, work breakdown structures and responsibility charting.										
29 I know all about my business' approach to risk management and, when necessary, put it into practice in my discipline.										
30 I have held a key role in a range of significant change management projects (eg relocating facilities to another country, mergers and acquisitions, restructuring of a business).										
ORGANIZATIONAL SAVVY										
31 In conversations and meetings with colleagues, I seek to identify the benefits and costs of particular options before arriving at decisions.										
32 I have been instrumental in the past in taking 'tough' decisions in the best interests of my business and/or function.										
33 I know how to make things happen with a clear focus on achieving agreed business objectives.										
34 I know that I'm resilient enough to cope with the ups and downs of organizational life.										

TABLE 3.1   *continued*

| | Commercial orientation self-assessment | DISAGREE | | | | | | | | | AGREE |
		1	2	3	4	5	6	7	8	9	10
35	I have a comprehensive network and regular connections with my colleagues in other functions.										
36	I am confidently able to challenge senior leaders when I believe their views and decisions are inappropriate for that business situation.										
37	I regularly undertake stakeholder mapping to consider how to establish even stronger relationships with senior leaders and key influencers.										
38	I know how to operate effectively with all the different leadership styles and demands that exist in my business area.										
39	I feel able to prepare a longer-term business plan for my business or functional area, taking into account all the different interests and points of view that exist.										
40	I can operate effectively despite the internal politics that exist.										

The checklist is not definitive, but is designed to help you:

- highlight your own L&D priorities;
- identify gaps in your business expertise;
- provide advice to colleagues who wish to improve their commercial skills;
- prepare a learning needs analysis for your business.

COMPLETING THE CHECKLIST

Please score each statement on the 1–10 scale by ticking the box that corresponds to the relevant number. '1' indicates that you disagree with the statement concerned. '5' indicates some agreement. '10' indicates total agreement. It is important to be honest so that your profile is accurate!

If, for any reason, a statement is not applicable to you, or you don't know, don't score that particular statement. Move on to the next statement.

Scoring your self-assessment responses

The maximum score for each section of the checklist is shown in Table 3.2. You can put your own score next to the maximum, and then calculate your percentage score. For example, the maximum score for 'Financial insight' is 100 points. If you score 65 points, then your percentage score is 65 per cent.

TABLE 3.2   Scoring your responses

Commercial orientation criteria	Your score	Maximum score	Your percentage score
Financial insight		100 points	
External perspective		100 points	
Internal organizational insight		100 points	
Organizational savvy		100 points	
OVERALL SCORE		**400 points**	

Interpreting your scores

For each part of the Checklist, **a score above 75 per cent** indicates that you are in excellent shape. It is now a question of making sure that you continue to develop your commercial skills, for example, by seeking additional responsibilities.

Scores between 50 and 75 per cent indicate that there are important gaps in your commercial skillset. You might consider preparing an L&D plan to address the filling of the gaps sooner rather than later.

Scores below 50 per cent suggest that, in that particular area, your commercial skills may be significantly underdeveloped. If you wish to follow a career in the people function, with increasing levels of responsibility, it may be appropriate to prepare a career plan so you can take practical steps to improve your overall commercial orientation.

www.crforum.co.uk (archived at https://perma.cc/R2RG-TBCR)

Developing your commercial orientation

The most effective development of commercial orientation really takes place on the job and in a real-time context. Hands-on experience is important, but organizations may be reluctant to place an inexperienced person in a position of full commercial responsibility. Experience can be built up gradually over time, perhaps by assigning ownership of a project at the outset, and then over time gradually increasing their responsibility as they move through different functions.

Here are some tips for improving, growing, building and/or developing this capability that have supported development across a range of organizations.

ASSUME P&L RESPONSIBILITY FOR A BUSINESS AREA

This is the best way of developing commercial experience, but may only be practicable for a small number of HR people within the organization who have the potential to progress to general management.

This involves being responsible for both revenue and expenditure and being focused on the "expenditure" side of the P&L. It also gives people practitioners the opportunity to set objectives and budgets and to manage to plan, reforecasting as necessary.

PROJECTS OR ASSIGNMENTS

Projects, assignments or secondments to other parts of the business can be effective in building experience of key skills such as budgeting, forecasting, objective setting and performance improvement, and developing an understanding of how other functions work, all of which will help to broaden an understanding of the business. The key element is the means by which the commercial benefits are delivered, not an obsession with 'delivery on time'.

PREPARE AND DELIVER A BUSINESS CASE OR PROJECT PLAN

This offers the experience of putting together a business case, obtaining funding for projects, and managing a budget as well as influencing senior management to achieve buy-in for ideas.

GET INVOLVED IN AN ACQUISITION OR DISPOSAL

Acquisitions or disposals offer many opportunities to get involved in commercial activities, from due diligence through to integration. Assigning responsibility for delivering the potential business improvements or efficiency gains identified during due diligence can help sharpen commercial skills.

For HR, outsourcing projects or post-acquisition integration projects provide excellent opportunities to develop skills such as how to evaluate a business, reduce costs and improve service standards.

EXPERIENCE IN A LINE MANAGER ROLE

People practitioners can enhance their commercial experience and credibility by taking on a line manager role for part of their career. This provides exposure to the dilemmas and trade-offs involved in running a business. The other benefit is that exposure to customers will be a part of the line manager role. This could be through attending sales visits, or being given relationship management responsibility for a particular customer.

This can help develop an understanding of who the organization's customers are, their needs, and the profitability of different customer groups. Some organizations also get key customers involved in training.

TRAINING AND SIMULATIONS

Many of the knowledge-based aspects of commercial awareness such as interpreting financial statements and ratios and selecting and applying diagnostic models can be learnt through training interventions. However, a large part of commercial acumen is about developing the right sort of mindset and attitudes, and training is unlikely to be totally sufficient to shift this as it's all about applying any new learning in real-life situations. How about working with the Finance team for a couple of days to understand the methods and application of financial analysis?

Linked to this, some organizations use off-the-shelf business simulations to assess the commercial capability of people practitioners. Alternately, in-house commercial business managers can lead people through case studies or scenarios which reflect the types of dilemmas, choices and consequences faced by commercial managers in real-life scenarios.

FINANCE BRIEFING

In some organizations as a part of the onboarding process into HR, quality time is spent with the Finance function to understand the business metrics of the business areas that the people practitioner is responsible for.

EXTERNAL PERSPECTIVE

Read the business sections of the press, such as the *Financial Times*. Quality journals such as the *Economist*, *European Business Review*, *Forbes* and *Harvard Business Review* are also good information sources. Remember that high-performing people practitioners are able to express a view about all business issues, not just those on the people agenda.

ANALYTICS-BASED TARGETS

Finally, if you are already on the people analytics journey then set a target in terms of the income generated, costs saved etc that your analytical interventions have identified, therefore demonstrating real commercial benefits for HR and the organization as a whole.

This isn't an exhaustive list, but as you can see, it's about growing an exposure to commercial situations that will enable the people practitioner to operate more effectively with their internal client by talking the language of the organization, rather than being obsessed with "HR speak". Coaching and ongoing mentoring will always be helpful as a support to any development that you decide to undertake.

The analytics agenda will ensure a more commercial perspective, but it will not enable the function to make the necessary transition on its own. It needs to be supported by a mindset that is naturally thinking "business first, people a very close second"!

KEY TAKEAWAYS FROM THIS CHAPTER

1   The people function has to focus on developing more of a commercial mindset that embraces the financial challenges of the organization. Do this and the business may start to perceive the function to having something to say in the strategic conversations that occur. Aspiring to "being strategic" isn't enough any more, and the function hasn't successfully made that shift over the past 20 years or so!

2   The commercial HR practitioner needs to be driven by the Six Cs (curiosity, credibility, confidence, courage, connected and capability) – these characteristics will underpin a more evidence-based practitioner that is focused on value creation for the organization they work for.

3   Shifting to a commercial mindset won't happen by itself; the self-assessment diagnostic is designed to make you consider what changes you need to make to become more commercially-orientated in the HR function.

4   The commercial mindset is at the heart of a data-driven approach as it is driven by business, numbers and an external perspective that will build credibility with internal clients/customers.

References

1   Korn Ferry (2017) HR heal thyself – Korn Ferry CHRO survey reveals serious gaps in HR talent including low business IQ, *Korn Ferry* [Online] https://ir. kornferry.com/news-releases/news-release-details/hr-heal-thyself-korn-ferry-chro-survey-reveals-serious-gaps-hr (archived at https://perma.cc/7E3J-BSLN)

2   Pillans, G and Kind, J (2013) *Developing Commercial Acumen for the HR Function*, Corporate Research Forum report, London

3   Chamorro-Premuzic, T (2018) Take control of your learning at work, *Harvard Business Review* [Online] https://hbr.org/2018/07/take-control-of-your-learning-at-work (archived at https://perma.cc/J7H2-QQB2)

4

Developing new ways of working

Having outlined the factors that are impacting on the need for the change and the necessity of becoming more commercially-orientated, we outline our thoughts about the infrastructure changes that have to be made. This relates to the way that the function operates, and what that means for the new people practitioner of today and tomorrow. This is all driven by data and more of an evidence-based approach that will change the focus moving forward.

This chapter will cover:

- **The people function structure**: We'll outline our thoughts on the change that needs to be considered in terms of priorities and the shift from being a Service Station to a Power Station.

- **The new people practitioner driven by data and technology**: We'll discuss what historical data has told us about HR capability, and what the new people practitioner competencies and demands will be, all driven by data and the ever-evolving technology that is impacting on HR at great speed.

The people function structure

HR in organizations today is the result of an age when the function needed to engage with employees across the whole lifecycle as they focused on producing outcomes that were the result of clearly defined, stable processes and procedures.

Time to undertake organizational design activity on the people function

The world of work has significantly changed, and yet the structures of most HR functions have not really evolved since 1997, when the Ulrich Model introduced the idea of shifting HR from an administrative role to a more strategic one.[1] Our contention is that HR is no more strategic now than it was in 1997. It has also struggled to adopt a more commercial focus, as outlined previously, which would have made a greater connection to the executive and business imperatives that need to be proactively delivered.

The problem may not lie with the model, but the way in which the HR profession implemented it. It seemed that rebadging the HR team as "business partners", building a service centre, throwing in some technology and calling it an HR transformation would deliver a new HR operating model. But the model was not meant to be cut and pasted into an organization without fulfilling due diligence, organizational and job design activity to ensure that an aligned business focused solution was created.

The core principles of organizational design, whichever model you use, have always revolved around ten areas that need to be comprehensively explored:

1 What is the strategic aspiration of the function that is being reviewed?

2 What data is available to help understand the current and possible future state of the function being reviewed? If data isn't available, then obtain some from a wide range of stakeholders, employees and leaders/managers.

3 What framework to create a revised or new function is going to be used, and why?

4 How does this framework complement the organization's operating model?

5 Which aspects are being reviewed? They should include structure, processes, jobs and people requirements.

6 What new talent demands are required to implement the change successfully? Change is always likely to bring skills gaps, so ensure that these are anticipated as part of the process.

7 What mindset shifts are required to ensure that the change is implemented successfully? In the HR/people world, this could be, for example, embracing, not fearing, measurement and the use of data to support change.

8 What metrics and measurements need to be put in place to measure the change, and ultimately the success of the change?

9 How will leaders at all levels be aligned in their behaviour to support the change and ensure consistency and transparency in their

communication of key messages associated with the change, both before, during and after the change process?

10 What are the risks associated with the change and how will this be managed and facilitated by leaders and key stakeholders?

A quick restructure of moving accountabilities and responsibilities is likely to fail, as this is merely "shifting the deckchairs on the Titanic". At the last structural change of the HR function that was undertaken, how many of these questions were comprehensively addressed? We'll leave you to consider how to revisit some of the gaps.

Creating value as a people function

The goal of the people function today will be to enable the development of a value-creating ecosystem, a shift that is a major change from "servicing" the employee lifecycle. This will be driven by technology, changing employee expectations and an increasing value creation focus, and hence the increased emphasis upon using data and analytics to demonstrate value.

Nalin Miglani outlined a matrix-based model to consider the technology vs value dilemma when considering strategic and operational changes.[2] The model is outlined in Figure 4.1.

FIGURE 4.1   Technology vs value-add matrix

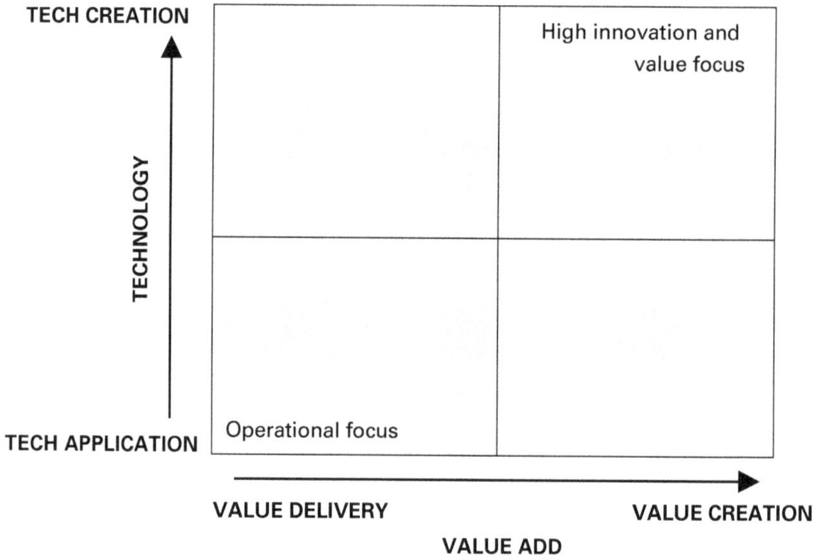

Adapted from Miglani, 2017

Some examples of how future changes could impact on the people function in terms of technology and "value add" are shown in Figure 4.2. This reflects some possible ways of categorizing challenges for the function, in this instance reclassifying work, networks and reshaping HR.

These templates provide a means of prioritization that have historically been obtained via:

- design thinking techniques such as journey mapping and storyboarding;
- stakeholder interviews;
- focus groups with key employee and functional groups.

How the people function evolves will be dependent upon the ability to clearly demonstrate a clear value to the business. This is why the clamour for analytics is growing.

From our experience of previous change-based transformations of people functions, below are some key questions to consider when reviewing current structures:

- What is at the core of creating value in your organization?
- How well does your organization create or apply technology?
- Where are the pools of talent that your organization needs to access?
- How do you create partnerships that enable your organization to access talent and create a competitive advantage?
- What are the forces of change in your industry over the next six months, 12 months, two years and five years?
- What are your competitors doing when it comes to new/refined products or solutions?
- What impact are these changes having on workforce capability demands (quantity and quality)?
- How can senior leadership anticipate these changes so that they are well prepared both offensively and defensively?
- What partners and vendors can support you in addressing the future of work challenges?
- Where are your business-critical roles? What financial value do they generate?
- What is your differentiation strategy when it comes to pay and performance-related incentives?
- What is your current organizational design process?

FIGURE 4.2 Transforming HR – some technology vs value-add examples

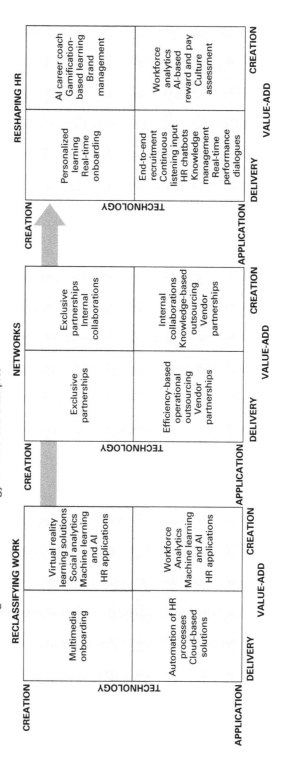

Adapted from Miglani, 2017

- What opportunities exist in the operationally-based function of HR to introduce or expand technological solutions as a way of increasing efficiency and improving productivity?

Is your people function a Service Station or a Power Station?

Currently HR seems to accept being a Service Station, a function that people can call on when they want or have a specific need. That's fine, but if the aspiration is to be more strategic/commercial, then that approach ensures HR will always fall into the operational support category.

The people function needs to move to being a Power Station (see Figure 4.3) – a function that (whilst not always high-profile) is a core necessity of life and is truly appreciated because of that fact. Consider the uproar when power cuts occur!

FIGURE 4.3   The people function as a Power Station

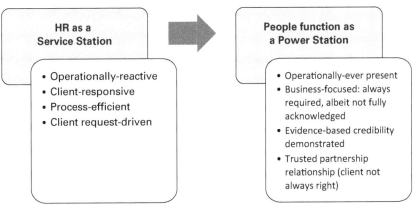

People functions become Power Stations when they are truly business-focused, share accountability for performance with line management and leaders, and focus on both the short and long term efficiency and productivity agenda. They are a consistent partner whose views, opinions, insights and challenges are consistently sought out because they are perceived to be an "added value" collaborator with the business.

They are proactive and focused on continuous improvement that focuses on tangible bottom-line improvements, growth or significant cost inefficiencies, all of which are underpinned by a robust business planning process that is stretching the boundaries and expectations of the business. Finally, the whole focus is upon delivering value to the internal and external customer.

All of these elements have an inbuilt futureproofing approach to ensure that their solutions remain fit for purpose, and that means that data- and analytics-based insights are a critical element of demonstrating the evidence that builds credibility with their internal clients. See Table 4.1.

TABLE 4.1   Service Station vs Power Station

Service Station (HR function)	Power Station (people function)
Informed: Told about decisions and expected to implement the people implications.	**Consulted**: Brought into business conversations and decisions because they are perceived to be adding value with their insight and opinions.
Reactive: Responds to situation and crises as they occur.	**Proactive**: Formulates plans/programmes to help the organization achieve its future business plans and goals, before being asked.
Tactical: Executes processes and task requirements.	**Strategic**: Creates goal-based programmes and initiatives that are focused on added value and measurement of value to the business.
Traditional: Works within the boundaries of traditional HR practices.	**Futureproof**: Takes a wider view of business issues and challenges (objectives, competitive landscape and financial goals) and identifies people-based solutions that are focused on problem resolution and add value.

The change journey that HR has been on has been slow, and two of the barriers to HR realizing its full potential are specifically related to recruitment-based issues. There is a perception among business leaders that HR is slow to change, with talent development and recruiting at the bottom of the list at a time when business is changing at such a rapid pace.

Additionally, organizations are seeking employees with high-level digital skills so they can make the most of opportunities around data analytics, AI, and automation. However, just 41 per cent of HR practitioners express concern about having enough people with the right high-level digital skills, compared to 54 per cent of all business executives. Similarly, 56 per cent of executives want more people versed in digital business models, but only 46 per cent of HR practitioners see that as a pressing need.[3]

This suggests a lack of agreement about the business challenges that executives see and how HR recognizes the urgency for action. It needs to get closer to the business leaders to truly understand their concerns, perhaps challenge them on their perception, and certainly create a plan of action to ensure that the function is proactively on board with a clear way forward.

The HR dilemma isn't an easy one. A clear commercial outcomes focus means that the label of being "strategic" or "commercial" will be irrelevant, because the people function will have demonstrated through data and analytics how they add value. This is something that we all aspire to, and something that a Power Station-type mentality can provide.

The new people practitioner (driven by data and technology)

Having outlined the digital world of work and the people challenges that emerge, it is important to understand the need for a different mindset in terms of profit, growth and productivity, rather than just focusing on cost management. That's what a lot of senior leaders would regard as being strategic.

The capability required by the people practitioner of the future needs to be considered against the backdrop of speed, transformation change and changing talent management requirements.

What does the data say about current HR capability?

Whilst there are a significant number of views and opinions about the capability of the HR practitioner, there isn't a wide range of published assessment data. The most comprehensive study of HR and learning and development practitioner capability was undertaken over six years between 2012 and 2018 by IBM Kenexa.[4] An overview was shared in 2014 by IBM, *Building a Smarter Human Resources Function*, but data collection continued after that published report.

The data focused on three areas:

- HR effectiveness: the views of HR and their stakeholders about the solutions provided by the function;

- HR capability: the acquired behaviours, knowledge and work experiences that an individual possesses in relation to the job demands;

- HR capacity: the innate talents (such as motivations, preferences and work styles) that an individual has, and their suitability to the job demands.

HR EFFECTIVENESS FINDINGS

The study asked 1998 internal key stakeholders (executives, senior and middle managers) from Europe and the Middle East about their perceptions of their HR functions. The questionnaire was developed from academic and project-based research as well as insights relating to HR transformation programmes that IBM Kenexa had been involved in over the six-year survey period.

The bespoke HR diagnostic questionnaire covered seven broad areas:

1 **Strategic context**: HR's development of a relevant and business-focused people strategy.

2 **Commercial context**: Awareness of the competition and the environment of the organization's industry, including planning strategies.

3 **HR solutions**: The talent initiatives HR had in place, such as development programmes, talent management, compensation and organizational culture change. This also included the evaluation of these interventions in terms of both effectiveness and the bottom-line impact.

4 **Line management**: The level of support provided to managers by HR regarding key people processes.

5 **Stakeholder management**: The level of service provided to various stakeholder groups such as, executives, employees, applicants and former employees.

6 **HR capability**: The knowledge, skills and abilities that line managers observed in their HR function/partner in their dealings with them.

7 **HR delivery**: How well HR delivered on its core tasks such as performance management, employee development, change initiatives and diversity management.

The results were as follows:

TABLE 4.2   HR diagnostic questionnaire results

Category	Result	Strengths	Development areas
Stakeholder management	73%	• Strong line management focus	• Executives' perception had room for improvement • Limited past employee focus

TABLE 4.2   *continued*

Category	Result	Strengths	Development areas
HR delivery	68%	• Strong compliance, cost management and employment issue support provided	• Performance based support and change management required increased support
HR solutions	67%	• Relevant career development and engagement support provided	• Technology focus perceived as weak with limited compensation options offered
Line management	65%	• Good overall support • Onboarding and honest feedback seen as strong	• Compensation support and attract top talent perceived to be areas for improvement
HR capability	62%	• Delivered on promises and helped solve people-based problems	• Weak data and analytics focus • Limited technological awareness
Strategic context	61%	• Strong role model for organizational values • Clear policies in place	• Weak measurement-based ethos • Too reactive to costs
Commercial context	58%	• Understands strategic drivers of the organization	• Planning lacks breadth and depth re: external influences • Weak business case approach

There were high levels of satisfaction regarding the more technical elements of being an HR practitioner (keeping up-to-date with legislative changes, providing value and input to people-based issues, and so on), but the more challenging areas of feedback revolved around:

• thinking differently about issues; considering more of an external perspective and providing more long-term and strategic insight;

• building a more robust commercial case for people programmes and initiatives; this would include assessing and evaluating the value of previous programmes, which would need to be aligned with business success metrics to be relevant;

- being an advocate for technological based advances/solutions that can increase workplace efficiency;
- underpinning just about everything HR does with business metrics and analytical insights that are linked to commercial business challenges.

HR CAPABILITY FINDINGS

Over a period of some 10 years (2009 to 2019), data was collected from various HR development programmes, capability assessment projects and some Transformation and Change programmes. These required some form of assessment of HR and L&D practitioners to assess their suitability for future roles or to identify development requirements to ensure that the people function was operating in line with its future strategic intent. This entailed research into current and future HR job demands through job analysis data, stakeholder priority ranking data, stakeholder interviews and feedback, job shadowing and observation and focus groups, amongst other data techniques.

Over the 10-year study period, this research led to the evolution of seven key demands, behavioural and technically-orientated, across the HR and L&D practitioner roles as well as understanding the levels required in a range of categories across the HR function:

- **commercial insight**: bringing business insight into HR issues;
- **breakthrough thinking**: making sense of problems and opportunities, and providing different ways of looking at challenges before making a decision;
- **impact with credibility**: persuading others and gaining support and buy-in for ideas;
- **facilitating relationships**: facilitating involvement and ongoing relationships in teams and across organizational boundaries to achieve shared business goals;
- **collaborative leadership**: leading, promoting and reinforcing a clear belief in one's own and others' capability to succeed for the benefit of the organization;
- **delivering value**: continuously driving forward significant improvements and changes in business results;
- **technical capability**: having technical competence in the areas of HR commercial awareness, talent management applications and HR consulting.

This framework acted as the basis of a range of assessment techniques such as assessment/development centres, 360-degree assessments, mini simulations and assessment-based interviews. There were of course different levels for certain key roles across the HR/L&D function, but we were able to examine the data that was collected to understand whether these practitioners possessed these key capabilities.

To that end, 1,078 practitioners across Europe and the USA were assessed via a number of the assessment and development methods highlighted above. The individuals were assessed in relation to their job level and demand. Table 4.3 shows the "level of fit" that was evidenced.

TABLE 4.3   Capability fit results

Capability area	Percentage fit with job demands	Comments
Facilitating relationships	76%	A strong collaborative and teamwork-based approach seen – the key question is whether HR is using that strength to their advantage.
Breakthrough thinking	63%	There is a clear ability to problem-solve, but a lack of business perspective was evidenced. Less HR speak would have helped.
Impact with credibility	42%	The focus was on influencing from an HR perspective, rather than looking at issues from a business perspective and putting themselves in the client's shoes.
Commercial insight	38%	There was an ongoing lack of external commercial insights being sought out or demonstrated.
Delivering value	33%	Delivery plans were not an issue, but the return on investment and methods to assess success were weak and lacked a depth of metrics.
Collaborative leadership	31%	As thought leaders in their discipline, there was a clear need to give more focused direction to clients and have the courage to challenge their assumptions from both an HR and a business perspective. This is one of the hardest forms of leadership, though.

TABLE 4.3   *continued*

Capability area	Percentage fit with job demands	Comments
CORE TECHNICAL DEMANDS		
HR consulting	66%	Strong interpersonal capabilities ensured that methods to engage with clients were effectively implemented.
Talent management	62%	Clear appreciation of core talent management techniques and applications. Lacked insight into how technology could enhance the approach.
Commercial awareness	41%	Knowledge of financial principles was weak and lacked any insight into how to apply them in the context of the HR world.

The results reflect a lack of overall behavioural capability to operate and optimize the opportunities to add value, which HR needs to capitalize on. A realistic expectation would be a 70 per cent fit when assessing capability against the job they are required to perform.

It's not all doom and gloom, as these results, albeit collected over a period of 10 years, help to highlight some terrific learning opportunities for HR employees. Some people in HR already excel in these areas, but targeted L&D interventions around gaining more competitive commercial insight, for example, can lead to better HR performance. According to David Creelman, CEO of Creelman Research, HR and L&D invest money in the rest of the workforce but not in themselves, and the time has come when their own growth and development is now of paramount importance.

This of course raises the issue of whether HR practitioners should have a "zigzag" career path that embraces both HR and a business discipline; the traditional HR practitioner who learns their professional capabilities and qualifications over many years may be a thing of the past. The commerciality of the HR function is critical, says the feedback obtained from business leaders, and crucial to developing the credibility that HR seeks; the route to that development may well be moving from business-related roles to HR and back again. Certainly, a number of organizations seem to be adopting that route already, certainly for a number of senior HR practitioner roles.

HR CAPACITY FINDINGS

During that same ten-year period, research into the capacity or attributes that support success in the HR/L&D practitioner mirrored the process that was undertaken to look into the HR capability behavioural and technical areas.

The data highlighted six personality characteristics that were found to be particularly beneficial for an HR practitioner's performance, independent of job level. These were extraversion, energy, emotionality, agreeableness, structure and openness to experience. By linking trait scores on personality assessment to exceptional performance in HR roles, a Job Fit profile was created, which enabled a comparison that could be made to compare an individual's profile in percentage terms for selection or development purposes.

In the period between 2009 and 2018, 1,524 HR and L&D practitioners from Europe, the Middle East and the United States were assessed. Based on the personality traits needed to fulfil the HR job demands, the HR practitioners were assessed in terms of their percentage fit with the optimal personality profile. Table 4.4 highlights the overview of the results.

TABLE 4.4   Personality profile level of fit

Job fit range	Level of fit	Number of HR population in range	Percentage of HR population
90% fit or above	Excellent fit	151	13.4%
85% to 89%	Good fit	179	15.9%
80% to 84%	Adequate fit	187	16.6%
75% to 79%	Development	198	17.6%
Less than 74%	Significant development	409	36.4%

Fit with the HR role focuses on social confidence, assertiveness, self-confidence, energy and drive, collaborative team work, personal organization, problem solving, and being a change agent. The bottom line is that from a trait perspective, just under a third of the population were an excellent/good fit for the demands of the role. However, of more concern is the finding that 36.4 per cent required significant development focus to be able to fully operate in the evolving HR role.

This does not mean that they were or are unable to perform in the role, but it meant that a significant level of "coping mechanisms" would be required. Furthermore, development of an individual's work styles is both hard to achieve and inevitably takes time. As we know, employees who poorly fit with their job tend to be less satisfied with it and with their supervisor and co-workers, less committed to the organization, and more likely to leave.[5] Such outcomes may also harm job performance, so having a good person-job fit appears to be in the organization's best interest.

Since personal traits can be difficult to change, the focus should be on selection in HR functions, rather than training employees to adopt specific traits. It is worth noting that personality is not the only characteristic employees bring to their jobs; other key predictors of good fit, such as knowledge, skills and abilities, should be considered as well.

How can I develop my current capability?

The data is saying that there is a gap in capability that needs to be addressed. The priorities revolve around commerciality, influencing and demonstrating the value of their interventions, through data and analytics. There are a number of areas that existing practitioners do very well – strong collaboration, solid domain knowledge of talent and HR practices, strong stakeholder relationships and so on – but is the people function using these strengths effectively to help address some of the areas of capability concern? From a job fit perspective, is the people function ensuring that the right people with the right behaviours are being recruited into the function?

The need for development and improvement allied to a change in mindset and behaviour needs to be embraced. Whilst we are promoting the need for the current HR and L&D function to focus on their growth and development as a priority, we are mindful that time and resources will always remain a constraint in this respect.

Mike Haffenden of the Corporate Research Forum says: "It's a question of not just knowing what you know, it's what you don't know that's important, and that's where HR constantly needs to challenge itself about what's new in the business and respond accordingly".

What does the new people practitioner look like?

Building on the research undertaken over the past 10 years into the demands of HR, and also considering the digital world of work trends that are driving new expectations of the people function, we believe that there are six key themes that will drive the future demands of the people practitioner in the people function of the future. These are shown in Figure 4.4.

FIGURE 4.4   The people practitioner of the future

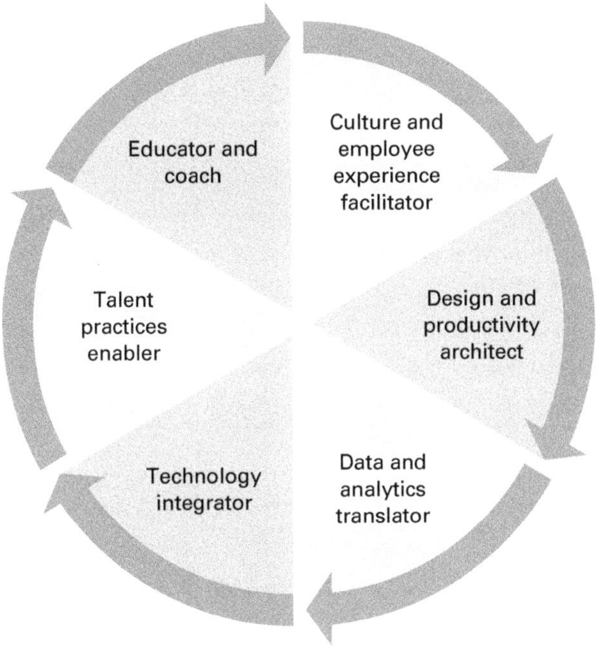

Let's explore each of these areas.

CULTURE AND EMPLOYEE EXPERIENCE FACILITATOR

Employee experience, as already highlighted in Chapter 1, will have significant implications for the way in which people practices are designed and implemented. Employee experience relates to the perceptions and feelings of the employees towards their job experience at work, whereas employee engagement is about the perceptions and feelings of the employees towards their organization. The outcome from an engagement point is that those who are positively engaged with their organization and its approaches are more likely to apply additional discretionary effort to doing their job and achieving their goals.

To ensure that these elements are aligned and suitably prioritized, it requires a culture where leaders and managers alike put themselves in the employees' shoes. That means, the people practitioner will need to:

- challenge leaders if existing practices, procedures and methods are constraining performance;
- facilitate with leaders culture-based challenges and changes;

- realign current HR offerings to cater for future workforce experience needs;

- facilitate dialogue with and between people, so that they can all contribute fully to research, design and delivery methods that need to be adopted to understand what the employee experience could look like in their organization (for example, facilitating design thinking-type sessions).

It's critical to remember that the employee experience journey looks at the lifecycle of the employee, and considers the experience that they "feel" at each stage. The aim of considering the employee experience journey is to ensure that all employees are engaged all along the way from candidacy through onboarding, performance, growth, and eventually exit. Disengagement has to be avoided at any stage.

DESIGN AND PRODUCTIVITY ARCHITECT

Low productivity is a persistent workplace issue in most organizations, and barely a month goes by without yet another major report highlighting the challenges of lower than expected productivity in both public- and private-sector organizations. Whether it is a "productivity gap" or a "productivity puzzle" the issue remains the same, insofar as a measure of productivity is about the efficiency of an employee, a machine, a factory or a business unit or indeed a process-based system that converts inputs into useful outputs.

The opportunity to make an immediate data-based impact on an organization exists, and as people are the main resources involved here alongside automation, the people function needs to focus far more time on this business challenge. That means the people practitioner will need to:

- examine productivity data to understand the issues and challenges that exist;

- work with leaders and managers to understand how business and people-based insights can be brought together to create a better more aligned solution;

- review and evaluate education and learning programmes to ensure that employees and managers are able to understand how to identify productivity and process issues before they become a crisis;

- ensure that technology improvements truly maximize and enable productivity outputs;

- undertake organizational and job design methodologies to identify workflow improvement opportunities.

Investments in technology are usually aligned with some form of efficiency improvement levels. Efficiency alone isn't always good enough, though, as you could be very efficient but still produce poor outcomes in terms of quantity and/or quality.

Whilst advanced smart technology (such as chatbots and artificial intelligence-based automation systems) are becoming a feature in the workplace, technology will continue to provide time for humans to do more of what technology can't yet do; things such as creativity, innovation, making critical judgements and demonstrating empathy and trust through dialogue.

DATA AND ANALYTICS TRANSLATOR

Data and analytics are at the heart of this new digital world of work. We explore ways to develop people analytics capability in Chapter 9, but it is important to understand that we are not trying to convert every practitioner into a statistical genius; far from it. What we do promote is that the future practitioner needs to be more numerate and be able to explore data and information to elicit insights that might not normally have been identified. This is based on a foundation of having a commercial mindset and thinking like a business leader in terms of ensuring that everything that is done has an impact upon the bottom line or (for public sector organizations) impacts on the purpose and efficiency of the services being provided.

Some practitioners may already be numerically proficient, but that doesn't preclude other practitioners from learning core techniques and methods that enable them to "add value" in a more analytical way. The translator role emerged from McKinsey observations[6] as more organizations explored technology, data and analytics in various large transformational projects and found that the data scientist role, the number cruncher, may not always be the right person to interact with the business.

The analytics translator role is about:

- focusing on their domain knowledge (HR, talent management and L&D) and using data to help business leaders identify and prioritize their business problems, based upon which will create the highest value and impact when solved;
- being comfortable with building and presenting reports and user cases;
- collaborating well with technical (analytics and statistics-based people) and senior management teams;
- managing projects, milestones and dependencies;

- being able to translate analysis and conclusions into compelling stories and actionable recommendations for management to take forward;
- being comfortable with data, metrics, measurements, analytical processes and prioritization.

Translators are able to help businesses increase the return on investment (ROI) for their data and analytics-based initiatives. They're instrumental in identifying the right opportunities to pursue, and can help ensure that everyone involved, from data analysts to business executives, work collaboratively to realize the promise that analytical insights can provide. The role is seen as being so important that Bernard Marr in *Forbes* suggests that we should forget data scientists and hire a data translator instead.[7]

It's for this reason that the capability gaps of commercial orientation, demonstrating value and creating impact and influence with senior leaders, becomes more important than ever as this role will, to our minds, be key to the success of the people function. But don't just take our word for it, as we look to marketing and their analytics journey which has preceded that of HR.

THOUGHT LEADERSHIP INSIGHT
Data translators – the must-have role for the future

*Michael D Lieberman, founder and president of Multivariate Solutions,
a research consulting firm*

As defined by Google, a data translator is a conduit between data scientists and executive decision-makers. They are specifically skilled at understanding the business needs of an organization, and are data savvy enough to be able to talk tech and distil it to others in the organization in an easy-to-understand manner. After many years of digesting many conference presentations, forming strategic alliances across skills sets in the research industry, and waving hello and goodbye to new fads, data torrents and the new "sexy" data scientists, I can offer a prediction about a lucrative avenue our industry may be pursuing.

Like the merging of qualitative research with quantitative analysis, the new data/analytics translator is a mixture of traditional research skills and the continuing expansion of bandwidth. There is now a plethora of open-source software available, as well as a tsunami of consumer and social media data.

So many tools, so much data. One message is coming through clear as a bell: clients and C-Suite executives want to hear the story.

Big data and the problem with predictive analytics

Predictive analytics is a cousin to research, focusing on investments, commercial and security applications of advanced analytics, including text mining, image recognition, process optimization, cross-selling, biometrics, credit scoring, and fraud detection.

At an international predictive analytics conference that took place several years ago in San Francisco, I met experts in their field. I was surprised to hear that many of those who regularly run optimization models for companies like Unilever, Proctor & Gamble and Levi's spend their working hours using Excel to ensure that Levi's, for example, does not send skinny jeans to dairy farmers in Wisconsin. Yet statistical know-how is in short supply among this group, as well as experience in constructing surveys or writing the narratives that constitute the core of research reporting.

Predictive analytics and research are two distinct fields. However, both industries employ data-scientists. Research firms regularly mine corporate databases in order to write up conclusions, and the project path these endeavours take is summarized in Figure 4.5.

FIGURE 4.5   The analytics translation process

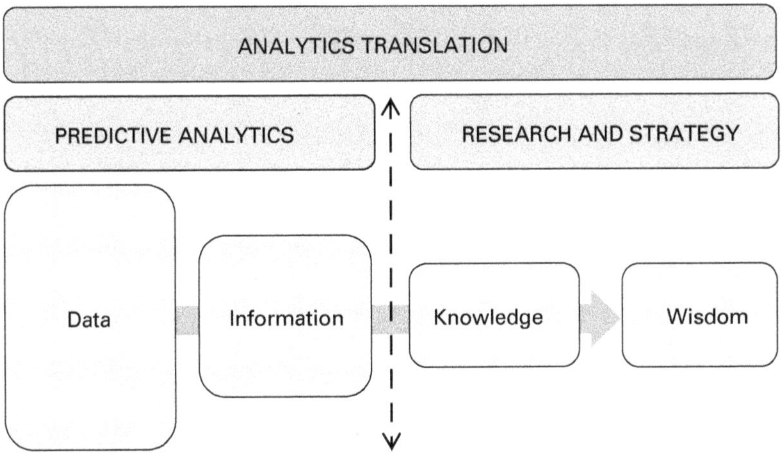

Predictive analytics professionals calculate results to maximize model efficiency; the data and information side of the chart. They are not equipped to present detailed yet summarized knowledge-based reports.

Research reporting skills, combined with sophisticated analytical firepower, position research professionals to interpret that data for the C-Suite. This considers the right side of the project path as well, that of knowledge and information. It also opens the door for a researcher to grow into the role of strategic consultant, now commonly referred to as an analytics or data translator.

Open-source power: the R-Project

For those who are not familiar with open source statistical software, R is a free-of-charge programming language for statistical computing and graphics supported by the R Foundation for Statistical Computing. The R language is widely used among statisticians and data miners for developing statistical software and data analysis. While there is a steep learning curve with R, marketing research professionals can certainly learn to use it.

In the past, one had to purchase expensive SAS licenses or many SPSS modules to achieve the firepower that is now available for free on the internet. There are many open-source modules contained in the R-Project. It now means that any research firm can partner with a data-scientist, and thereby offer to its clients not only a research report, but the capability to mine corporate databases with a sophistication provided by predictive analytics companies.

Each of the above-mentioned algorithms can be utilized in day-to-day research. Training for these additional skills is also open-source. Dozens of free, short, online courses can train anybody on the basics of how to analyse and distil analytic output.

Ubiquitous tools: Excel

When I perform a conjoint analysis (a survey-based statistical technique used in market research that helps determine how people value different attributes that make up a product or service), I always give my clients the simulator in Excel. Why? Because unlike speciality software, everyone has Excel, and its capacity is huge. The published limits on Excel spreadsheets are 1,048,576 rows by 16,384 columns. In other words, over 16,000 variables with more than one million data points – and that is for one workbook! Databases can easily be separate workbooks. Furthermore, all Excel files can be brought into SPSS for data management, and then imported into R for the superpowered statistical analysis.

Exchange of these large files is simple via data exchange services such as Dropbox. In short, now even boutique research firms have the ability to receive and analyse large client databases that, only a few years ago, required too much space.

Bringing analytics translation into the mainstream

Thus far, we have demonstrated that the tools and bandwidth for marketing researchers to perform predictive analytics or database mining are readily available today, and will be increasingly so over time.

So: how might the research industry best exploit this new frontier? Researchers are experts at constructing questionnaires and summarizing results, whereas predictive analytic people, by contrast, are not. While they can certainly calculate a dataset, when it comes to summarizing findings and presenting them to an executive, the researcher wins hands-down. Why? Because researchers are natural data translators.

Summary

We can indeed do it all. We take the data, process it with high-power, open-source software; we summarize the results and provide our clients with the ability to leverage strategic thinking. We fuse sophisticated predictive analytics capabilities with research-based story-telling prowess to offer cogent and compelling conclusions. We are data translators, the "must-have" role for the future, and one that I'm now doing not just for Marketing, but also for HR as well!

As for the HR community, if Marketing can do it, then you must be able to as well. It's a mindset shift, but one that makes you a close ally with the executive leadership when you show insights that were not previously considered.

www.mvsolution.com (archived at https://perma.cc/6ADV-QVGG)

TECHNOLOGY INTEGRATOR

HR technology will be a crucial enabler for the people function moving forward, in terms of defining and supporting new technology-based process design. This will support the desired employee experience that is being talked about. There will be a need to provide a clear focus on efficiency, effectiveness and engagement throughout all the people practices. This will be increasingly relevant as the continued automation of efficient 24/7 talent and people practices through for example, chatbots continues to advance at speed.

Underpinning this will be the change management process, as digital-based transformations will be ongoing and will require people practitioners to be able to master these transitions as a part of the change.

The Corporate Research Forum (CRF) March 2019 report *Harnessing the HR Technology Revolution* highlighted a number of key technology challenges.[8] These were underpinned by the need to build a digital workforce, with people practitioners also uplifting their own digital capability, and put more emphasis on developing the digital savviness of the workforce. David Creelman and Geoff Matthews, authors of the CRF report, said:

> The HR technology space is vast, confusing and rapidly changing – and will remain so. However, its transformational effect means it cannot be ignored – HR leaders need to be tech savvy if they are to be effective and credible in the future.

The key challenges for the people function revolved around:

- **technology management**: HR must take more control, and actively manage stakeholder relationships rather than leave the IT function to facilitate its use;
- **external connection**: it's critical to remain aware of external developments in technology;
- **change and continuity**: this will be increasingly important to get the speed of implementation right, adopting technology neither too quickly nor too slowly for users;
- **technology capability**: it's important to make sure that users have the skills, policies, principles, and information about how to use new technologies;
- **differentiation**: HR will need to focus on creating a differentiated employee experience to attract talent across the different generations now operating in the workplace;
- **capability upskilling**: reshaping and upskilling the HR function with the capabilities for future success is a key imperative;
- **data and analytics**: HR will need to learn how to leverage data to deliver powerful and relevant insights with outcomes and recommendations that drive future success and business impact.

As a result of this, the people practitioner needs to have a greater understanding regarding what is happening in the whole area of technology; this is about what developments are coming HR's way and the impact they can have upon the workforce's capability to deliver to their customers. They need to become more involved in technology and see what it can enable the people function to achieve, in terms of business outcomes and data-based insights.

The development of their digital capabilities through pilots or user-testing new technologies will enable them to learn through first-hand experience as to how to use the technology and offer pragmatic feedback. This will also ensure that they understand what the user experience is like when using HR technologies, as they will start to shape employees' changed perceptions about the people function as a whole.

What is clear is that there is a need to have an HR technology strategy in place, or at least form a part of the main people strategy that outlines what HR will be doing regarding future technology interventions over the next 12–18 months.

Technology in the HR industry is changing the way traditional people-based policies and practices are being carried out. That means that all practitioners must understand how these technologies enable the function to focus on those "added-value" practices that deliver greater value at an enterprise level.

TALENT PRACTICES ENABLER

HR needs to continue to attract, retain, develop and maximize the performance of the organization's talent at all levels. At the heart of the challenge is the need to obtain and demonstrate "value for money" and it's important to remember that, the majority of roles in an organization are undertaken by solid and competent performers – not necessarily the organization's superstars or high-potentials.

The rise of automation is raising expectations about what technology can do to improve and enhance elements of the employee lifecycle. However, there do seem to be four key fundamental practices which seem to be at the heart of a solid and differentiating talent management strategy:

1 **Recruitment, selection, assessment and feedback**: It remains crucial to generate objective data about an individual's capability that allows the organization to both understand the strengths of that employee and to better differentiate their investment, by focusing on those elements that add the greatest value to the organization.

2 **Performance management**: The need to connect with the employee becomes really important, as dialogue opportunities come under even more work pressure than ever before. The ability to improve an individual's contribution to the business through mutual goal setting, coaching/

feedback and reviews remain a vital part of everyone's responsibility and drives the workforce's experience at work, their level of engagement with what they are being asked to do, and their commitment to the organization's purpose.

3 **Learning, development and coaching**: Underpinning the employee experience raises the opportunity to improve an individual's capabilities and behaviours so that they are able to increase their performance. The personalization of learning, through technology, is vital to ensuring that the employee takes as much responsibility for their development as the organization does.

4 **Succession and talent planning**: As the speed of disruption increases, the ability to be able to have a clear and focused understanding of the organization's talent becomes more crucial. This is about looking at both future business-critical roles, succession planning, and also having a clear appreciation of the resourcing demands of an organization over a six- to 12-month period through workforce planning. Both are challenging to execute, but with more reliable and relevant data this can change.

As a result of this, the people practitioner needs to:

- Be able to clearly identify the expected business outcomes of any talent management process.

- Challenge the business to ensure that there are clear lines of accountability across all levels of the organization. This is not only about employees and leaders taking greater responsibility, but ensuring that these practices are adopted and reviewed critically, with data to ensure that business impact is being realized.

- Ensure there are clear lines of ownership from the business for the expected business outcomes that the practices should drive. Talent management, after all, exists to solve business problems.

- Retain a balance between simplicity and complexity when designing talent practices; it's all about obtaining leaders and management's buy-in and developing their ability to implement the solutions.

- Ensure there is an expectation to measure the ROI of the talent practice and their role in identifying and collecting data that can subsequently be used to assess and evaluate the viability of the process.

- Ensure that the business always focuses on the best rather than just "making do"; the importance of standards is crucial to driving performance from the workforce.

EDUCATOR AND COACH

If you're an experienced HR practitioner, you probably think coaching is just another name for what you've already been doing for years, namely helping managers and leaders increase their capabilities and knowledge in dealing with people-based issues and requirements. This support will remain a vital element to help executives, leaders and managers achieve their potential in their organizational leadership-based role.

External business coaches usually work exclusively with high-potential or senior leaders, but the practitioner may well work with every manager and supervisor at various levels of an organization which in itself makes the coaching role very challenging. The ongoing speed of change in the people practices and the advent of more technology means that the coaching role will take on an increased importance to ensure that the investments made in technological infrastructure are both understood and implemented effectively by the management and leadership teams.

As a result of this, the people practitioner needs to:

- be able to address the people-based issues and opportunities that occur, as well as drive a more detailed understanding about how a leader or manager could improve their performance by reflecting on their approaches and methods in the workplace;
- have the courage to give direction, guidance and support to leaders and managers, some of whom will be more senior and perceived to have more experience than the practitioner;
- facilitate conversations with tact and credibility to ensure that the underlying messages are clearly understood by the coached;
- motivate leaders and managers to take personal action, by creating compelling stories and messages that convince them to make changes in the way they operate;
- generate a climate of collaboration, where perceived barriers are broken down so that there is a clear agenda focused on improving business performance;

- ensure that they are commercially credible from a business point of view as well as being up to date in terms of talent management/HR domain knowledge.

There we have it: the people function is facing some of the most exciting challenges it has had to face for some time, and for the practitioners in the HR and L&D functions, the time to shine is here now. The context for analytics has been outlined, and we now move on to how to start working with data in your role.

KEY TAKEAWAYS FROM THIS CHAPTER

1 Shaping the people function is complex, but needs to follow the principles of good organizational design – merely copying other frameworks and models from other organizations in isolation isn't going to work in the complex world that we now find ourselves in.

2 Focus on being a Power Station, a function that is fundamental to business performance, and not merely a Service Station that can be used (or not) when clients want.

3 Available data indicates that there is a gap in capability in the people function that needs to be addressed. The priorities revolve around commerciality, influencing and demonstrating the value of their interventions, through data and analytics. Never forget yourself when it comes to learning and improving your capabilities; it's vital for the people function of the future.

4 The practitioner of the future will demand new approaches and methods that focus on driving forward the design of the employee experience, improved productivity and enable high-performing talent practices to be implemented. All of these are supported by an increased awareness of technological advancement, application of data and analytics that prove the value of the interventions, and a continued emphasis on the education and coaching of leaders and managers in those people practices.

References

1 Ulrich, D (1997) *Human Resource Champions: The next agenda for adding value and delivering results*, Harvard Business School Press, Brighton, MA

2 Miglani, N (2017) Look outside…for the future shape of a HR organization, *Medium* [Online] https://medium.com/future-of-hr/look-outside-for-the-future-shape-of-a-hr-organization-7b4267518397 (archived at https://perma.cc/U23Y-XQ7R)

3 Goldstein, J (2018) Igniting HR for strategic business partnerships, *Accenture* [Online] www.accenture.com/gb-en/insights/operations/hr-intelligence (archived at https://perma.cc/F8BC-V5AD)

4 IBM (2014) *Building a Smarter Human Resources Function: The data reveals room for improvement*, IBM Software

5 Kristof-Brown, A L *et al* (2005) Consequences of individuals' fit at work: A meta-analysis of person-job, person-organization, person-group, and person-supervisor fit, *Personnel Psychology*, 58, pp 281–342

6 Henke, N, Levine, J and McInerney, P (2018) Analytics translator: The new must-have role, *McKinsey* [Online] www.mckinsey.com/business-functions/mckinsey-analytics/our-insights/analytics-translator (archived at https://perma.cc/38DK-YN8Z)

7 Marr, B (2018) Forget Data Scientists And Hire A Data Translator Instead?, *Forbes* [Online] www.forbes.com/sites/bernardmarr/2018/03/12/forget-data-scientists-and-hire-a-data-translator-instead/#783f93bc848a (archived at https://perma.cc/Z58Y-SHJX)

8 Creelman, D and Matthews, G (2019) *Harnessing the HR Technology Revolution*, Corporate Research Forum report, London

5

Working with data

The importance of the commercialism of the people function, and the need to look at scenarios from a business perspective, has been clearly reflected so far, and based on that foundation, it is now time to explore the people analytics space and the various elements that need to be considered.

This chapter outlines the importance of working with data and information and how that translates into working knowledge and wisdom. Knowledge is a complex phenomenon that needs to be managed within organizations for it to be able to be passed on. The challenge for organizations is twofold – firstly, to create a persuasive business case to work with all this newfound data, and, secondly, to manage all the new knowledge created that can ultimately assist people in making better business decisions.

This chapter will cover:

- **From data to information to knowledge**: Understanding the different types of information available is vital to the start of any analytic process. Here we describe the options that are available in your search for data and information.

- **But we don't have any data!** Lots of HR functions highlight a lack of quality data as the rationale for not currently embracing the analytics challenge. The desire for 100 per cent accurate quality data is not a feasible one, and basic or partial data can still lead to insights that make the organization think differently about its workforce.

- **Looking at data through a different lens**: It's not just about gathering new data all the time. Your existing data can provide all sorts of insights; you just need to consider examining the data in a different way. We provide some ways of doing that.

- **Building business cases with data and technology**: The commercial people function needs to ensure that it builds business cases orientated towards outcomes that drive improved performance, using relevant language.

From data to information to knowledge

Most of our time spent in HR is devoted to the communication of people data, information and ways of obtaining it. However, less time is devoted to understanding how this information can become knowledge within the organization and how we can reap insights from it. As a consequence, our research has highlighted that there are even more challenges when trying to understand the different types of people and business data available within the organization that are relevant to draw insights from.

It is important for us to understand the difference between data, information and knowledge.

From data to information

We are all familiar with the term "data", and at some point in our lives we have all dealt with it in a document or spreadsheet. But taken alone, a piece of data does not convey any meaning. For example, the number 12.8 is a piece of data, but what does it tell us? The number must be given context in order to make sense of it. In other words, the weakness of data is that there is no meaning when it is taken in isolation.

We can say that data is a set of discrete, objective facts. In an organizational context, data is most usefully described as structured records of transactions stored in the form of technological systems such as databases, software or what we now term as the cloud. If there is no context to data or relationship to it, we cannot make sense of it, and that is the problem we run into with organizational data. That's why words that are emphasized with numbers is the goal to aim for.

When we talk about "information", there is a context to it. Information is a systematically-arranged set of data that has meaning; for example, by putting 12.8 in a context such as "the turnover for people in grade 7 and 8 in the IT sector in the UK is 12.8 per cent", we enable this data to make more sense.

We define information as data that makes a difference[1] – an explicit fact that is available and we know about it.[2]

FIGURE 5.1   Sources of information

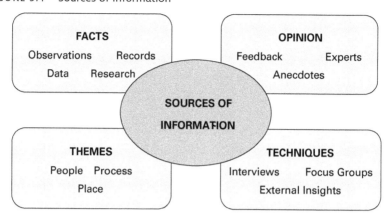

However, there are many sources of information (see Figure 5.1) and these all have a bearing on the breadth and depth of research required when determining what is impacting on the business problems that you are trying to resolve.

The complexity of knowledge

Knowledge is a complex phenomenon that is gained through experience and expertise in a particular domain or discipline. Knowledge is totally different from data and information because it's mostly hidden, until it is shared.

Although the key differences between data, information and knowledge may seem clear, it is essential for HR to understand how to gather the right data and information to be able to obtain insights through knowledge. Each person has different knowledge that is clearly different from the information that we have and the data that we get.

Knowledge becomes embedded not only in documents or shared databases but also in organizational routines, processes, practices and norms. Because of the fluid nature of knowledge, it is changing continuously, and organizations must create new streams of knowledge on a regular basis to remain competitive. This is especially relevant as we continue to develop new automated knowledge practices and processes – for example, chatbots answering core HR knowledge-based questions.

Focusing on effectiveness rather than efficiency

People analytics can play a key role in ensuring that all the available data, information and knowledge within the organization is clearly mapped. We foresee organizations becoming an ecosystem of learning and newly accessible data, as technology systems will shape new streams of knowledge. However, a lot of organizations do not build a culture where learning and change is at the heart of the digital workplace.

Information and knowledge can enable us to increase efficiency, not just effectiveness. Being effective is about doing the right things, whilst being efficient is about doing things right. Intelligence is the ability to increase efficiency, whereas wisdom is the ability to increase effectiveness. Today, by using technology and data, HR can gather intelligence and insights to increase organizational efficiency, but that is only half the story. The difference between efficiency and effectiveness is that which differentiates wisdom from knowledge, information and data. This is reiterated by the Continuum of Understanding[3] (see Figure 5.2) where the focus is drawing on data, information and knowledge to build wisdom in an organization which ultimately would ensure that a better quality of decision-making is being demonstrated across an organization.

Although data, information and knowledge can provide us with insights to make decisions, it is our capability and wisdom that will allow us to make effective decisions.[4] We sometimes refer to this as "intuition", which is the highest form of intelligence.[5]

FIGURE 5.2   The continuum of understanding

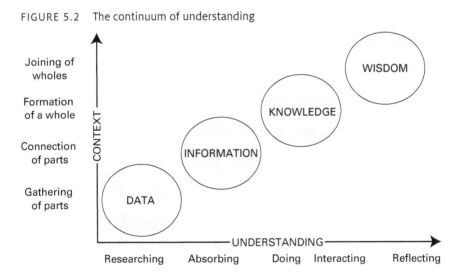

A tech and touch approach

Putting all this into context, there are some excellent people analytics-based software systems that can provide insights and intelligence through artificial intelligence, machine learning and/or automation. Such technology will never be able to generate wisdom and intuition; characteristics that differentiate man from machine, and a core reason why we believe that people analytics should be a "tech and touch approach": technology with a human touch. It is important for the people function to not only create a culture of using data to make decisions, but also assist the workforce to develop its ability to use data and information appropriately.

The key learning is that gathering as much data as possible is not the key to understanding and resolving a particular business challenge. Many different sources of information are available, and sometimes by collecting more and more information you may leave yourself with more questions than answers and may not be able to see the "wood for the trees".

Focus on what is available. It may not be a complete data or information base but sometimes it's better to analyse some partial data or information that you know is correct, albeit only 60 per cent of what you would like, rather than wait for all of your data to be fully accurate and complete. You will have a long wait if you want a complete data base!

But we don't have any data!

The one certainty is that no one is going to be able to provide any analytics-based insights without any tangible data, people and ideally business data. Capita's June 2019 report highlighted that almost half (46 per cent) of organizations in the UK still rely on "instinct and gut feel", rather than hard data and insight, when it comes to assessing and identifying skills requirements.[6] This is despite the fact that the vast majority (83 per cent) of HR and recruitment leaders regard data and insight as critical to improving recruitment and talent acquisition, and 81 per cent admit that they need more visibility into current skills within the workforce.

The worrying trend though is that senior business leaders point to HR and recruitment as the business function that has made the least progress in using data and insight to optimize and measure performance – 24 per cent of business leaders report that it is the worst at collecting, analysing and using data!

The following two learning scenarios reflect the need to change mindsets across the HR function, as this is the foundation of the shift to an analytics or data-driven approach to people and business challenges. Both of these scenarios are real, and reflect the need for a commercial mindset that focuses on:

- the business problem that we are trying to solve;

- the data that is available to ensure that we make the most relevant, effective and financially viable decision or recommendation to the business.

LEARNING SCENARIO
Time is money – a mindset shift for HR

The scenario

It was a workshop for an HR team in an organization of around 500 employees. The idea was to "up their game", and the workshop was designed to challenge and drive new behaviour from the HR team, which was made up of a head of HR, a couple of HR business partners (HRBPs) and some HR officers.

All was going well until we came to the section of the workshop that related to data and analytics in HR. Immediately the mood changed, and a clear message was conveyed that:

- their people and organizational data was all over the place;

- they didn't have any reliable data;

- it would be best to move on with other topics!

The challenge back

My response revolved around the fact they must have had at least one accurate and reliable data point – salary – which was conceded. We then explored what current issues existed in the organization, and quickly got to the current challenge of workforce absence levels, currently 12 per cent for the month of March. This had been fed back to the executive team the previous week. The response from them was one of interest, and thanks for keeping them informed!

My assertion was that the wrong data had been shared; 12 per cent didn't mean anything to them, hence the polite response they received. I talked about the idea that "time is money", a critical fact that a lot of HR practitioners forget. For example, an employee with a salary of £40,000 actually costs a UK organization around £50,000 per annum if you include:

- statutory pension contributions being made by the organization on the employee's behalf;

- statutory UK National Insurance contributions;
- a proportion of the cost of the workspace for that employee;
- a proportion of the cost of providing technology to the employee;
- a proportion of the cost of ongoing training and development.

If we then assume that the average UK employee works around 250 days per year (this organization didn't work at weekends), the daily cost of an employee with a salary of £40,000 per annum is about £200 per day. (Note that this is probably an understatement, but it's always best to underestimate than overestimate and create figures that may be perceived to lack reality.)

The absence challenge

The spreadsheet for absence was quickly unveiled, and the team then started to calculate the actual costs of their 12 per cent absence figure for the month in question, and in fact for the first three months of the year. Having calculated the daily cost of those employees who had been absent, a new piece of data emerged, the cost of the absence was in the region of £180,000 for just three months; more impactful than 12 per cent!

There was a desire to immediately inform the executive team of this analysis (please note it was basic mathematics!), but before doing that the team were asked to critique the cause of the absences to see if there was anything else that could be understood. They identified that 35 per cent of all the absences were from a flu virus, and so when reporting the new insight to the executive team three observations were made:

- The absence had increased to 12 per cent of the workforce that month.
- The cumulative cost to the business of workforce absence for the first three months was £180,000, plus as-yet unquoted opportunity cost in relation to work/processes not completed, sales not executed, new income opportunities not crystallized and so on.
- An option for the future was to consider vaccinating all the employees against flu (if they wanted), at the organization's expense. The high-level overview was:
  - cost of vaccination (500 employees × £20) = £10,000;
  - time off for on-site vaccination (500 employees × 30 minutes) = £20,000 projected cost;

o   cost of absence of £180,000 – cost of vaccination of £30,000 = cost savings of £150,000.

The outcome

The executive team suddenly saw absence in a completely different way due to the cost implications being highlighted in a business format by HR. They immediately focused on carefully monitoring the wellbeing of the workforce over the subsequent three-month period.

Additionally, they asked for future HR insights to be highlighted using cost rather than percentage increase/decrease, as these were more meaningful and relevant to their understanding of specific people and business issues.

The learnings

- Provide meaningful insights that relate to the business leaders by using their language, in this instance cost, rather than continue to use the methodology that has historically been used by HR.

- Consider the data that is being shared with others; whilst percentages may easily highlight trends and shifts (upwards/downwards), does that data truly describe what is actually happening?

- Talk the language of the business at all times; it's about being commercial in your outlook.

- Analytical insights don't always require complex algorithms to demonstrate a meaningful insight; basic mathematics and a spreadsheet can on occasions provide all the insight that is required.

www.hrcurator.com (archived at https://perma.cc/9MSH-BJWF)

The key learning here is that in a lot of cases, all you will need is cost of salary to start your data-driven based conversations. Dr John Sullivan, an international HR thought leader, constantly talks about how HR's opportunity to change comes from showing the business the money. That all starts with the salaries of the workforce.

The next example refers to a core HR operational activity: releasing an employee. Again, a cost/data-based approach can be considered in these situations to question the quality of the decision-making process.

LEARNING SCENARIO
Time is money when it comes to employee relations and reputational risk issues

The scenario

This sports media organization had a dispute with an employee regarding a redundancy/performance related issue that had been ongoing for some time. The individual had claimed that this was a decision that was underpinned by discrimination. The complaint had been independently investigated by the organization internally, but the situation had now reached an impasse.

The organization had offered £25,000 with a non-disclosure agreement (NDA) to settle the disagreement and close the situation. The employee had declined the offer and the organization's CEO refused to negotiate any further, so the only option now open was for the case to go to an employment tribunal, where disputes between employers and employees are legally resolved in the UK.

The process

Prior to the decision not to increase the offer to the employee, timesheets had revealed that between the employee's line manager, the HRBP and the HR director that had been involved with the complaint, over 65 hours of time had been used to try and identify a solution to the problem. That equated to around £21,125 in terms of cost – salary, plus a proportion of costs relating to organizational contributions.

A date was established for the tribunal and that required further internal preparation time of around 55 hours at a cost of £17,500, and the use of external legal barristers for their preparation time, at a cost of £20,000. The tribunal hearing lasted two days, with the time cost of HR involvement at £9,500 and the external barrister at a cost of £20,000.

The outcome

The organization's case was dismissed by the employment tribunal, and the employee was awarded £42,500 plus costs.

Whilst £25,000 had been offered earlier, discussions at the time had indicated that £32,500 would have been accepted by the employee. If the situation had been resolved at that time, the cost to the organization would have been £21,125 + £32,500 = £53,625.

As it turned out, the case cost to the organization in terms of time, external costs and tribunal fees was around £130,625. In the debrief with the CEO, the question was asked: "Was it worth pursuing the claim given that an extra £77,000 was paid by the organization?" This was particularly relevant, as the reputational risk of the organization was also somewhat tarnished because of the publicity that the tribunal created.

The learnings

- Never forget the internal cost of the time taken to resolve situations. Organizations tend to write it off or forget all about the fact that "time is money".

- Intangible costs such as reputational risk should never be forgotten.

- All HR practices and processes can be underpinned by a more commercial focus in terms of time and efficiency.

- Even core HR domain knowledge, in this case employment law/employee relations, is not immune to a more commercial focus, which in this instance could have driven a different approach to the decision-making process.

www.hrcurator.com (archived at https://perma.cc/9MSH-BJWF)

Both of these scenarios are commonplace in organizations across the globe, where previous habits and routines have driven the way that the HR practitioner has operated. There is nothing wrong with the approach, but the key question to ask yourself is "Are these types of approaches fit for purpose in today's digital world?" We think not, especially when a data-based perspective could have altered the approach adopted in both instances.

Every organization is a data business of some kind, and apart from being more commercial in outlook, approach and questioning, there is the issue that leaders and managers can become almost too data-focused. As David Creelman, HR thought leader, regularly outlines, there is a need to ensure that: "leaders become good consumers of data".[7]

He goes on to say that a bad consumer asks for a lot of data, takes a brief glance at it and then decides that's not what they want, it's not really useful, or they didn't really need it at all, at which point they throw it in the bin. A bad consumer is also one who, when asked what data they need, says: "just give me everything", without thinking about the burden that puts on the analytics team.

The reason why it is important to manage this type of request is that "data dumps" take up considerable amounts of wasted time and effort without any focus on the original problem that needs to be solved. Additionally, it is challenging to consider what data may be needed, and hence the "give me everything you have" request is a common one. Managing expectations and working through the problem together with managers and leaders is crucial to changing this habit, as they need to understand that asking for numbers without any clear idea of how they will use them undermines the capability to make more informed decisions based on data.

Whether you perceive that you have "no data" or "too much data", the key issue here is that there is no easy alternative to scoping out at the beginning what data is required, and for what purpose.

Looking at data through a different lens

We've talked about how thinking in a more commercial data-orientated way is the future of the people function. As Bernard Marr outlines: "The average HR team is sitting on a data goldmine"[8]. That means that an important starting point for any HR practitioner is to look at the existing data that is available to them, and gauge how they approach that information in their daily tasks.

Analysing your data is important for many reasons. For example, it helps people practitioners to:

- understand what is happening with regard to its people practices from a data perspective;
- understand what the real business and people challenges are;
- appreciate where the successes and improvement areas are, and, more importantly, why;
- enable comparisons to be made to understand patterns, trends and themes that can be explored.

You don't always need new data to undertake any of these elements – one of the most powerful aspects to consider is to review existing data and see if there is another perspective that could bring greater meaning or insight to an issue.

This next case study covers such an example by using employee engagement survey data. By thinking differently about the data and considering a different question to be answered, a different view was reached that drove new organizational behaviour and outcomes.

CASE STUDY
*Investigate the data you have by questioning what it is saying – it can
provide persuasive insights*

Business problem

This case study originates from a European financial institution, highly experienced in
the implementation of their employee engagement process across all their business
areas and support functions. It had created significant momentum, led by the CEO and
the executive team, over a number of years.

Looking to the future, the organization had refined its strategy for the next five
years driven by a digital approach in a rapidly changing world. This meant that the
future focus needed to revolve around service, digitalization and a skill shift to meet
future needs, underpinned by simplicity, commitment and wider co-operation across
the organization. This highlighted the one item within the employee engagement
survey that was always the lowest-scoring and where efforts to improve had had
minimal impact.

The digital transformation would only work effectively when a culture of
collaboration was actively demonstrated, as the technological advancements being
talked about would mean clear cross-selling opportunities and "one stop" banking
instead of multiple contacts. The CEO was looking for a clear data-based reason to
push collaboration as a pre-digital transformation initiative.

Reviewing the data

The most recent collaboration-related data item showed a positive response of 57 per
cent, a neutral response of 23 per cent and a negative response of 20 per cent based
upon 13,278 responses from across the organization.

A review was undertaken with the data "re-cut" to look specifically at the 57 per
cent of the workforce (7,568 employees) who had experienced positive collaboration
across the organization, and the 20 per cent of the workforce (2,745 employees) who
had not seen positive collaboration in their jobs. What impact did it have on their
perceptions about the whole organization? Were there any themes that highlighted a
positive rationale to be more collaborative, other than that it's the right thing to do?

The recut data highlighted the differences in perception that existed across the
workforce when positive and negative/lack of collaboration was seen:

- **Engagement**: Where positive collaboration was seen, engagement was some
  6 per cent higher, for an organization with an already high level of engagement.
  Where negative/lack of collaboration was seen, engagement was 16 per cent
  lower.

- **Enablement**: Where positive collaboration was seen, employees felt 9 per cent more enabled to be able to serve customers and take the initiative to resolve issues and explore opportunities with them. Where negative/lack of collaboration was seen, enablement was 23 per cent lower.

- **Opportunities to develop**: Where positive collaboration was seen, this theme was some 17 per cent higher. Where negative/lack of collaboration was seen, this was 12 per cent lower.

- **Customer experience**: Where positive collaboration was seen, customer service was only 5 per cent higher, but where negative/lack of collaboration was seen, the perception of service was 19 per cent lower.

- **Future alignment**: Where positive collaboration was seen, the workforce felt more aligned to the future by some 18 per cent. Where negative/lack of collaboration was seen, this was 18 per cent lower.

The essence of the feedback was that positive collaboration meant that the employee experience at work was even more positive than where silos and a more insular approach was evident. This gave the executive team the focus to drive collaboration as a key theme for post-survey activity and this was supported by forums, breakfast meetings, a suite of learning focused on behavioural change in collaboration, and scorecard measures designed to drive change.

Outcomes

Key outcomes as a result of this data and the subsequent activity were:

- Collaboration in year 1 increased by 9 per cent to 66 per cent.

- In year 2 this had further increased by 6 per cent to 72 per cent.

- By reviewing the data on the survey and aligning it with the learning data that was separately available, 78 per cent of the highest scoring business units had undertaken micro-learning activities (reading short blogs on collaboration, watching short videos about improving collaboration, downloading simple tools to support collaborative behaviour, etc). This has led to a change in focus regarding learning, with a more personalized micro-learning approach now being adopted in a number of other behavioural development areas.

So, whilst the clamour for new data, both breadth and depth, is important, don't forget the data you currently have been looking at. See if there is another way of looking at the data differently, either by asking a different question or seeking a different analysis of the data that you have.

Another version of this is to consider what data is missing. As the following learning scenario outlines, not having specific data in itself can sometimes provide an insight or an area that needs to be explored further.

LEARNING SCENARIO
Sometimes the data you haven't got tells you more than the data that you have got!

Mark Abrahams, chartered occupational psychologist working with data scientists at Launchpad Recruits Ltd and head of research at MyWorkSearch

Missing data can often be meaningful.

For example, a particular question on an engagement survey may have a low response rate. This may be because the question is either poorly worded or that respondents have real concerns about responding truthfully. Job applicants may leave some fields on an application form blank because they do not have that qualification, or it doesn't apply to them.

In analytics, missing data needs to be considered carefully. In order to ensure a more complete dataset, some data scientists will replace missing data using a technique called data imputation, using a value that represents the mean or other typical responses to an individual question, without always considering whether this is sensible or indeed meaningful. For example, a job applicant who does not provide a Grade Point Average (GPA) score for their degree might have been educated in a country where GPA scores are not used – filling in their missing score with the group average, therefore, is meaningless.

This is where the HR practitioner and the data analyst need to work together to ensure that sensible conclusions and interpretations of data are being made; data alone doesn't have all the answers!

The learnings

- Sometimes the missing data tells you more than the data that you do have. Try to understand why that data has been omitted – is it for another possible reason?

- Collaborative working between HR and the analyst or data cruncher is vital to ensure that only relevant data-based techniques are used when analysing.

Building business cases with data and technology

A key challenge for HR today is the ability to build a business case for investments that provides the business, and the executive leaders, with sufficient detail and confidence to enable them to support a people-based proposal. It is therefore crucial to demonstrate how people-based initiatives can transform how the organization operates and performs. This activity attains even greater significance than before, especially when every other function in your organization is also vying for that same financial invest-ment. That's where data can be used to build a persuasive investment case.

Articulating a powerful business case means that you need to be able to speak the language that resonates with the business, and the senior leaders who are making that decision.[9] That means commercial, viable numbers and predictions that make realistic sense. We believe that there are three key stages to consider – see Figure 5.3.

FIGURE 5.3   Building a business case

Stage 1: The diagnosis

This revolves around:

- Establishing the need for the initiative that you are suggesting. Identify the critical business challenges and business processes that could be optimized, and/or opportunities for change. This builds the context and the value proposition for the initiative.

- Identifying the external insights and data that can help build some data regarding the issue. For example, if you are recommending a revised project change methodology, review the external data that outlines the cost of failed projects.

- Identifying the internal business challenges that will be impacted by the initiative, for example, improving productivity, reducing absenteeism, etc. Whilst it is always preferable to have specific detailed numbers, sometimes that's not possible, and forecasts based on well-thought-through stated assumptions can help to build confidence in what is being suggested.

- Identifying as many details and data points as possible when identifying the causes. For example, if you are seeking a new employee engagement survey process, quantify the extent to which each issue contributes to the lack of engagement. This will enable you to use that data later to justify the cost of each part of the solution.

Stage 2: Outlining the proposed solution

Now that you have communicated the need for your initiative, it is time to explain why the solution you are suggesting can resolve the problems that you have identified:

- Be as specific as possible about what is required. Outline what will be changed, added, and removed and how that will be accomplished.
- For each step, describe what resources you will need and how they will be allocated, along with how the step will contribute to the solution. This builds a clear cost/benefit analysis, justifying each cost and describing the proposed savings.
- Provide a timeline for project execution and completion. Describe the implementation plan and each component of the initiative.
- Establish the end date and the follow-up procedures and metrics to measure project success so that senior leaders can understand the anticipated return on the proposed investment.
- Outline what the senior leaders will have to do as key stakeholders of the initiative.

Stage 3: Determining the desired results

This is about demonstrating what the initiative will achieve for the organization in terms of performance improvements. This will require you to:

- Outline what effect your initiative will have on the original business challenges that were outlined in Stage 1 quantifying the anticipated performance improvements.
- Identify the internal impact created by the initiative, outlining the return on investment (ROI) predictions. These will reflect organizational improvements and efficiencies, with data to support your views such as productivity data, reduced turnover, etc.

- If there are external benefits then quantify them with data trends drawing on external insights. For example, if the new recruitment process will be perceived to improve the employee brand, work with the marketing function to outline what that benefit looks like in terms of tangible performance data.

- Identify the clear takeaways that will resonate with senior leaders in terms of resolving some of their business challenges and pressure points.

- Finally outline a picture of what the organization will look like after the initiative has been implemented; making the intangible more tangible.

This framework will work when you relate to the senior leader's business priorities and pressure points. Be as specific as you can, using actual or pre-dicted data and numbers that are available. Enlist the support of other func-tions as they can help you identify stakeholder pressure points and get a better sense of the initiative's impact throughout the organization.

The case study below outlines an approach that was adopted for that organization and the situation that the HR function faced at the time. It utilized the three-stage approach, although the focus was totally on ROI, as requested by the executive at the time. Whilst the calculations look complex, it's no more than simple maths.

The approach was driven by working with the learning and development (L&D) experts and the business managers in the organization who would be involved in the implementation of the programme. They outlined the approach that was required and the capability focus that was crucial to the senior leaders who would sign off the initiative.

CASE STUDY
Building the projected ROI business case for a development programme

Business problem

This case study originates from the UK region-based business of a global multinational conglomerate where the management development process within the Operations part of the business was being reviewed. It had an informal approach to management-based succession that was heavily reliant on performance management data and the spreadsheet-based approach to succession planning.

Other issues associated with the same problem were:

- Development opportunities across this part of the organization were perceived to be limited; the engagement survey item for the past two years had a score of 51 per cent and 47 per cent against a global benchmark of 69 per cent.

- Key talent who had been lined up for key operational roles had left for other organizations. Their exit interviews named lack of opportunities, no clear development support and coaching and no perceived organizational career path as the top reasons for their departures.

Solution

Research and feedback from the internal review team identified a need to instigate a new change process that drove development across the operational management business in terms of both current and potential operational managers, and would be underpinned by:

- a development centre to assess the capability and potential of future operations managers;

- a new capability framework focused on high-performing management behaviour;

- self-managed personalized learning;

- line manager coaching to support behavioural change.

The business challenge was that there was agreement from the executive team about the way forward, but they were concerned about the external costs that were going to be incurred, especially for the design and delivery of the development centre. Accordingly, a business case was requested, and an ROI framework of ten steps was developed to assist in that process:

1 Cost of development centre design and delivery: **£1,750 per participant**.

2 Average salary of participants on the programme: **£42,500 per annum**.

3 Competencies and job relevance (how much value is placed on behavioural competency-based capability): stakeholders assessed this at 80 per cent, which equated to **£34,000** (80 per cent of £42,500).

4 Predict the desired competency-based capability (to perform in the future operations manager role): stakeholders assessed this at **7 out of 10**.

5 Rate the current average competency-based capability of the participants (based upon appraisal and 360-degree data): 5.5 out of 10 which equates to **78 per cent proficiency** (5.5 ÷ 7.0).

6   Rate the desired average competency-based capability of the participants six months after the event: 6.5 out of 10, which equates to **93 per cent proficiency** (6.5 ÷ 7.0).

7   Assess the financial value of participants' current competency-based capability: 78 per cent proficiency of £34,000 = **£26,520**.

8   Assess the financial value of participants' competency-based capability six months after the event: 93 per cent proficiency of £34,000 = **£31,620**.

9   Assess the financial value/difference between before and after the development event: £31,620 − £26,520 = **£5,100**.

10   ROI for the programme: £5,100 (value) − £1,750 (cost) = £3,350/£1,750 (cost) × 100 = **191.4 per cent**.

The investment in the programme would provide two times the return on the investment that was being requested here. As a result of this, the project was signed off and implemented as originally outlined.

Outcomes

Key outcomes driven specifically by this project were as follows:

- Initially, 55 participants were assessed to "kick-start" the programme. Over the subsequent twelve months, 30 per cent of them were promoted into new more challenging operations manager roles, and within eighteen months that figure had increased to 55 per cent.

- The perception regarding development opportunities changed through this development programme. Management and employees become more focused on L&D, and the organization provided the infrastructure to ensure that change could happen. The subsequent employee engagement survey item regarding this specific perception changed from 47 per cent to 56 per cent in year 1, 63 per cent in Year 2 and 69 per cent in Year 3. The initial operations management programme was regarded as a key feature in shifting attitudes and behaviour.

- At the same time, retention had significantly improved. Prior to the programme more than 20 key individuals with operational management potential had been lost to other organizations, with an indicative cost of around £1 million including replacement costs, training for replacements and productivity reductions. Following the introduction of the programme, only 13 key talent potentials were lost over a three-year period, with anticipated savings of over £1.5 million following the introduction of the programme.

Business case learnings

Learned over many years of building business cases for people-based interventions, these are some tips to consider when creating your business case, with a numerical and added value emphasis:

- **Show the money**: Show the total revenue impact of your project, and ensure that the language you use reiterates its impact in percentage terms or numbers.

- **What does the data say**: This is where the whole data-driven approach is so important in terms of defining success in terms of numbers and metrics that are of relevance and interest to the executive decision-makers. Tell the story of the data by using the business language that interests them.

- **Show the impact on other strategic goals**: Executives are focused on corporate performance levels, so ensure that you outline any associated improvements in productivity, efficiency, revenue growth by quantifying them with projected numbers increases!

- **Focus on solving business problems, not just people problems**: Remember that executives spend all day talking about business problems, so show the impact of the proposed people practice/initiative on business challenges, where possible, not just your functional people challenge.

- **The doing nothing syndrome**: It's important to place a cost on any likely major failure if you want to get the attention of executives, but also remember to show that delaying a decision, or doing nothing, could make a problem much worse.

- **Futureproofing**: It's important to focus on the future in terms of where your competitors will be. If you can include some forecasting or predictive component into your assessment, it will demonstrate that what you are proposing has a today and future orientation to it.

- **Innovation**: Assure your decision-makers of the innovative elements of your proposal or highlight the competitive advantage that the solution will bring in your sector. Alternatively, highlight the risk of falling behind your competitors if the solution is not adopted.

- **Scalability**: Reassure the decision-makers about how implementation can be scaled up from an initial pilot by using data that highlights the scale of making the initiative organization-wide.

The principles behind building a business case can be utilized in other decision-making processes. The learning scenario below outlines how the business case approach can widen the thinking that people may give to a challenging issue.

LEARNING SCENARIO
Using a business case type approach to rethink a critical decision

Business challenge

This example comes from the division of a large European logistics organization. Whilst working with their HR leaders on a project proposal, they became distracted by a request from their CEO: "How much will it cost to release one of my senior executives who I don't perceive to be performing anymore?"

The discussion focused on the terms and conditions of the person's contract, which specified six month's notice to be paid. This meant €200,000 in this instance (salary €400,000). The recruiting costs associated with hiring an executive were then discussed and set at €10,000 in upfront fees and €140,000 retainer fee for the first year. The proposed figure that was going to be shared with the CEO was therefore €350,000.

The discussion at my suggestion, was then focused on not only tangible costs, albeit a wider emphasis, but also on intangible costs given the seniority of the position. The discussion then went in a different direction and derived a completely different answer based upon a business case-type approach to the request.

Tangible costs

The tangible costs included:

- Contractual obligations: €200,000.

- Replacement hiring costs: €150,000.

- Impact on the executive's team: Reports indicate that between 15 and 41 per cent turnover occurs as a result of the executive moving. In this instance there were nine people in the executive's support team; conservatively, two team members were regarded as being at risk. Cost to replace based on €60,000 salary per person (recruitment fees, productivity learning, training costs etc) – €240,000.

- Organizational project stakeholder implications: A key reason for project failure is lack of executive governance and alignment with business strategy.

This role ran three major change-related projects. An anticipated 12 per cent of project cost is wasted, and with cost of project budget per annum c€45 million, possible performance loss of €5.4 million.

- Upfront onboarding and learning costs: €30,000 (a month's salary for learning, meetings to acclimatize, etc.

Intangible costs

The intangible costs included:

- Loss of knowledge capital: Cost difficult to quantify.
- Loss of customers relationship: Cost not known.
- Disruption to productivity due to increased inefficiencies and lack of local leadership: Cost difficult to quantify.
- Loss of social networks and relationships (today, organizational network analysis could be utilized to assess value): Cost not known.
- Negative external visibility regarding executive departure: Cost difficult to quantify.
- Negative impact on employee engagement: Cost difficult to quantify.

This was not a complete list of intangible costs, but these were thought to be of greatest relevance to the business given the position that it was in at the time.

Conclusion

The actual figure shared with the CEO was €6 million plus a series of other possible intangible costs that could be impacted by the loss of a senior executive. The impact and credibility of the HR team was significantly enhanced, not because of the number they produced, but because of the breadth and depth of thinking that had been demonstrated by the team.

The decision to release a colleague, at whatever level, whilst hopefully based on performance-based evidence, always has a number of emotional aspects that come into play, and to be able to control that by broadening the elements to consider in such a decision is vital. The business case approach had outlined some predictions of what could happen, and ensured that the widest considerations were given to the decision being made.

The executive was retained with a clear performance plan put in place to determine improvements in organizational performance.

www.hrcurator.com (archived at https://perma.cc/9MSH-BJWF)

This learning scenario reiterates the need for commercial awareness when considering issues and business challenges. The methodology is about trying to predict the consequences of taking certain actions, hence its applicability to other situations that a people practitioner may face.

Building a business case for a people analytics team

A key challenge for HR today is to create a business case for people analytics that ensures buy-in from the variety of stakeholders within the business. It is important to ensure that people analytics is an initiative that is owned by the whole organization.

The three-stage process previously outlined in Figure 5.3 can help shape the methodology to identify some of the people resources costs and business benefits of adopting such a strategy.

ENABLING HR TECHNOLOGY

There may need to be an additional business case for HR technology solutions to support and optimize the people analytics team's capabilities. Look at the data; an organization of 10,000 employees has approximately three years of data, and every month each employee creates approximately 50 data points. Some of these data points don't change and are generated through payroll, attendance and other such activities. This could be first name, last name, gender, date of birth, position, job history, employee identification number, line manager name information/structure, salary, performance review, bonus payments and so on.

So, 10,000 employees multiplied by 36 months multiplied by 50 data points equates to 18,000,000 data points that you may need to work with. Using Microsoft Excel with this breadth and depth of data is unlikely to be fully effective, and subsequently the analysis will take a lot of time and effort. For example, Microsoft Excel can specify 12.5 per cent attrition for an organization and whether it is going up, or going down or is twice as high as a year ago. But the key question is whether this is good or bad.

Ultimately, that means that it is not easy to translate and use this quantity of data points, whereas supportive technology can enable the people function to see the trends.

ROLE OF PEOPLE PRACTITIONERS

People practitioners will play a vital role in this agenda. With their new-found capabilities, they can add context to the information that is generated by the technology systems. For example, they can add insightful commentary such as "This is disappointing, but with imminent automation in a number of key business areas that will impact on a number of support roles, there is a strong likelihood that less people will be required, so as a result high attrition at this stage may be more acceptable".

By providing this business context, people practitioners can derive actions to mitigate or improve the situation based upon the data insights. Consequently, they can measure whether these actions have the desired impact, and can then start to develop a business case for the people function.

It will become increasingly important to develop a business case to introduce and sustain people analytics across the organization. At the same time, it will be vital to build capability for all people practitioners to understand how analytics can be used to drive true added value that is based on factual data and insights. That will ultimately change the perception of the HR function into a people function that is driven by business profit, interacting with technology, and driving, not just reacting to, the digital world of work.

In the future, smart cognitive technology will be able to translate data points into information, and inform us about any trends with the necessary rationale and analysis readily provided. But we feel it is essential to be able to continue to provide context and derive clear focused actions underpinned by impact-based success metrics. As technology evolves, it may eventually take over this role completely. Nevertheless, we believe it will always remain a successful marriage between technology and human intuition.

KEY TAKEAWAYS FROM THIS CHAPTER

1 Data alone does not provide all the answers. You need to have clear context to make sense of the numbers, and that's what information and knowledge provides.

2 Data, information and knowledge can provide us with insights to make decisions, but it is our own capability and wisdom that will allow us to make more effective decisions.

3 Be focused about the breadth and depth of information and data that you need to collect. Have a plan regarding what you need to know – sometimes, too much data will mean that you can't see the wood for the trees.

4 Understand that, sometimes, less is more. You may want a complete data base, but sometimes it's better to analyse some partial data or information

that you know is correct, albeit not everything that you wanted. You could have a long wait for perfection when it comes to data!

5   Time is money; it's the one piece of data every organization has access to (salaries and time), so there's no excuse any more when it comes to the "we don't have any quality data" debate.

6   The commercial mindset is again crucial, to challenge and review existing practices and ways of making decisions. Having more of a numerical orientation is vital to that behaviour.

7   Data and analytics-based activity is not always about looking at new data sets and making judgements. Consider existing data sets that are available, and consider other ways of looking at that data by asking different questions. Also consider what data is not available – what does its absence say to you?

8   Building powerful business cases means that you need to be able to speak the language that resonates with the business and the senior leaders who are making those investment decisions. That means that commercial, viable numbers and predictions that make realistic sense will need to be provided.

9   The business case methodology is about trying to predict the consequences of taking certain actions, and with a more numerical commercial orientation it has greater applicability across a range of other situations that HR and L&D face. The new people practitioner will play a vital role in moving this agenda forward.

References

1   Davenport, T and Prusak, L (2000) *Working Knowledge: How organizations manage what they know*, Harvard Business Review Press, Brighton, MA

2   Alavi, M and Tiwana, A (2002) Knowledge integration in virtual teams: The potential role of KMS, *Journal of the American Society for Information Science and Technology*, 53 (12), 1029–37

3   Cleveland, H (1982) Information as Resource, *The Futurist*, 37–39

4   Ackoff, R L (1989) From data to wisdom, *Journal of Applied Systems Analysis*, 16 (1), pp 3–9

5   Kasanoff, B (2017) Intuition Is The Highest Form of Intelligence, *Forbes* [Online] www.forbes.com/sites/brucekasanoff/2017/02/21/intuition-is-the-highest-form-of-intelligence/ (archived at https://perma.cc/6YVG-NGDZ)

6 Capita People Solutions (2019) The insight edge in talent acquisition: How data and insight can deliver the skills needed in a hybrid workforce, *Capita People Solutions* [Online] https://content.capitapeoplesolutions.co.uk/whitepapers/insight-edge-talent-acquisition (archived at https://perma.cc/X286-85WP)

7 Creelman, D (2019) When They Say 'Just Give Me Everything,' Don't, *TLNT. com* [Online] www.tlnt.com/when-they-say-just-give-me-everything-dont/ (archived at https://perma.cc/R533-SCTN)

8 Marr, B (2018) Why Data Is HR's Most Important Asset, *Forbes* [Online] www.forbes.com/sites/bernardmarr/2018/04/13/why-data-is-hrs-most-important-asset/ (archived at https://perma.cc/5STD-H3QW)

9 Dearborn, J and Swanson, D (2017) *The Data-Driven Leader: A powerful approach to delivering measurable business impact through people analytics*, John Wiley & Sons, Chichester and New York

PART THREE

People analytics delivering value

6

A people analytics framework

Having considered the data that needs to be gathered, we now focus on how data, information and knowledge can be translated into insights by looking at a framework that reflects the different levels of complexity involved in people analytics. Whilst there is a demand for specialist skills to deal with the more complex statistical correlations, calculations and predictive-orientated hypotheses, the basis of people analytics is mathematics, and a lot of analysis can be done by using a commercial mindset and exploring the data that is available with a more numerical orientation.

This chapter will focus entirely on:

- **A framework to move from reporting to analytics**: Many models or journeys are talked about, but it is very clear that there is no one prescribed way to shift from a reporting base to the use of analytics in any organization. There is certainly a framework to build on, and that will be described as a means of helping outline a route to becoming a more data-driven function.

A framework to move from reporting to analytics

Before we explore the development of analytics approaches and how they are being used in organizations, let's deal with the elephant in the room: what do we call this whole area of analytics? HR has managed to make the simple complicated by calling the topic by a variety of names: people analytics, workforce analytics, HR analytics, experience analytics, and more. There is no right or wrong answer, but these phrases are used interchangeably, and for us some clarity is needed to ensure that everyone knows what they are referring to.

Crunchr, a cloud-based provider of people analytics and workforce planning solutions, explore the different definitions in their paper covering the differences between HR and people analytics.[1] According to them:

- **HR analytics** captures and measures the functioning of the HR team itself – for example, analysing key performance indicators (KPIs) such as employee turnover, time to hire, etc. These analytics are predominantly relevant to the HR team.

- **Workforce analytics** is broader, encompassing the entire workforce, and allows for the future inclusion of automation, AI and robots-based data. Workforce analytics, therefore, is more descriptive when it comes to creating a holistic workforce strategy.

- **People analytics** aims to encompass HR, the entire workforce and customer insights. People analytics inculcates the approach of measuring and analysing all this information and knitting it together to improve decision-making and business performance.

We have used the phrase "people analytics" for the purpose of this book, and whatever the definition, the purpose is to ensure that the use of data and analytic tools will identify insights that enable faster, more accurate, and more confident quality-based business decision-making.

Throughout all the case studies and examples that we explore, the focus must always be on ensuring that whatever activity you are undertaking, it is aimed at demonstrating the value that the people function can generate. That will need to be underpinned by:

- focusing on business priorities;
- leveraging your analytics-based finding through clear messaging and storytelling;
- using analytics to help inform the decision-making process, not as a substitute;
- understanding that perfection when it comes to data isn't required for a successful analysis to be undertaken;
- building a point of view that not only understands the past, but also optimizes the present, and attempts to predict the future when it comes to performance improvement.

Before describing the journey, we wanted to start with an example where a leader's judgement was made without the benefit of data. Whilst the decision was well intentioned, the subsequent data that was obtained highlighted the fact that it was intrinsically flawed.

CASE STUDY
The $35 million mis-investment

Business problem

A CEO made the decision that he wanted to "fix the pay issue once and for all" within his business. It was an international brand known for luxury and service, but many employees felt undervalued and unappreciated, and were dissatisfied with their current compensation. The solution was simple.

The solution

The CEO announced that the company was going to provide a 15 per cent raise for all 2,000 employees. This equated to an investment of more than $35 million dollars in annual payroll. The announcement was made six months prior to the next yearly employee survey. To the leadership team's dismay, the subsequent survey showed a decline in employees feeling recognized and rewarded of more than 7 per cent, which was statistically significant for a population that size. How could a significant increase in compensation leave employees feeling less rewarded?

The failure came in how it was communicated and presented to the organization. Many employees left comments on the employee survey along the lines of, "I'm a top performer on my team, and I received the same raise as everyone else". The truth was that in most cases, top performers were already paid more, so 15 per cent on their base salary was actually a larger amount than their co-workers received. However, this fact was clearly lost on many employees.

More importantly, the negative impact the raise had on perceptions highlights something important about employee psychology. Equity theory states that employees anticipate and desire to receive a return on their work equal to that of what they invest in terms of knowledge, skills, ability, loyalty and effort. This wasn't taken into consideration when rolling out the raise. The organization made no connection between performance, results, or value and the pay increase itself. At best, it felt like a random but nice increase in pay. At worst, it reinforced an already held belief that the organization didn't notice, recognise or reward high performance.

The key factors within a company that engender feelings of being recognized and rewarded are:

- manager feedback linked to specific accomplishments;
- managers supporting employee growth and development;
- employee empowerment through involvement in decisions that affect their work.

The 15 per cent raise was generous, but the way the organization communicated it to employees did not address any of the three factors that were at the root of the original dissatisfaction. It left many still feeling unnoticed or unappreciated, just with a bigger pay cheque.

Perceived fairness in pay is about more than just a monetary amount. For most organizations, the correlation between feeling the individual is paid fairly for their contributions to the company and the actual amount paid is almost zero. Employees need to have some understanding of how their pay is determined, how they can affect their pay (by taking on more responsibilities, creating more value and/or improving work quality, being a top performer, etc), and there needs to be a sense of procedural justice and equity within the company so that employees trust their accomplishments will be recognized and rewarded appropriately within the company.

Key learning

This was an expensive lesson for a company that invested an additional $35 million in annual payroll, only to see employees left feeling less recognized and appreciated. However, it is a lesson that can benefit others who want to influence employee perceptions around compensation and recognition.

Courtesy of Perceptyx: www.perceptyx.com (archived at https://perma.cc/WHC9-4FMT)

The example reiterates that whilst it is the leadership's role to make decisions, if in this instance the existing data and insights had been considered, the impact of the decision could have been more positive. For us, this highlights why the use and application of data through people analytics is crucial to making better informed decisions.

To understand how organizations build their people analytics capability, we used the Crunchr Maturity Model for People Analytics (see Figure 6.1), developed by Dirk Jonker, people analytics expert and founder of Crunchr. We refined it to include the importance of the all-embracing commercial mindset that we believe is vital to any data-based analytics activity.

We wanted to understand the challenges that organizations face during each level of activity, the key capabilities required by the people function during these levels and how to move from one area of activity to another based upon their learnings. Using the Crunchr Maturity Model, we were able to understand where these organizations are, where their ambition is and what kind of challenges they face when they move from one level of activity to another on their analytics journey.

It is important to point out that the journey towards systematic analytics in Box 4 is predominantly a sequential journey which starts with opportunistic reporting, and evolves. This maturity model ensures that a solid

FIGURE 6.1   Building a people analytics capability model

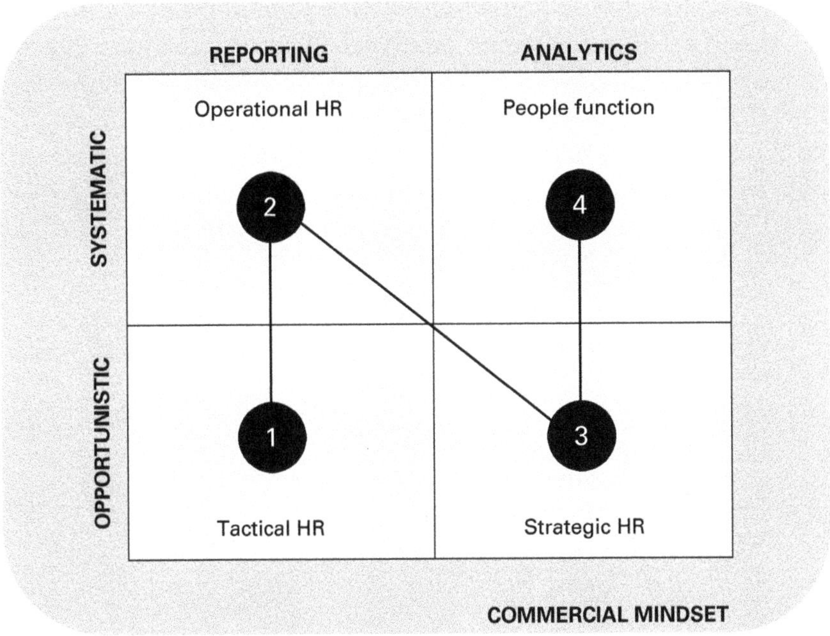

Adapted from the Crunchr Maturity Model for People Analytics

foundation is created, where business questions, capabilities and data are always in balance. However, not every organization will need to conform to the sequence.

Reporting

Reporting translates data into information; for example, comparing data sets to calculate employee turnover. In the reporting stage there is often no context, nor does it result in taking any actions; this is about just providing information. This can be done in two ways, either in an opportunistic or a systematic way.

Organizations tend to start in Box 1 (see Figure 6.2); this area symbolizes an opportunistic way of gathering data and translating it into information. Organizations that are on their analytics journey might have been at this point a few years ago; organizations who are embarking on their journey may be operating in this area of activity today.

OPPORTUNISTIC REPORTING

Usually this links back to local business leaders who have local challenges and questions. They will approach the local HR business partner (HRBP) and work with the tools that they can access to obtain the numbers that underpin the request that is being made of them. That inevitably means that a lot of manual spreadsheets and ad hoc work is required to fulfil the request.

Sometimes the analysis carried out may not be fully accurate, as most organizations will have their own reporting methodologies that can restrict access to all the data that is required.

FIGURE 6.2   Opportunistic reporting

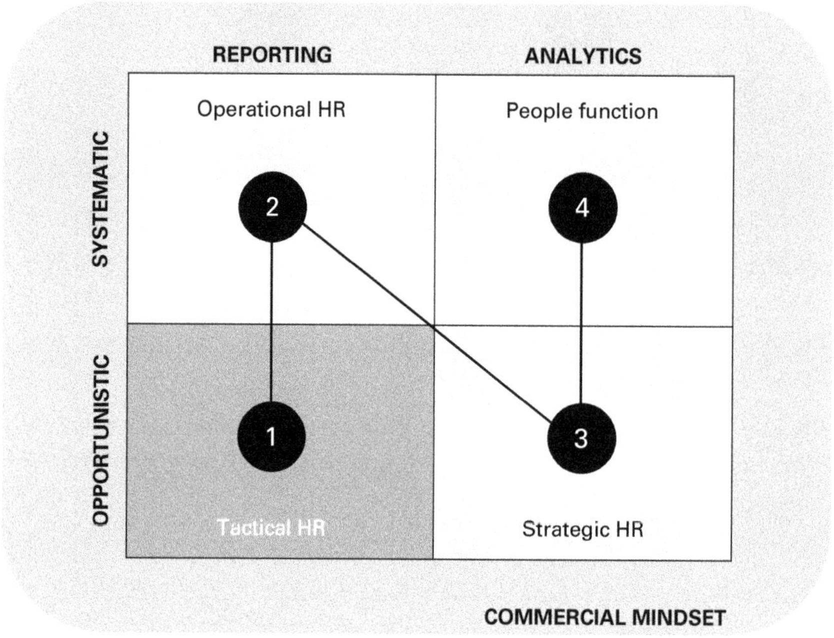

Adapted from the Crunchr Maturity Model for People Analytics

At this stage, there are no harmonized definitions, metrics and measures; however, people in the HR function are doing their best to get the right information. Compiling, integrating and synthesizing this data does not look attractive, though, as it takes a lot of time and effort to undertake the manual calculations and ensure that there are no evident mistakes. As definitions are not harmonized, this may be based on many local different HR systems that are not integrated, adding a whole layer of complexity to the issue.

A host of Human Resource Information Systems (HRIS) are available to use. Most of these systems are disparate from other organizational software so that HR administrators end up gathering data from a variety of systems and work with spreadsheets to report information in a meaningful way.

The first case study explores an issue where there was a demand for business-critical people with certain capabilities, and where there were real challenges recruiting and retaining the people that joined the organization. The situation required an opportunistic approach to the one that had been adopted by the organization, which had minimal reporting frameworks in place; firmly in Box 1.

CASE STUDY
Using business-led metrics drives the desire for more people data (part 1)

Business problem

This case study originates from a global multinational conglomerate headquartered in Europe and revolves around its technology solutions business which focused heavily on project delivery to generate sustained income and growth. Against the need for growth and maintenance of demanding large contracts with established private and public sector clients, the turnover of project and programme managers had increased significantly over a two-year period.

The new recruits that were being selected were struggling to perform despite their established project management credentials for which they had been recruited. Additionally, there was a comprehensive projects based infrastructure in place, focused training and onboarding processes, all designed to advance the professionalism and practice of project management.

The solution

Research was undertaken internally and it was clear that there was too much reliance placed on previous project management expertise and experience in the recruitment process. Clear ownership by line managers of the recruitment process was in place, but the level of evidence that the process provided was inconsistent.

This led to the development of a new multiple assessment process that included a new bespoke multiple-choice project management test, a psychometric assessment aligned to a high-performing project manager researched benchmarks and a structured behavioural interview. Detailed guidelines and interview training were undertaken, with separate guides created for each role, ranging from top-level programme directors to associate project managers. Each guide provided the interviewer with a suggested list of probing questions aimed at establishing the candidate's capability.

To support this, a Quality of Hire (QoH) metric was developed to assess the viability of the new process against an organizational benchmark/expectation, to ensure that the initiative was consistently implemented across the business. The metric for this organization (most QoH metrics are bespoke) was:

Average job performance of new hires + Percentage of new hires reaching acceptable performance levels in six months + Percentage of new hires retained after 12 months

These percentage figures (out of 100) were then divided by the number of criteria areas to provide an indicative benchmark to assess progress against. Stakeholders of the process were looking initially for a 75 per cent benchmark, formed as highlighted below:

New hire job performance (3.5 out of 5.0) – **70 per cent** + New hires reaching acceptable performance levels in six months (75 out of 100) – **75 per cent** + New hires retained after 12 months – **80 per cent (target)**

Prior to the new method being introduced, the QoH standard was measured at 38 per cent, based on the previous 12 months' recruiting activity.

Outcomes

Key outcomes from this initiative were:

- QoH metric benchmark at the end of year 1 increased from the pre-initiative score of 38 per cent to 69 per cent, up 31 per cent.

- In year 2 the QoH metric benchmark was up a further 8 per cent to 77 per cent. In year 3 it was at 84 per cent, up 7 per cent on the previous year, and went to 91 per cent in year 4, another 7 per cent gain.

- As a result of implementing a more evidence-based approach to recruitment, the business leaders sought a more behaviourally-based career development framework that incorporated a series of simulated development centres and learning initiatives designed to improve both current and future project management capability.

- This in itself led to the development of the Talent Scorecard approach, which is summarized in Part 2 of this case study, later in this chapter.

The use of an HR metric in this case study highlights the value of introducing a measurement framework in Box 1 of the model. HR metrics are indicators that enable HR to track and measure performance on different aspects of people process or practice, and can ultimately support the prediction of future people performance over time. However, not all HR metrics are created equal.

Dr John Sullivan, international HR thought leader, suggests that there are five elements that drive an effective metric in HR:[2]

- **quality**: the error rate or quality of the output of a process;
- **quantity**: the numerical output of a given process over a specific period of time;
- **time**: the speed or elapsed period of time within which a specified action or process is completed from start to finish;
- **money**: the cost or revenues associated with or produced by a specified action or process;
- **customer satisfaction**: the degree to which the outcome of the process matches the expectation as defined by the customer of the action or process.

The development of HR metrics provides a useful framework that creates a systematic approach to the measurement of people-based process and/or practice outcomes.

SYSTEMATIC REPORTING

At this level, our research shows that requests for people information are becoming increasingly important to the business. As these reports take time to compile, HR needs to become more efficient and systematic in their focus and production. Everyone wants to understand (for example) attrition, so a situation could occur whereby everyone is asking for a monthly dashboard with the KPIs relating to attrition.

The challenge is that everyone may well be doing it their own way. HR needs to start to work across the organization to harmonize definitions, to streamline and organize their data, and this takes some protracted effort to consolidate libraries and embed the consolidated information into, ideally, a global HR system.

At this stage, many organizations implement systems such as Workday, Oracle Fusion or SAP Success Factors, globally or at least at a regional level. It's at this stage that organizations are seen to move from Box 1 to Box 2, where reporting can become much more systematic through the use of technology to automatically produce core HR dashboards with standardized definitions. This means that any business-led ad hoc requests can be provided with minimal time delays.

FIGURE 6.3   Systematic reporting

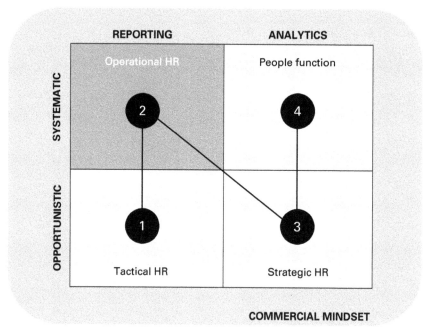

Adapted from the Crunchr Maturity Model for People Analytics

For organizations operating in Box 2 (see Figure 6.3), HR should be able to answer these simple questions:

- What is the age profile across our workforce?
- How many employees are aged 65 or above?
- What is the average pay of male and female employees?
- What's the pay differentiation between male and female employees?
- What is our attrition for employees who just joined the organization at middle management, senior leadership and executive level roles?
- How much is budgeted and spent on employee branding, and how does that relate to last year's expenditure and budget?

If you are able to access data that can answer these questions relatively simply then you are likely to be operating, or able to operate, in Box 2.

The next case study outlines that shift from Box 1 to Box 2, driven not only by changing internal business needs, but also external demands – in this case from the financial services sector regulators.

CASE STUDY
Admiral Group underwrites better data management

Admiral Group, a leading financial services company within the UK with businesses in seven countries, globally partnered with a business analytics provider to transform its employee data management and workforce planning activities across multiple locations. With a global workforce of around 10,000 employees and 7,000 in the UK, Admiral Group has offices around the globe. From locations in the UK to Canada and India, the company required powerful data management tools to organize its operations.

Solution application

Admiral is using SAP technology to gain insights into the performance of key business areas and identify areas for improvement. This process includes examining attrition and absence reporting information and data about its core business areas and analysing this to make informed decisions. A vital function of the new system is to ensure products and services are up-to-date and compliant with the latest regulations.

The solution also allows Admiral's HRBPs across geographical areas to work together closely with key divisions of the business, gaining access to performance and employee information in real time. The data allows managers to make quicker decisions, and has helped automate many manual tasks in areas such as IT, facilities and the company's data warehouse.

Alex Deem, systems manager at Admiral Group, comments: "We needed a solution that could bring together departments and ensure accurate decision-making across the whole business. We are already transforming the way we work by giving managers access to real-time workplace performance data, giving us useful insights that allow us to improve our business for the long term."

Nick Felton, senior vice president of MHR Analytics, says: "For a long time, data has been the backbone of the insurance sector, and Admiral understands the vital role it can play when making important business decisions. Now, it's even more vital for many reasons, not least the need for insurance companies to comply with new regulations like International Financial Reporting Standards (IFRS). Insurance products need to be updated continuously, and it is only with the smart use of the data they own that insurers can remain competitive."

FIGURE 6.4   Bringing together disparate data through technology

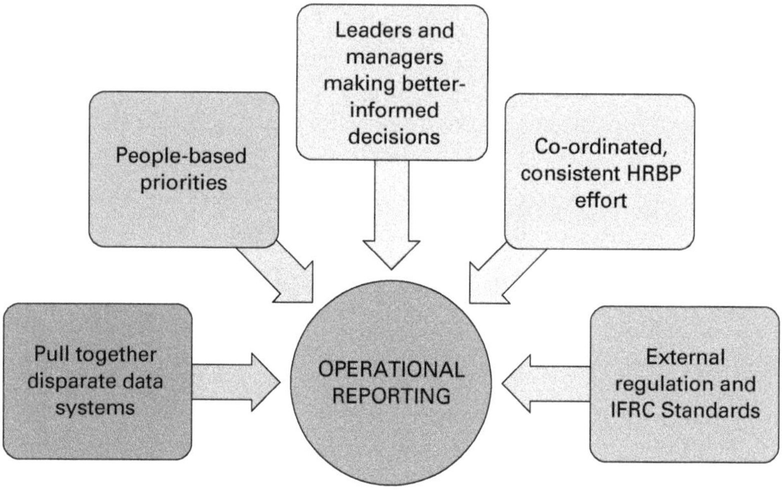

Figure 6.4 summarizes the impact that the new system had on the Admiral Group.

Courtesy of MHR Analytics: www.mhranalytics.com (archived at https://perma.cc/3LJA-PRQP)

With the shift to using a unified technology system, access to data becomes easier and enables managers to become self-service users.

Analytics

The shift to developing a more evidence-based HR function via the application of analytics from Box 2 to Box 3 is the most challenging transition for people functions. There is a strong desire to be operating in Box 3 (see Figure 6.5), and even Box 4 as soon as possible, but our research has found that organizations are still struggling with basic definitions. So, the trick for moving from Box 2 to Box 3, from systematic reporting to opportunistic analytics, is to create focused organizational momentum for change and make better informed data-based decisions.

This usually entails the formation of business groups across a business, where a pool of individuals and stakeholders from both the business and HR investigate the route to making the necessary changes. Key questions can tend to revolve around:

FIGURE 6.5   Opportunistic analytics

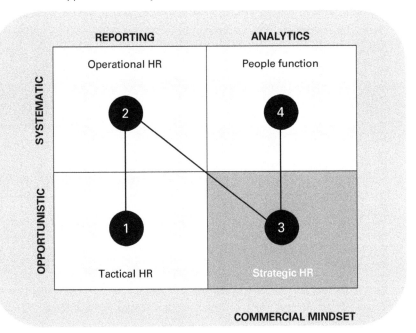

Adapted from the Crunchr Maturity Model for People Analytics

- Why is the attrition in business-critical roles increasing?
- Why has that happened?
- What can we do about it?
- What is the impact on business performance?
- How can we quantify the challenges and the opportunities that this issue has created?

This is when the business starts asking the "so what? now what?" follow-up questions, and that is when HR has a tangible business reason to undertake more complex analytics.

OPPORTUNISTIC ANALYTICS
This is where businesses and their leaders may now request a more analytical response to their business demands. This is where you may need to provide an analytics-based appetizer to the business, in the form of small experiments to show how different or better-informed decisions could be made using a more evidence-based approach. This remains an opportunistic

approach because HR may not have all the necessary data available to immediately answer the question, but will be required to draw information and data from wider sources and channels to make sense of the challenge.

The case study focusing on HR metrics earlier in this chapter was opportunistic by nature, and it instigated the desire from the business for a more structured approach to researching, collecting and understanding people-based capability data in a business context. The second stage of this project, which focused on more of a human capital-based approach to assessing and understanding an employee's skills in relation to their cost/value, was a crossover between Box 2 and Box 3.

CASE STUDY
Using business-led metrics drives the desire for more people data (part 2)

Business problem

This case study is part 2 of the story about a global multinational conglomerate headquartered in Europe, and relates to its technology solutions business. Improvements to the recruitment of project managers had raised the issue in the eyes of the business leaders about how data could provide more comprehensive insights and inform better decision-making throughout the range of people related processes and practices that were adopted.

Assessing its 1,500-strong workforce based on robust and effective assessment approaches such as psychometric testing, structured interviews, assessment centres and criteria based sifting tools would be ideal, but resources, timing and costs precluded this being an option. The challenge was assessing the whole workforce in a consistent and robust way so that reliable data could be provided to inform development, reward, future potential and resource capability decisions. This would continue the advancement of the professionalism and practice of project management across the business.

The methodology and process

It became apparent that there was a lack of insight into the capability of the workforce at an individual, team and business level and given the budgetary constraints it was decided that a new process called the Talent Scorecard was to be adopted. This method is designed to facilitate a structured approach to assessing individual's capability and talent via a scorecard approach.

This meant that assessment of the crucial job-related performance areas would be undertaken and could, if required, relate this to their value or worth to the organization. It enabled the organization to:

- provide an overview of an individual's capability;
- identify an individual's value to an organization;
- identify possible development needs;
- differentiate between different individuals in terms of capability and their development.

This was based on the collection of existing people data and, where areas of data were not available, a structured facilitated process to collect these in a consistent and reliable format. The simple framework is based on:

capability / employment costs × 100 = Employee Value (EV)

The approach was as follows:

1 Job demands: Five job families/talent frameworks had been identified and 18 specific job profiles for the whole organization were put in place as the basis for the assessment.

2 Key capability demands (behaviours, knowledge domains, experience) for each job profile had been identified.

3 Psychometric profiles had been obtained for the employees so they could be assessed against researched "job fit" profiles for critical project management roles and support roles.

4 Individual demographic data (salary, bonuses, benefit costs, workspace costs and so on) were downloaded from the HRIS.

5 For other criteria areas for which data-based information was not available, frameworks for assessment were created relating to behavioural competencies, potential, business contribution and culture fit.

6 Facilitated sessions were then run with line managers to obtain individual assessments for their team to ensure that differentiation occurred between individuals in their team (not all high, medium or low ratings) with a range of rating and ranking methods adopted to obtain data-based assessment across various capability areas. The facilitation process was complemented with HRBPs and learning advisers so that future assessment using this method could be run in-house.

7 Feedback from individuals about their capability was also obtained.

8 Calibration sessions then were run to ensure that across various business areas and teams that there were no significant inconsistencies or anomalies being seen in terms of approach.

9 Data collection was completed and line managers were briefed regarding the results/feedback for their team and the individuals within them. Sample results are shown in Table 6.1.

10 Sessions were then run with all individuals to focus on career, technical and behavioural based development moving forward – some with the support of HR and learning and development (L&D).

How data drove different conversations

By reviewing the results of Team A in Table 6.1, you can see an overview of the process in terms of the framework that was adopted to collect a consistent data base on the workforce capability. The real added value that emerged was that the data drove different conversations regarding individuals. For example, the line manager of Team A was surprised to see that Employee E had the highest Employee Value (EV), whereas Employee H had the lowest.

Further investigation revealed that Employee E, a recent graduate, had made a significant impact within the project team and, whilst still lacking experience and a level of detailed project management-based process knowledge, had developed a level of capability that had supported the potential expectations for that employee. Given that the rest of the team had a minimum of five years of projects-based expertise, Employee E had made significant progress. The conversation revolved around a need to reward that progress, in other words reduce their current EV assessment, as a retention strategy for that individual. The data suggested that Employee E could be a potential retention risk. Development opportunities were outlined to Employee E, but their remuneration was not changed; they subsequently left two months later to join a competitor with a higher remuneration package.

Looking at Employee H, this was a highly experienced project management practitioner who was regarded as an industry expert. The data revealed whether the organization was prepared to pay for that expertise, given that other capability areas were at a lower level than other colleagues in the team. The outcome was that their expertise was needed to be more widely used if value was to be fully obtained from the individual. A new role emerged in the organization that focused on their knowledge and associated product/process expertise across the business as a whole.

The key was that the consistent format of data was providing different insights for consideration that enabled comparisons, the identification of relative strengths and development needs and focus at all times on the business imperative in terms of getting value for money from individuals.

TABLE 6.1   Talent scorecard sample

1. Name	Competencies (out of 400)	Personal characteristics (out of 100)	Knowledge (out of 100)	Experience (out of 100)	Potential (out of 100)	Business contribution (out of 100)	Culture fit (out of 100)	Talent score (out of 1000)
A	252	68	60	62	55	60	60	617
B	271	78	75	70	68	75	57	694
C	272	59	68	62	72	64	60	657
D	247	66	70	64	64	60	62	633
E	217	70	53	50	66	55	68	579
F	218	62	59	54	50	50	54	547
G	285	67	69	68	64	68	60	681
H	246	58	79	66	52	62	62	625

The calculation could stop at this stage: The financial value aspect of the process is aligned to those organizations who want to assess the human capital value of their people.

TABLE 6.1 *continued*

2.

Name	Salary	Performance bonus	Organization's 12% NI contributions	Benefits (including pensions)	Organizational overhead as % of salary (18% used)	Total costs
A	44,800	9,040	6,461	2,600	8,064	70,965
B	47,800	12,240	7,205	2,600	8,604	78,449
C	38,800	7,769	5,588	2,300	6,984	61,441
D	49,800	8,483	6,994	2,850	8,964	77,091
E	30,000	5,002	4,200	1,850	5,400	46,452
F	39,000	5,643	5,357	2,450	7,020	59,470
G	46,800	10,539	6,881	2,700	8,424	75,344
H	58,000	8,550	7,986	3,100	10,440	88,076

3.

Name	Talent score		Total costs		EV
A	617	÷	70,965	×	0.87
B	694	÷	78,449	×	0.88
C	657	÷	61,441	×	1.07
D	633	÷	77,091	×	0.82
E	579	÷	46,452	×	1.24
F	547	÷	59,470	×	0.92
G	681	÷	75,344	×	0.90
H	625	÷	88,076	×	0.71

(Organizational overhead as % of salary column and EV multiplier of 100 applied.)

Outcomes

Apart from the quality of dialogue that the data drove, other key outcomes from this initiative were:

- The audit provided a clear data base regarding all of the workforce's capability. This in turn enabled:
  - individual development to be taken forward across the business based on data insights;
  - organizational initiatives to be identified regarding skill development gaps that existed in relation to perceived future client demands (eg digital practices, technology infrastructure knowledge);
  - workforce and succession planning to be taken forward based using tangible data and analytical insights, rather than the intuitive approach that had been adopted in the past.
- Across the business, retention had significantly increased, with vacancies falling from 11 per cent in year 1 to 4 per cent in year 2. This was perceived to have saved the organization in the region of £1.1 million in recruiting and wasted training costs.

Key learnings revolved around the need for transparency in terms of how the data was being used. The involvement of the employees to appreciate the rationale and the desired L&D outcomes that were being sought was regarded as key. It became clear that the process had raised the capability of line managers not only to have difficult conversations, but also to feel more enabled to discuss development and coach individuals on improvement methods.

The case study demonstrates how utilizing data can drive different conversations, especially if the analytical rigour behind it is challenging existing perspectives that may be held on people issues.

If the business asks how many new hires have left the organization in the past 12 months, it is vital that HR demonstrate the loss to the organization in a language that is both relevant and impactful to the business leaders. That means that HR should express this impact in lost revenue – so you need to correlate and link your data with revenue numbers. As these numbers are unlikely to be within your core HR systems, this data will need to be obtained from the accounting and financial systems in place.

This is an experimental approach as it's a project which may take longer due to the lack of easy access to the data required. However, an answer can be obtained, as shown in the case study below.

CASE STUDY
Reducing the number of failed hires

Context

A UK organization that hires 600 people every year was facing issues with the quality of their new hires. The business had asked HR to look into this matter. As the business had asked HR to do the analysis and to dive deep into the problem, this focused upon Box 3 of the model (see Figure 6.5). As this was an opportunistic analytics activity and because the organization was shifting to Box 3, they had all the data items and information available to review. Building this business case took them just two hours, whereas historically this could have taken up to three months to do a similar exercise.

The project demonstrated a huge benefit, as HR could now immediately inform the business of:

- the number of people that left within the first 12 months;
- the percentage of people hired that left – 49 per cent;
- the average tenure – 4½ months.

This was a key business problem because the time it takes to be fully proficient and productive was known to be nearly eight months. The information now available led to an insight that could be shared with the business leaders – 49 per cent of the people that are hired would never become productive.

Further data insights

Going a step further, HR needed to quantify the extent of the business challenge. This revolved around the wasted salary and recruitment costs. By assessing the financial data, HR observed that the total cost of failed hires was £2.4 million every single year. The context behind this piece of data was that the organization needed to drive profits in order to cover these losses; so how much revenue was needed? The answer was that the organization needed to make £13 million a year to cover the cost of failed hires.

HR were quickly able to understand the business context, translate key data points into information and then into insights. As a result of that, the business requested further support from HR to show the future direction and take proper action to reduce the risk that this hiring dilemma was creating.

Because the business had shifted from Box 2, all the information was ready to be used. HR probed the data to identify that the highest failed hires were being seen in the engineering and IT departments. Using the developing capability of HR at that time and the technology tools available, HR worked with IT and further found that people were leaving either after one month or after the sixth month. That meant that the data was saying that not only was there a selection issue, but also an onboarding challenge and a retention/development issue to be addressed.

HR probed deeper into the data by analysing the recruiting channels that they used. Because HR had access to a more systematic source of information, they were able to provide recommendations for the IT department in terms of changes to be made. One of the recommendations was that they should not use the "Careers" section of the website for their recruitment, because the data showed that it yielded 31 per cent of the failed hires that were being seen. HR recommended that LinkedIn should be used as an alternative, and they continue to monitor the interventions and the data that is being provided to gauge the success of the changes that have been made.

Courtesy of Crunchr: www.crunchrapps.com (archived at https://perma.cc/2ZH8-BUCR)

As the case study outlined, it was an initial project that created further interest and an appetite for further investigation from business leaders. At some stage, all analytics teams or HRBPs will be faced with these challenges as they prove the value of a more data-based approach; thereafter demand will increase.

Our research shows that there are still few organizations who have fully shifted their analytics-based operations into Box 3 (see Figure 6.5). A trend that will be evident is the need to demonstrate the proof of concept by way of experiments or "one-offs". These projects need to reflect a critical business problem that requires executive or senior leadership consideration. The first chance to impress is so vital, and it's important therefore to focus on the need-to-know, rather than the nice-to-know.

The next case study focuses on Box 3 activity driven by a professional data scientist, Dr Max Blumberg, who was focusing on solving a sales performance issue. It includes a clearly structured approach to identifying data insights with elements of Box 4 in terms of predictive analysis.

CASE STUDY
Growing sales using people analytics at Rentokil Initial

Dr Max Blumberg, founder of Blumberg Partnership

Business problem

Founded in 1925 and listed on the London Stock Exchange, Rentokil Initial provides pest control and hygiene services across 70 countries with over 36,000 employees.

There are three global brands and some local brands in several other countries. In 2018, Rentokil had revenues of approximately £2.4 billion. Dr Max Blumberg was approached by the Rentokil CEO at the time, Alan Brown, who had started a period of examining operations and in particular sales expertise and performance. This is the story of how Max utilized a people analytics-based approach to identify sales performance improvements.

Sales results and turnover at Rentokil Initial were highly variable among the 700 global sales people. Some regions were overachieving their targets easily, while others were consistently underachieving. The CEO was keen to explore this using an analytical approach, in contrast to the anecdotal information he was receiving from the various managers and directors in the business.

Feedback from other leaders was highlighting people-related topics, so the focus was on the sales workforce itself rather than territory alignment, market opportunity or competition. A more methodical approach to assessing and improving sales performance was being sought and so Max was asked to undertake the analysis.

Approach

Initially, Max interviewed sales leaders in different regions around the world in a bid to isolate a hypothesis that might explain the sales performance issues. Following these initial interviews, it was clear there were different hypotheses depending on who he spoke to. These included:

- effective sales training delivered at the right time will develop the technical confidence needed for successful sales performance;
- better recognition tools will increase seller motivation to deliver higher performance;
- a globally consistent recruitment process for sales staff will deliver higher performing salespeople.

Max set about gathering data relevant to his hypotheses in a multi-pronged approach. This involved:

1 A detailed literature review of all the work that had been undertaken on sales performance in various industries, to understand whether examples existed of similar sales challenges elsewhere.

2 An analysis of the HR practices at Rentokil Initial. Given the range of hypotheses and ideas presented to him, Max wanted to clarify the various processes and policies that existed for each of the main HR functions, including recruitment, compensation, management training and leadership development.

3 Feedback from the workforce. A survey was used to investigate employees' perspectives of the HR processes in the company. People were asked to score the efficiency and importance of each HR process to sales performance. When the survey results were analysed, it was clear that recruitment was viewed as the most inefficient yet most important HR process (see Figure 6.6).

This analysis allowed Max to focus on a single hypothesis – that a globally efficient and consistent recruitment process with clear criteria will improve sales performance. Max continued his investigations and next looked at whether the most commonly used selection tests correlated with sales performance. Only small correlations between the two most frequently used tests and sales performance were found and he recommended that these tests be discontinued. This recommendation was implemented.

Next, the team collected and analysed another new set of data, gathered from surveying the sales force, to identify the specific attributes that were most highly correlated with sales performance. These attributes were grouped into categories such as conscientiousness, interests, interpersonal skills and cognitive ability.

The next step of the analysis involved looking for a selection test that would accurately identify these identified attributes. The team undertook a literature review to source validated and relevant tests, and also conducted an extensive review of the selection tests available in the marketplace. In the end, six externally sourced tests that appeared to meet the criteria needed to improve sales performance were chosen.

Using these six tests, Max undertook a study among 270 sales people in the UK and US. Each person took all six tests, and their results were analysed against their sales performance. This became a complex and sensitive exercise; partly due to the need to work with six vendors across the many global assessment platforms in Rentokil at that time, but also because of a significant level of concern among sales professionals taking the tests and their sales leaders about how the results would be used.

Using this seller assessment data set, various statistical analyses were undertaken to identify which traits could be linked to high sales performers. The analysis revealed that one test in particular, a personality assessment, had a strong relationship to sales performance. Max predicted that the use of this assessment would identify an above-average sales person with a high degree of accuracy. Using the UK sales population, Max then converted that into financial value. Should the assessment be adopted and implemented, he estimated that in the UK alone there would be a potential increase in sales of £1.5 million per annum.

From these and further analyses, Max was able to make a very specific recommendation to implement one external test for the selection of all future salespeople worldwide. He also made detailed recommendations for the redevelopment and global standardization of the recruitment process, as well as the implementation

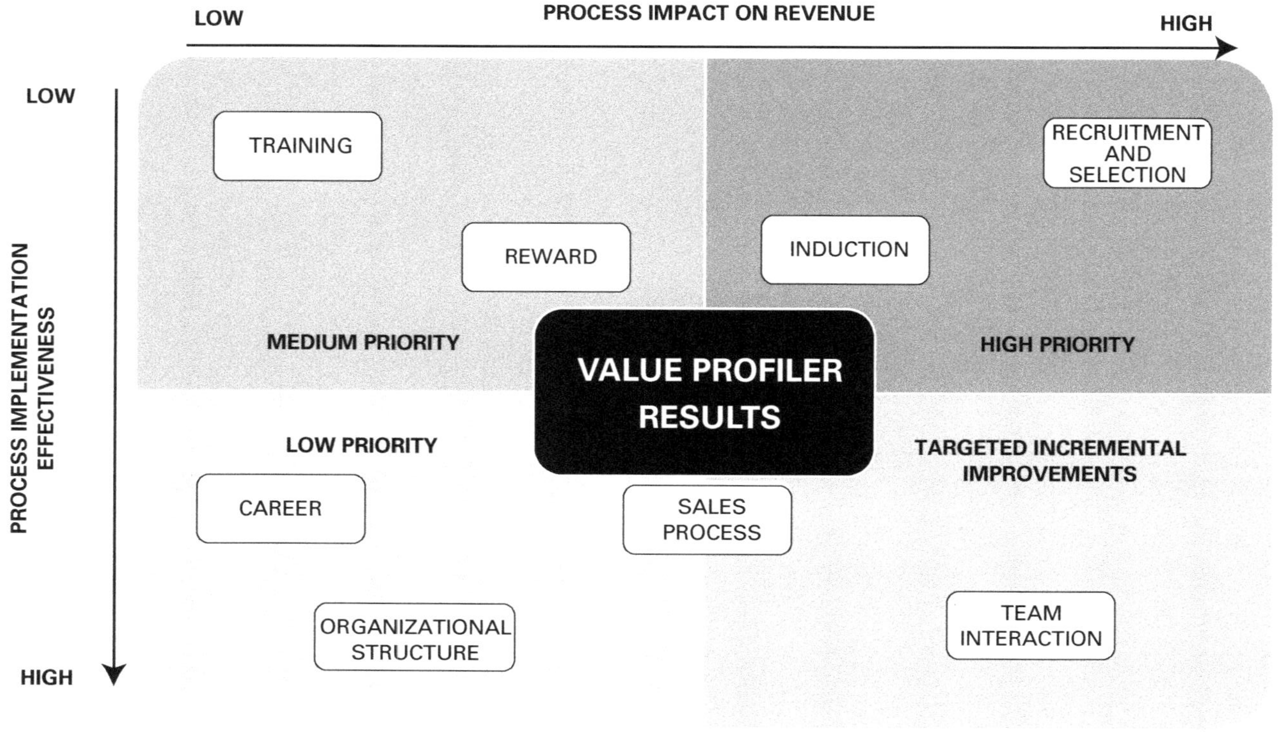

FIGURE 6.6   HR processes plotted by inefficiency and importance to sales

of new induction programmes and associated recruitment and induction training for managers.

Implementation and outcomes

There were strong governance principles established throughout the project with regular checkpoints with three core groups of stakeholders:

- The global executive team and sales directors: This group required ongoing one-to-one meetings as well as some team meetings at every stage of the project, to ensure that they not only understood the insights from the analyses and associated recommendations, but also were clear about the decisions that were required.
- Works councils, especially in Germany and France: This audience was briefed and managed carefully. The works councils were made aware of the benefits of the project to those countries' businesses and to the individual workers within them.
- The sales force: Communications with the entire sales force were handled through regular newsletters and emails. When needed, personalized communications were sent to salespeople asking for their participation in the surveys outlined earlier. These private emails strengthened the message that the collection of personal data would be treated with a high degree of confidentiality.

Communication was only part of the story, as implementation of the recommendations required extensive planning within the recruitment function as well as the associated HR functions, such as induction training and sales enablement. Specific elements of the plan included:

- procuring the selected assessment;
- implementing the technology needed to manage one global assessment test, which resulted in implementation of a standard global recruitment process;
- training in interviewing techniques to align all hiring managers with the new recruitment process and selection criteria.

Furthermore, the plans needed to be implemented worldwide. To achieve this, the team used a phased approach starting with the US and UK, moving on to Europe and concluding with the rest of the world. The implementation plan took one year to roll out fully to all countries.

The entire project took over two years to complete. The first year provided clarity around the business problem and enabled data collection and analysis. The second year was focused on the implementation of the recommendations. With the CEO sponsoring the project and effective stakeholder management and involvement of sales professionals throughout, the project had a high chance of adoption and success.

FIGURE 6.7 The human capital value profiler framework

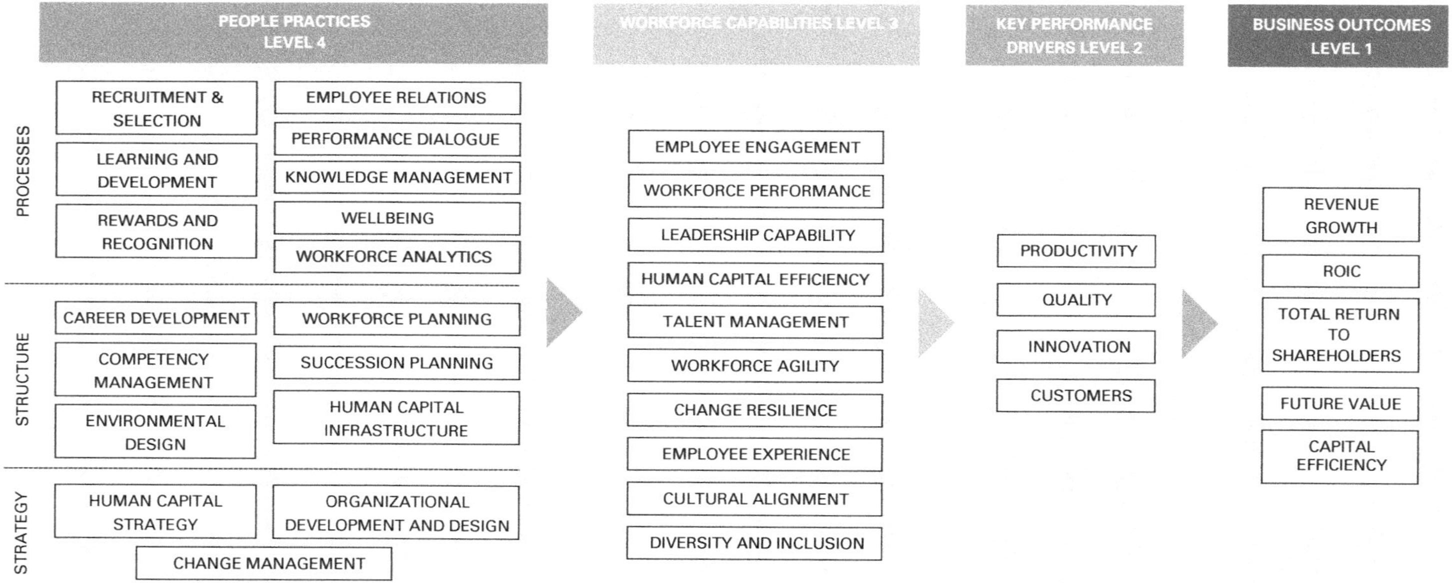

© Blumberg Partnership

In the year following the project, sales improved by over 40 per cent and the return on investment from the project was over 300 per cent. In conclusion, this project demonstrated a clear and direct business impact in terms of increased sales. It was successful because of the high-level sponsorship, effective stakeholder management and the use of a strong methodical approach to analytics.

Key learnings

Successful analytics projects require these key elements:

- strong sponsorship from senior leaders and a clear business problem to solve;
- well-researched hypotheses which then need to be validated and verified as part of the analytical methodology;
- an iterative process of collecting data, analysing it and discovering insights will lead to the identification of a clear recommendation, in this instance a single selection test;
- good communication with each stakeholder group;
- recommendations backed up with strong statistical evidence and a quantified financial impact, in this case improved sales.

www.blumbergpartnership.com (archived at https://perma.cc/8AJC-H4YC)

The project methodology that was adopted is clearly defined, and was based on a value profiler framework as shown in Figure 6.7. From a human capital perspective, making the right people process decisions, in this instance sales-based, delivers the workforce capabilities that an organization needs to enable its key performance drivers (KPDs), which drive the organization's desired business outcomes.

Conversely, if managers make poor people process decisions, the organization will not have the workforce capabilities and KPDs that it needs to achieve its desired business outcomes. The key point here is that desired business outcomes depend strongly on the quality of decisions that managers make about people processes. The analysis that was undertaken identified the priorities that needed to be refined and changed to improve the performance of the sales team.

SYSTEMATIC ANALYTICS

Organizations move to Box 4 (see Figure 6.8) when they can perform more complex analysis for queries that not just one business leader is requesting, but that almost all business leaders are now requesting. An example could include the need to monitor retention challenges and specifically failed hires who had been with the organization between three and 12 months. Some organizations may want to have little nudges or proactive signals that highlight possible loss of employees.

This is at the more complex level of analytical activity, and it may take some time to establish the criteria behind such a system. The key to this is obviously a robust technology system which is basically a nerve system that constantly seeks out data opportunities, risks etc and flags them to the relevant end users, proactively making suggestions on how to solve the performance issue that has been identified.

FIGURE 6.8   Systematic analytics

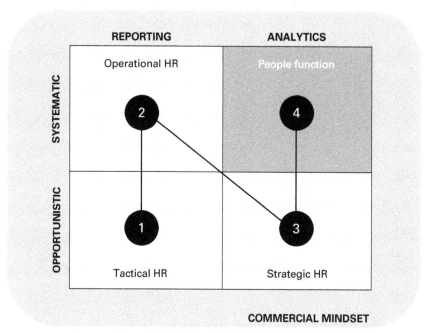

Adapted from the Crunchr Maturity Model for People Analytics

It's a decision support system that organizations aspire to create and whilst at the moment there is no one holistic technology system out there that can do that, this type of solution will emerge over the next few years. We believe that the people function must be at the epicentre for this integrated and holistic process to work efficiently across the organization.

Shifting from reporting to analytics

Any transitions across the model have a clear reliance upon the capabilities of HR, on the quality of the data and on the sophistication of the technology platform being utilized. A summary of the key characteristics in these areas across the model are in Table 6.2.

One of the key challenges is that most of the current HR capabilities today are relevant for Box 1-based activity. These include the HRBPs that have a local business client perspective, but they are still learning about data structures and tend to just work with Microsoft Excel using their graphs functionality to try and tell a story.

HR needs to upgrade their commercial capabilities, and this is something that we believe is a real challenge:

- In Box 2, HR needs to start thinking almost as a data engineer with a strong diagnostic focus.
- In Box 3, HR needs to think like a business consultant.
- In Box 4, HR needs to think like a data/computer scientist and business architect.

There is the opportunity for HR practitioners to develop their capability. We know from some organizations that becoming highly data-orientated is achievable if that mindset shift is made in terms of recognizing the change that the people practitioners of the future need to make. It's about having that commercially-orientated mindset, and it will be a journey that can take some time to fulfil. A framework for development is included in Chapter 9 that can help you to change the way that you can operate, certainly to Box 3 level.

The challenge here for HR practitioners is that they are always looking for that "silver bullet" that will simplify the whole process and enable them to provide an insight without all of the hard work. A common model used in analytics is the "Data – Insight – Story" model. The model is based upon looking at the data, drawing insights from that data and then telling a convincing story. See Figure 6.9.

It's a useful framework, but reviewing rows of numbers and data in isolation won't always provide you with the compelling and inspiring insights that you desire unless you adopt a more structured analytical process. The key is identifying the business problem that needs to be investigated and

TABLE 6.2   Characteristics on the journey

Level	HR capability	Data	Technology
Opportunistic reporting	• Users are mainly HR administrators. • Will use Microsoft Excel and try to analyse the data and present the information in the best possible way. • Unlikely to possess the skills to work with more complex software solutions like SPSS, Python R or Tableau.	• Data is disorganized and scattered. • Unlikely to have clear definitions and metrics throughout the organization on any job level or functional departments. • May be disparities in terms of how criteria is described (for example, should an organization include interns, students and gig workers into their full-time employees calculation).	• Unlikely to be any specialized HR reporting tool. • Majority of the data is being stored locally, possibly in Excel spreadsheets.
Systematic reporting	• Users are mainly HRBPs with better developed skills who will want more detailed information. • Stronger numerical orientation will be required at this level. • Will be comfortable with unexplained numbers and challenges. • Will consider creating a roadmap for a people analytics strategy. • Consulting capabilities become vital to research, analyse and feed back data-based storytelling. • Focus on insights that drive tangible change and improved performance. • More complex calculations undertaken by analysts or data scientists.	• Likely to be a standard library of definitions that have been agreed across the whole organization. • Clear and consistent definitions mean that benchmarking data points across different regions, countries, functions or business units can occur. • Data likely to have been cleansed, thereby providing more consistent and robust data to work with.	• Likely to be an integrated HRIS at least at a regional level sometimes at the local level. • There may be a range of tools or solutions in place to help with more complex HR reporting.

Level	HR capability	Data	Technology
Opportunistic analytics	• Some HRBPs may be active in this space depending upon their numerical capability. • Likely to be considering the adoption of a data scientist (buy, borrow or build) or analyst with complex statistical capabilities. • The scoping of business issues and storytelling-based feedback falls firmly to HRBPs to facilitate.	• Data becomes much richer and varied. • Ongoing data cleansing likely. • Solid base of people data exists with access to business performance data, customer satisfaction, financials and other lines of historic information available. • Will have established and synthesized demographic definitions. • Likely to have historic data over at least two or three years, that is suitably organized to make accessibility easier.	• Building on the HRIS in place, likely to be using or accessing workforce analytics-based technology. • Supporting tools in place to maximize data analysis.
Systematic analytics	• Main focus will be on data scientists and analysts with complex statistical capabilities. • Again, the scoping of business issues and storytelling-based feedback falls firmly to HRBPs to facilitate. • With the rapid advent of artificial intelligence (AI) and machine learning interventions, access to data engineers, computer scientists, and architects may be required.	• Multiple quality data sources now involved. • Increased automation of data means that caution needs to be demonstrated; automated technology data may have been constructed differently to normal parameters.	• Organizations will be seeking to make a permanent connection between finance, business performance and core HR systems to maximize the available data sets. • Increasingly exploring AI and machine learning-based systems to provide data across people practices. • Accessibility will need to be automated to support a future-based AI enabled decision-making support system.

FIGURE 6.9   Data – Insight – Story model

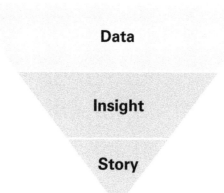

explored, so that you can focus on answering some of these key business questions:

- How can we improve the profitability of the organization?
- How can we improve the revenue generated by the organization?
- How can we improve the cost base of the organization?
- How can risk be mitigated or reduced?
- How can we make the organization more agile and responsive to external forces?

These are real business issues, so it's important that HR identifies some of the pressure points for the organization, translates these as lost opportunities in terms of lost revenue, reduced costs, increased risk and so on, builds a hypothesis and prepares the data that enables this to be explored.

Reporting is anchored in Box 2, and analytics that can examine relevant people practices and its associated data is based in Box 3. The embedding of that methodology can then lead to systematic-based Box 4 level activity, with regular insights being generated by the infrastructure that will ultimately be led by the people function.

Dirk Jonker, people analytics expert and CEO of Crunchr, believes that as companies follow the rules of the maturity model, without taking short cuts, all foundational aspects of systemic people analytics will grow. The initial scattered data will become rich and of good quality, people practitioners will develop their business consulting capabilities and organizations may well then establish an advanced analytics centre of excellence, putting technology in place to make the people analytics function super-scalable and democratize the insights to the full organization.

KEY TAKEAWAYS FROM THIS CHAPTER

1 Each of our case studies reveal their own specific learnings based on their journey, but the key trends revolve around having a strategy, being mindful of the organization's culture, developing an approach that fits with the business demands/interests and ensuring that the capability to undertake the analysis process is in place across all your HR practitioners.

2 There is no "one size fits all" approach to implementing analytics into your people function, but it is underpinned by capability, data and technology.

References

1 Crunchr (2019) The difference between HR Analytics and People Analytics (and why it matters), *Crunchr* [Online] https://blog.crunchrapps.com/blog/the-difference-between-hr-analytics-people-analytics-and-why-it-matters (archived at https://perma.cc/SB6K-3HWE)

2 Sullivan, Dr J (2003) *HR Metrics: The World Class Way – How to build the business case for human resources*, Kennedy Information, Bristol

7

Business insights from people analytics

People analytics is not just about finding interesting data and information and raising issues that have materialized for leaders and managers. Data is being used to understand every part of a business operation, and people-analytical tools, techniques and processes are being embedded in some organizations, driven by the increasing adoption of cloud HR systems.

In this chapter, we expand on the people analytics capability model (Figure 6.1) by sharing a series of case studies about how organizations are either starting their analytics journey or are already under way and looking for further operational improvements. We have dedicated this chapter to providing practitioner business insights from the application of people analytics in an organizational context.

This chapter will focus entirely on:

• **Providing business insights through people analytics:** Learning from those who have gone before is vital. We will demonstrate how data and analytics methods have been used to show the value of the people function in a range of different organizations.

People analytics: providing business insights through analytics

People analytics is a journey, not a destination. Organizations across the globe are on this journey, which starts with basic workforce reporting and moves through to analytics driven by mathematics, and then more complex statistics powered by data science and technology.

It has proven difficult for HR to upgrade its capabilities to fully handle the demands that people analytics makes on the function. This is primarily because this journey requires a mature usage of data and its integration from a multitude of systems and processes. Most data systems within organizations are disparate, where the definitions and key matrices are not harmonized. It takes time for HR to achieve a certain level of analytical maturity, to develop skill sets and the data-driven commercial mindset to use data to support decision-making. Nevertheless, today's modern people analytics technology may have a solution to this problem, as these cloud-based software solutions enable the integration of all these disparate systems into one system and can provide real-time insights that link to business performance.

People analytics has opened the door to a new people function driven by the digital future of work. Strategic HR leaders need to focus on developing a strategy that encourages knowledge transfer across business functions and fosters collaboration so that data and learning in this discipline can be taken forward. Combining data insights with the human touch, the people function has a real opportunity to take the lead in creating a data-driven culture that can both improve business results and demonstrate added value in business terms.

Types of analytics

There are four core types of analytics:

- **Descriptive analytics**: These describe what has already happened, or what is currently happening. This is about taking historical data and summarizing it into something that is understandable.

- **Diagnostic analytics**: These reveal the underlying cause of the events presented by descriptive data. If you know the cause, you know where to focus your efforts to mitigate the problem.

- **Predictive analytics**: These focus on what might happen in the future, based on the details of past events. Statistical models and forecasts are used to answer the question of what could happen. Models are built on patterns that were found within descriptive analytics.

- **Prescriptive analytics**: These analytics provide recommendations about what to do, based upon predictions and what has happened in the past. These are all based upon evidence-based insights.

See Figure 7.1.

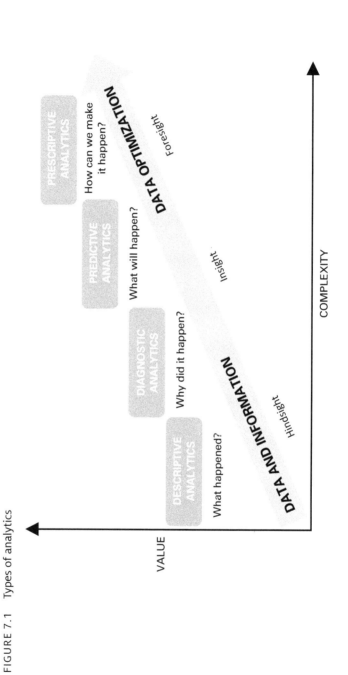

FIGURE 7.1   Types of analytics

Our intention is to share a series of case studies which reflect the distinctive journeys that a number of different organizations have undertaken as they have strived to become more data-driven and relevant to their organizations. These case studies are not the answer in themselves, but they show:

- a range of different and similar approaches to the challenges that they faced;

- some examples of the different types of analytics that can be used;

- the fact that opportunities have played a critical role in their journey; some driven by the business and some by proactive HR leaders;

- the fact that the culture of the organizations meant that certain approaches have been tailored, to ensure that there was an acceptance of what they were trying to achieve.

None of the organizations would suggest that their way is the only way for other organizations to approach analytics, but they have been very keen to share their learnings in the hope that it can support and guide others to be successful on their journey.

The British Heart Foundation (BHF) is at the very start of their analytics journey, and their case study reflects the approach they adopted for their organization and the challenges that they face as they move from Boxes 1 and 2 to Box 3 (see Chapter 6) over the next few months.

CASE STUDY
Putting our hearts and minds into people analytics at BHF (starting the journey)

Sarah Cousins, senior organizational change specialist at BHF, and Kirsten Edwards, head of analytics at Empathix Ltd

The BHF is a charity formed in 1961 in the United Kingdom, with the primary focus of funding scientific research into heart and circulatory diseases and their risk factors. Through investment in research centres of excellence in top-tier universities including Oxford, Cambridge and King's College London and other related activities, the BHF is a major funder and authority on cardiovascular research, education and care. More than 7 million people are living with heart and circulatory diseases in the UK. The BHF are committed to beating the heartbreak these conditions cause to families and loved ones every day. They want to create a world free from the fear of heart and circulatory diseases.

The BHF employs nearly 4,500 paid employees and over 20,000 volunteers working together to help beat heartbreak forever. It is a complex organization including research, fundraising and retail, which manages approximately 750 charity shops. The life-saving work done by the BHF seems to be reflected in the attitudes of its people, and they were awarded the top-rated workplace in the not-for-profit sector by Indeed in April 2019, as well as winning three HR Excellence awards in July 2019.

Context for change

The people and organizational development (POD) team at the BHF wanted to echo the organization's rigorous evidence-based approach to research funding in their people practices. Consequently, they have embarked on a significant cultural and procedural shift towards being a more intelligence-led organization through the use of people analytics and insights.

The BHF have just begun the journey, and this case study examines their first steps. What is fresh and innovative about their approach is the way the BHF have integrated people analytics into their people strategy design, the collaborative style they have adopted to incorporate input from across the organization and the courage they have shown in exploring the field of people analytics. This perfectly aligns with some of the BHF's values and behaviours which include being brave, informed, curious and working together.

The people experience

When the BHF started work on its new organizational strategy for 2020 to 2030, its leaders already knew that they needed to continue towards a more evidence-based approach. With improvements in technology and data, it seemed many organizations were considering how to use all kinds of data and intelligence together to gain meaningful insights, make better decisions and ensure greater impact.

While the BHF did this well in certain areas, they could see the potential to do so elsewhere, to ensure the best use of their precious resources. The process to develop the BHF strategy was driven by teams drawn from across the organization, each researching one theme of interest, using internal and external insights. Teams drew on external insights such as academic research and examples of best practice, and internal insights such as interviews with key stakeholders and employee surveys. This theme carried through to the subsequent development of a new people strategy, which had to build on past successes such as the implementation of several modules of the cloud-based Workday People System, and be flexible and adaptable to meet new challenges and prepare BHF for the future of work.

The team knew the importance of ensuring that a golden thread ran from the organizational strategy through the people strategy, which was renamed the "people experience", into their plans, their measures and their actions. The organizational strategy included an ambition to "lead with intelligence", and the POD team knew that they needed to do this better themselves, as well as support the organization to do it.

It was clear that leaders and managers wanted to use Workday and other sources to gain insights and make better decisions about their people. The BHF wanted to use their new system to its full potential to derive comprehensive reporting and insights, and although they didn't have all the data they would have wanted, they had enough to get started. POD wanted to understand their people better so that they could make the right decisions about where to focus their efforts. Colleagues, both staff and volunteers, wanted to know that the BHF was making the best possible decisions about how to use its resources, and that their own feedback about the organization was being used as part of that decision-making.

Taking all this into account, the team decided that insight was so important that they made it one of their five "people experience priorities". Alongside the work to embed this priority into the people experience and people planning, the POD team started the work of encouraging a mindset and behaviour shift. They held a session with an external consultancy, Empathix, who were able to explain the field of people analytics in an easily accessible way. There was a lot of enthusiasm and interest in the session, which was attended by the director of people and organizational development, other POD leaders, diversity and inclusion, and members of the strategy, organizational development and people systems analytics teams.

Scoping the change – the conversation

Something Kirsten Edwards of Empathix noticed as an external consultant was that the language of research is familiar at BHF – after all, that is what they do, as they fund lifesaving research into heart and circulatory diseases. But how does this translate into their own organizational practices, and what happens when they put themselves under the microscope? This was the question that was asked in the first workshop with the POD team.

What was also striking to her in the session was the breadth of organizational representation invested in genuinely wanting to understand people analytics and the value it could add. The diversity of thought and skills in the workshop was refreshing to see, and the fact that a people analytics discussion was taking place as a key part of the formation of the people strategy design was inspiring.

Starting on the front foot enabled an open discussion about the analytics that might really enhance the BHF's people experience. Included in the discussion was an exploration of what it was that they really wanted to know, what trends or patterns might exist, and how this knowledge might help them to achieve their goals.

The POD team explored various business challenges and scenarios, including broad HR issues such as recruitment, talent management and turnover, plus the operational realities of employees and volunteers working together. The BHF is the leading charity retailer, so considerations around the stress levels of store leaders, shop staffing and linking shop turnover and performance with training and other items were explored. The team really opened it up to start to discuss what links, trends and patterns might exist.

At this point it is interesting to reflect on analytic literacy. Discussions like this are critical to the success of people analytics projects, and must be carried out in such a way that everyone understands what is going on and has the chance to give their input. Most people in this discussion were not statisticians, not data scientists and certainly not AI developers. In the room there were people who really understood the business challenges, business opportunities and business strategy of the BHF when it comes to people and organization design.

From that discussion, opportunities for people analytics began to crystallize. It became evident that it is possible to use analytical models to help steer, adjust and drive business strategy, take the gut instinct out of decision-making and move towards an evidence-based practice. Once the analytics are in place, they can further help to monitor the success of the people strategy and help the BHF to prosper, enable the POD team to build solid business cases for action and encourage sound, responsible investment.

This session helped the key players to think about how they could lead the way to a more insight led approach. As the POD director said: "Part of the challenge is asking the right questions and getting everyone to be curious and question things in a more analytical way".

After the session, POD leaders started talking about using insight more, helping people to understand what it meant and what it might mean for people. The next big step was introducing the new people experience at the POD away day which included breakout sessions from Kirsten at Empathix, to help a wider cross-section of people understand more about people analytics.

Reflections so far and future plans

BHF is still building the foundations for a more evidence-led approach to people decisions, as well as supporting the organization to become more evidence-led themselves. They have a strong and ambitious people experience, which is being built into plans and measures to support the BHF to achieve the maximum impact.

At the same time, people's mindsets are shifting and becoming receptive to the idea of being more insight driven. They know that they have a long journey and they need to continue to work hard on the basics of collecting and reporting on data, but they also understand that they do already have insights that they can use. The BHF plans to continue to support their people by upskilling them to be more evidence-led and apply the insights they gain to ensure the best results.

Key learnings

For others reading this and considering a similar path, the BHF has the following recommendations:

1 Be led by your values and culture in your approach – the BHF's values and behaviours include being informed, being curious, working together and learning. The BHF needed to harness these to understand the potential of people analytics.

2 Be brave – this is one of the BHF's key values, and they've really needed it to step into a world which at first glance is all about maths and statistics! When they got there, they realized there was more to it, and those first steps were the hardest.

3 Start somewhere – it's easy to think that you don't have enough data to think about gaining insights from analytics. But unless you start somewhere, you will never make any progress, and you no doubt have more than you think.

4 Take people with you – this is a cultural change and everybody can play a part in moving towards an evidence-based approach. People need to understand why this will be of benefit to them in their roles and to the organization, and to start to see the steps they might take to get there.

5 Learn together – this is a fairly new and expanding field so senior people can often be on a level playing field with junior people. Learning together helps gain insights and ideas from all levels, and makes it more likely that you create an approach that will work for everyone.

The BHF team is excited to learn more about how people analytics and people-based insight can help them to make better people decisions. As a charity, the BHF always need to ensure they are using their donors' money and support wisely and making the best use of resources. By basing their decisions on firm evidence, they know that they are making progress towards their hope of beating heartbreak for everyone affected by heart and circulatory diseases.

www.bhf.org.uk (archived at https://perma.cc/95A9-33JP)

The BHF example reiterates the need for:

- a clearly defined strategy that is aligned with the business and the rest of the people function;

- an evidence-based approach to research, as a lever to ensure that the people function also changes its approach to people-based interventions;

- a high involvement strategy, to ensure that a range of different stakeholders and interested parties were involved and provided their insight into what was required moving forward.

Next, Swarovski shares its analytics journey from reporting to undertaking analytics-based projects and activity over the past two years or so, as it moved from Box 1 to Box 2 to Box 3 (see Chapter 6). It has a clear business focus behind the analytics team and the added value that it is delivering to the business.

CASE STUDY
Swarovski: How to build a people function with business impact

Swarovski is a family-run, independent company, which was founded more than 120 years ago in Wattens, Austria, during the technological advancements of the second Industrial Revolution. Now run by the fifth generation of family members, Swarovski has become a leading group of global companies committed to stable growth and maintaining its place at the forefront of design, creativity, and technological innovation.

Throughout its history, Swarovski has been aware that the long-term success of the company is inseparable from the wellbeing of its clients, employees, the environment, and society as a whole. This is an integral part of Swarovski's heritage, and is embedded today in the company's established global sustainability agenda.

The company is split into three major industry areas: the Swarovski Crystal Business, that primarily produces crystal jewellery and accessories; Swarovski Optik, which produces optical instruments such as telescopes, telescopic sights for rifles, and binoculars; and Tyrolit, a manufacturer of grinding, sawing, drilling, and dressing tools, as well as a supplier of tools and machines.

Today, the Swarovski Crystal Business is one of the highest grossing business units within Swarovski, with a global reach of approximately 3,000 stores in around 170 countries, more than 29,000 employees, and a revenue of about 2.7 billion euros (in 2018).

The journey

In 2015 the challenges for Swarovski were that they had very limited availability of global data, technology and processes. The HR reporting team at that time was using manual data-based input received from individual countries and as a result the reporting team was not able to execute high-quality real-time reporting, let alone think about strategic people analytics. That is when their journey towards Digital HR commenced.

At the beginning of the Digital HR journey the team defined four building blocks. They wanted:

- transparency within their organization about all people-relevant data;
- simple and easy-to-understand processes that enable everyone to adopt new ways of working;
- an enabled and empowered workforce with state-of-the-art process support and be able to use data to make decisions;
- insights about their most valuable asset: their employees.

These four building blocks they defined in collaboration with senior executives in the business and in HR.

The roadmap

In Q3 of 2015, the team planned the strategic roadmap for digital HR and people analytics, keeping in consideration these four building blocks. The epicentre of this process was a two-week workshop with all top HR executives and selected business executives, where they defined what Swarovski wanted to achieve from a long-term point of view.

One of the key themes revolved around developing a data strategy that would steer Swarovski into the future; the data they wanted to manage globally, manage locally and prepare their foundation to move into the people analytics arena. This provided them with the necessary buy-in from their executives.

By the end of 2015, the time had arrived to roll out globally processes, systems, new ways of working and therefore a whole transformation programme. The roll-out in Europe was in the summer of 2016, in Asia the summer of 2017 and in the Americas, the summer of 2018. This created the foundation for the team to have access to consolidated global HR data; business data was already available on a global level.

Creating a people analytics function

At the beginning of 2017, Swarovski didn't have a people analytics function. At that time the HR leadership team decided the direction they wanted to go with people analytics. So, they clustered their journey in seven building blocks (see Figure 7.2).

The first three pillars (strategy and culture, analytics sophistication and capability) encompassed the areas that are required from a change management point of view for an organization that is really living and breathing analytics. The last three (data, technology and processes) are the hard part of what is required in the analytics journey. The people analytics team's focus was primarily on the first three, as they saw these as the critical success factors.

FIGURE 7.2   Swarovski people analytics building blocks

	STRATEGY AND CULTURE	ANALYTICS SOPHISTICATION	CAPABILITY	OPERATING MODEL	PROCESS	TECHNOLOGY	DATA
Baseline in 2017	There is a collective will in HR to do more, but without the ability to execute.	Only basic HR reporting on classic headline HR KPIs such as headcount – significant manual intervention and time effort required.	Basic reporting capability and data visualization skills. Excel is dominant tool.	No HR analytics team.	Irregular and reactive HR reporting.	Automation to enable regular data consolidation, but with a manual element.	HR data can be aggregated with effort, but still difficult to match with business data – large data cleanse/ transformation effort required.
Ambition for 2022	Business leaders see the value in HR analytics and have commissioned research from HR.	Focus on predicting HR outcomes (exit, promotion, hiring success, future headcount); integration of external data.	Strong HR analytics team in place. Business partners bring evidence to key conversations for decision-making with leaders.	HR analytics is centre of excellence, same status as L&D, talent, compensation, etc.	Business leaders identify ideas / hypotheses to test and commission research from HR.	Analytics module within HR system activated, configured, operational and linked to other internal systems such as retail.	HR data is collated in real time and easily combined with business data as required. There is some 'pre-packaging' of analytics.

MAKE THE ORGANIZATION WORK/ CHANGE MANAGEMENT FOCUS

MAKE THE SYSTEM WORK/ TECHNICAL FOCUS

These seven blocks encompassed Swarovski's people analytics maturity assessment where they captured their baseline on a scale of 1 to 5. Swarovski initial maturity assessment in 2017 came out between 1 and 2. From a strategy point of view this was a good initiative, because the corporate HR team and CHRO saw the future in people analytics and the people function. Today, all the people analytics activities are based on these seven pillars, and the people analytics team regularly reviews how they are improving in them. Swarovski's ambition is to move to 5 base points on all seven pillars soon. The model also evolved over time and more dimensions were added.

Swarovski started their analytics journey from reporting full-time employee (FTE) headcount topics that were operational in nature (see Figure 7.3) and later moved to advanced reporting, where the HR analytics team drilled down and analysed data to look back at why issues occurred.

Both these initial stages included data from a single source extracted from their HR systems. These approaches limited the HR analytics team to a descriptive and diagnostic approach of only considering the past and reflecting on what went wrong.

Today, Swarovski is getting data from multiple sources and was moving into the people optimization and business optimization space where they use predictive models through technology to predict people outcomes. With business optimization, they predict the impact of measures on business-relevant key figures such as sales (top-line) or production efficiency or quality (bottom-line). It is not only predicted what will happen, but also what concrete actions are needed for best results. These strategic projects contribute directly to the company's success and are carried out together with top management. Each people analytics team should aim to focus on these projects because it has the greatest impact on the organization.

Oliver Kasper, director of people analytics and digital HR, is very clear in his thinking. You do not need to get everything right first. You can start with business optimization projects even when the pure reporting at the end is not fully working yet. This might seem a bit counterintuitive, but business optimization initiatives have the highest business impact and therefore return.

The three-year roadmap

By 2017, the HR analytics team designed a three-year roadmap for achieving their mission to fulfil their vision: "All people decisions at Swarovski are informed by data and analytics". The journey was broken down into five categories – data foundation, data culture, operational, tactical and strategic:

1 **Data foundation**: By the start of 2017 the HR analytics team had a great data quality foundation from their digitization project, which was set in motion in 2015. As they maintained good data quality, they didn't require much data

FIGURE 7.3   Swarovski people analytics journey

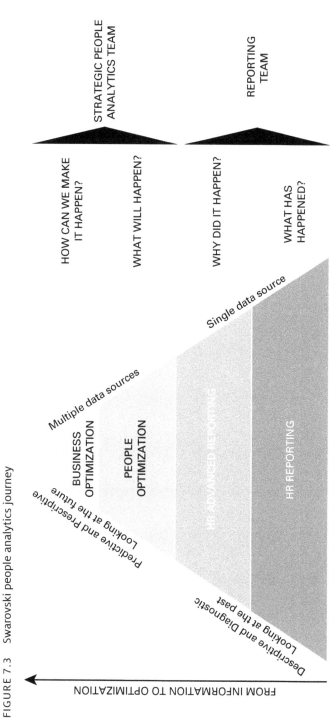

STRATEGIC PEOPLE ANALYTICS TEAM

REPORTING TEAM

HOW CAN WE MAKE IT HAPPEN?

WHAT WILL HAPPEN?

WHY DID IT HAPPEN?

WHAT HAS HAPPENED?

Single data source

Multiple data sources

BUSINESS OPTIMIZATION

PEOPLE OPTIMIZATION

HR ADVANCED REPORTING

HR REPORTING

Predictive and Prescriptive
Looking at the future

Descriptive and Diagnostic
Looking at the past

FROM INFORMATION TO OPTIMIZATION

cleansing activity. However, a requirement for them was to keep their data quality up to scratch.

2 **Data culture**: From a data culture point of view, Swarovski developed an e-learning people analytics curriculum that focused on developing competencies of their global HR and business community to move into analytics. The second key feature for developing a data culture was establishing communities of practice. The third was the monthly meeting with corporate HR and global HR business partners (HRBPs), getting them on the journey and getting HRBPs to discuss this agenda with business executives to bring them on the people analytics journey. This formed the cornerstone of their success.

3 **Operational**: On the operational side, the HR analytics team planned an operational reporting library, to automate reporting and to embed analytics into Swarovski's global HR processes.

4 **Tactical**: This relates to the definition of dashboards on key processes and the definition of key performance indicators (KPIs). The focus in this area needs to be on implementation of the results, rather than spending excessive time on their definition.

5 **Strategic**: From a strategic point of view, the first area included developing an executive scorecard. The people analytics team included input from several executives to develop this. Using the scorecard, the people analytics team partnered with global HRBPs to manage the HR function in a new and different way. This proved to be a boost for them moving forward to business optimization and getting buy-in from executives. After this initiative, the people analytics team received a lot of requests for detailed analytics on the executive scorecard. Based on its success, they started large-scale business optimization initiatives with top executives in two main areas:

   o driving better sales with people analytics;

   o improving production efficiency and quality with people analytics.

   These initiatives are large-scale strategic prescriptive projects, and with this people analytics entered the business optimization arena.

See Figure 7.4.

Essential to move from HR to people analytics

The elements that contributed to Swarovski's success were

- the engagement of HRBPs;
- the support provided to the HR managers to help them understand the overall agenda;

FIGURE 7.4   Swarovski people analytics roadmap

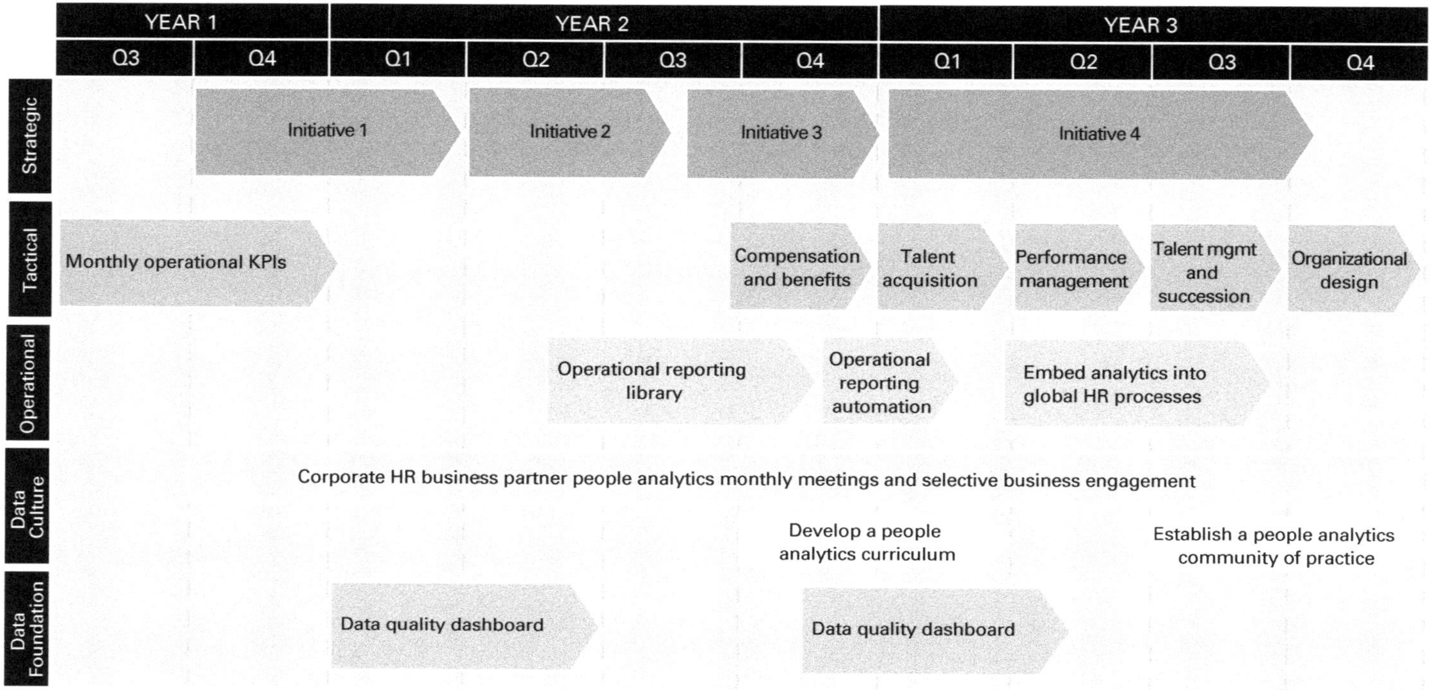

	YEAR 1		YEAR 2				YEAR 3		
	Q3	Q4	Q1	Q2	Q3	Q4	Q1	Q2	Q3	Q4

Strategic

Initiative 1   Initiative 2   Initiative 3   Initiative 4

Tactical

Monthly operational KPIs

Compensation and benefits

Talent acquisition

Performance management

Talent mgmt and succession

Organizational design

Operational

Operational reporting library

Operational reporting automation

Embed analytics into global HR processes

Corporate HR business partner people analytics monthly meetings and selective business engagement

Data Culture

Develop a people analytics curriculum

Establish a people analytics community of practice

Data Foundation

Data quality dashboard

Data quality dashboard

- the smart process in place to collect and keep the data in good quality and shape;
- sound expertise in business investigation and a strict focus on business challenges.

These were the four key ingredients that led the HR analytics team to move into people analytics. All this was supplemented with the right culture, and an amazing team with the right skill and mindset.

Oliver Kasper, director of people analytics and digital HR, believes that you need to have a great team and that you need to focus on having the right people in the right positions, especially in the beginning. He thinks you need to have business acumen, storytelling and consulting skills combined with HR knowledge, analytics knowledge and psychology knowledge. He believes that you need to have people inside the organization that can do all this from a people analytics perspective, but be aware that, as with any project, you need the right talent in place to be successful.

www.swarovski.com (archived at https://perma.cc/FFS3-WNRH)

The Swarovski example reiterates the need for:

- having a clear plan of action;
- ensuring that the data is of a suitable breadth and depth in terms of quality;
- a comprehensive approach that was adopted to ensure buy-in and acceptance across the business of the approach that was being implemented.

King shares its analytics journey over the past few years, as it again moves from Box 1 to Box 2 and starts to focus on Box 3-based projects. It's an organization full of data scientists, so expectations to use and analyse data are high and their story maps out how they approached the challenges that these expectations created.

CASE STUDY
King – even Candy Crush is on a people analytics journey

Pablo Borges, senior people analytics manager at King

King is a leading interactive entertainment company for the mobile world. They have developed more than 200 fun titles and offer games that are enjoyed all around the world. Their franchises include Candy Crush, Farm Heroes, Pet Rescue and Bubble Witch, with over 258 million monthly active users (as of Q2 2019) across the web, social and mobile platforms.

King has game studios in Stockholm, Malmo, London, Barcelona and Berlin, along with offices in Malta, San Francisco, Chicago and New York, and employs about 2,000 people (up from 600 people 5 years ago). King was acquired by Activision Blizzard Inc (Nasdaq ATVI) in February 2016, and operates as an independent unit of the company.

Context for change in HR: starting the journey

By the end of 2016, the HR team had developed in line with business growth, with core functions in place and technology systems that enabled operational reporting. Business leaders were able to obtain insightful data from the games that King developed and use that data to improve the games. The business has over 100 performance analysts and data scientists, but when it came to the workforce, the leaders were not getting that same data-orientated approach. One employee used to do advanced reporting mainly on the top priority of HR at the time – recruitment, but that employee left in early 2016. It was in 2017 that a people analytics function was created; a team of one!

Rather than immediately undertaking lots of data analysis, a clear process was undertaken in terms of connecting with the business leaders and understanding their priorities and appreciating the HR team's views in terms of core people challenges. The HR technology team had been working for a number of years with the Workday system so the basic data quality was good, with core dashboards covering headcount, turnover and so on, but there were gaps when it came to recruitment and learning. Visier's analytics system was also available to support that analysis.

Employee turnover was identified as a priority and a quick win, so the initial project was looking at exit survey data. The positive response from the business highlighted that they wanted that sort of insight regularly for their business area. This created a demand that exceeded the bandwidth of the people analytics team, and so an intern with data science skills was recruited. They were able to create more relevant and impactful dashboards, which again created more interest in this whole area. Interns have subsequently been recruited full-time into the team, with additional interns joining to supplement capacity and skills.

Continuing the change

Given King's data-based orientation, there is always scrutiny on the numbers. This meant that the wider HR team needed to feel more confident about using data and see how it could benefit them in their relationships with the business. It also meant that some of the work pressure could be facilitated by the HR team rather than the analytics team.

There was a range of numerical capability across the HR team. Some were really interested in the topic; they understood it and saw the value of it. However, there was a larger group who were not as engaged or as comfortable with the data. A small development programme was developed to drive a more data-driven approach to HR for the HRBPs across the business. Day one covered core data techniques in Excel and the second day was one-to-one-based, focusing on specific local challenges and data opportunities. The largest concerns revolved around their ability to get clarity on the ask, how to get their data insights correct, and how to build their credibility with the local business leaders.

Ongoing support and calls with the people analytics team have continued to drive a change in approach and behaviour. The outcome of the training was that the HRBPs felt more able to challenge business leaders, to work with the HR data that they were familiar with and to guide the business in the area of people data.

Following on from that, there is now a good self-service operational reporting platform with standardized metrics and dashboards in place, and core capability across the HR function with the central people analytics team available to provide expert prioritized support. Their work has now evolved into analytics-based projects looking at talent and organizational based challenges that are collaboratively undertaken with high stakeholder involvement so that they take responsibility for post-insight implementation.

The candidate experience in recruitment continues to be an important feature of King's business. For example, the recruitment director was concerned about the time it took to recruit people into the business. The analytics team's investigation revealed process inconsistencies from the data, with some candidates having an excessive number of interviews which were having minimal impact on the ultimate hiring decision. A pilot process that structured the process more robustly has been undertaken, and, if successful, will be rolled out globally. As a result, considerable operational time and money could be saved, as well as improving brand reputation in the recruitment space.

Looking to the future

There is a clear desire to ensure that the workforce feel a human connection with the organization, and the use of data can provide insights that may not normally be forthcoming. Further data and analytics-based projects remain the focus of the people analytics team, with support being provided across the organization with other data-based challenges. The team's aim is to become more strategic in its positioning, with projects and will inform and provide data and analytics-based input into the new people strategy as that evolves.

Key learnings

Pablo's reflections on the key learnings from the journey so far, are:

1   The initial stakeholder research and buy-in process was crucial to the success and interest in people analytics.

2   Understanding the business in terms of what it does and the roles that exist is very important. Analysing people and their data mean that a good awareness of roles will bring the data to life, and ensure that there is a real appreciation of the issues that are emerging, for example the different job demands between creative, customer service and data engineer roles.

3   Education of the HR community is vital to ensure that they can identify possible business/people issues and deal with the more routine data-based dashboard requests. They remain the key interface with the business leaders.

4   Identify what skills you need in your analytics team; you may need data scientist-type skills initially but as the analytics team evolves, more consultative project management capabilities may be necessary.

5   Don't be scared – data is fun. However, data can only take you so far; it will provide insight and information, but remember that we still need a human element in whatever decision we make. King's mantra when making games is to have a balance of art and science, and the same goes for people analytics – a balance of heart and science.

http://king.com (archived at https://perma.cc/PK5L-9SJD)

The King case study emphasizes:

- the way analytics were taken forward in King;
- the fact that the whole HR function had to change and refine the way it operates;
- again, a comprehensive approach to upskilling the HR community on an ongoing basis to ensure that the practitioners were supporting the central people analytics team activity.

This case study looks at the impact of machine learning-based data interventions and the business impact that it had on an organization in the Middle East, where an external provider adopted a Box 4 approach in an organization that had a Box 1 productivity-based reporting infrastructure in place.

CASE STUDY
Machine learning, AI and Productivity in Dubai

Dr Tommy Weir, founder and CEO of enaible Inc

enaible is one of the new breed of artificial intelligence (AI) and machine learning companies. Built with AI at their core, they are turning organizations' underutilized system data into a standardized productivity score and personalized, prioritized leadership recommendations.

Based in Dubai and Boston, USA, enaible maximize productivity so that every worker has an opportunity to succeed.

The productivity question

This case study revolves around a government agency in Dubai, United Arab Emirates with approximately 3,000 employees. Between 2011 and 2015 they experienced impressive year-on-year productivity growth, even reaching 15 per cent per year, which was phenomenal. This is credited to shifting the customer interface from being heavily manually-orientated to an online system.

Subsequently, starting in 2016, their productivity growth flattened out. Yet, they were faced with future volume growth. This led them to ask: "How can we handle our future growth without increasing our headcount?" In other words, how can we become more productive?

Their desire was to grow year-on-year productivity by 10 per cent or better to reverse the downward trends. The real focus was to decouple output growth from headcount growth. They simply could not believe that the only way to grow was always to hire more people.

The executive leadership team concluded that the best way to address this challenge was with an AI-productivity engine. They wanted to derive value and impact from their underutilized data, much like they did before, but this time using AI. The underutilization of data is a common feature that is seen across most organizations; yet they had the courage to act on it.

The productivity puzzle

enaible ingested workflow system data from their ERP, Outlook, HRMS and custom-built systems for their priority departments; these represented about a quarter of their total workforce. Then the data was pre-processed and the data from multiple systems were pieced together like a puzzle so enaible's proprietary Trigger-Task-Time™ (T-T-T) algorithm could analyse the data and seek out trends, themes and insights.

Most organizations only see their employees from a system usage perspective, whereas enaible shifts the focus to see from the eyes of the employee. Their T-T-T algorithm uses time-stamped data to comprehensively observe, individually and collectively, the employees' real work patterns and the related impact on the intended outcomes. The Trigger starts the work, and it contains the collective and specific characteristics of the workflow; the Task is the actual piece of work that an employee does, and Time is the duration and time of day of the task. The algorithm also considers an individual's behaviour, work patterns and interactions with others.

There is no need for manual task identification or time and motion studies. Built into enable is an automated task classifier based upon the O*NET task taxonomy, and the T-T-T algorithm contains a continuous ideal time calculator that determines the fastest, sustainable time for every Trigger-Task combination (in this case example, there are 7,400 Trigger-Task combinations). In productivity science, this is a breakthrough as it negates the commonly used average times, which lack granular specificity and fail to accurately represent employees' work.

This results in the enable productivity score, which is comprised of:

- **Capacity utilization**: How much of the available time is used (volume worked at ideal time adherence)?
- **Consistency**: Do employees work the same way each time, or do their patterns change often?
- **Quality impact**: What is the impact of employees' quality on others' productivity, including the company's?

The process data outcomes

enable ingested 480 million rows of data from 12 separate systems. The Trigger-Task-Time™ algorithm observed 7.5 billion data points and 700,000 hours of time-stamped data to identify the ideal times for each of the 7,400 Trigger-Task combinations.

Some of the key productivity findings, based on the four initial functions, were as follows:

- Only 1.1 per cent of work undertaken by the workforce led to its intended result.
- There was a 261 per cent like-for-like task variance. Initially this was thought to be the difference between outliers and poor performers, but in actuality the lack of ideal time adherence is across all employees, meaning at times they hit the ideal time, and at others they're shockingly slow. This is in like-for-like work where there are no external rationales for it.
- Upon the initial run of enable, 58 per cent of the employees' productivity trends were declining and 42 per cent were improving.

Key productivity improvements include:

- 270,000 hours of increased workforce capacity through ideal time adherence;

- 65,000 hours of non-value-add work being replaced by automation due to poor process design.

The management team has fully embraced using AI to grow productivity. It provided a transparent and objective view of productivity, which immediately engaged both the leaders' and employees' attention.

Capacity utilization was an area that caught the leadership team by surprise. Historically, they had been benchmarking the volume of work done by employees. But given the variability in ideal time adherence, the actual capacity utilization was different from what was thought to be. For example, in one department of 81 people, they averaged 13.2 tasks per hour, taking one minute thirty seconds per task. That meant that the employees in that team were only working twenty minutes of each hour!

Combined with the leaders' interest in the enable score, there was a real desire for guidance and direction about what to do to turn the insights into productivity impact. This is where the second usage of AI features in enable: the Leadership Recommender™, which is a recommendation engine that provides each leader and manager with ongoing personalized and prioritized actions that they can take to maximize their employees' productivity.

Future impact

This government agency is continuing to use enable as a SaaS product, with the goal to grow productivity by 15 per cent per year and realize a $75m comparative payroll savings over the coming two years.

Dr Tommy Weir believes that "machines learning and humans leading will change the way we lead". enable is challenging the very meaning of leadership by using AI to advance human potential. "People will always work, so it's time to really use AI to help leaders get better and grow employee productivity."

www.enaible.io (archived at https://perma.cc/EB47-TWZQ)

This machine learning and AI-based case study emphasizes:

- the impact that these new technologies can have on an organization in terms of the availability and depth of data-based evidence;
- the scope of insight provided by the analysis;
- the business impact created by focusing on productivity improvements;
- the need to ensure that we as people must continue to work collaboratively with this new technology to realize the best results possible.

The next case study looks at how Experian almost broke all the rules when introducing and then embedding analytics into the organization. This is one of the most exciting examples, as the analytics team are now productizing analytics-based solutions that means the dream of making HR a profit centre is becoming a reality. They are operating at Box 4 level and have not necessarily fulfilled a structured journey approach; the focus has been entirely on being opportunistic with business leaders to prove the concept.

CASE STUDY
Experian – The people analytics journey so far

Olly Britnell, global head of workforce analytics and HR strategy at Experian

Experian plc is a consumer credit reporting company with approximately 17,000 employees operating across 37 countries. Experian collects and aggregates information on over 1 billion people and businesses across the globe. Additionally, Experian also sells decision-based analytic and marketing assistance to businesses. Its consumer services also include online access to credit history and products meant to protect from fraud and identity theft.

Context for change

Experian's people analytics journey started in 2014. Prior to that, the business had a very disparate set-up in terms of regional management information and reporting. There was limited governance and central coordination, which led to inconsistencies of approach.

Olly Britnell, now global head of workforce analytics and HR strategy, set out a long-term vision that was to deliver innovative HR solutions, in line with the type of business Experian is, that could solve critical HR challenges; so effective that they could be commercialized externally. That in itself was a huge aspiration for any HR function, especially as reporting based data was still difficult. Whilst the core Oracle system was in place, there were multiple platforms set up for talent, reward and learning and so on, which meant that to get a simple global headcount number, or a global attrition number, was about combining in Excel to get to that single "source of truth".

In the early days, the small global analytics team were consolidating data and dealing with business requests for information. Some insightful analysis was undertaken by the team during this period. However, capability-wise the mix of the team was more technically focused rather than on interpreting data and storytelling around the results. Additionally, there was a lack of challenging the HRBPs in terms of what was required.

In terms of the capability of the wider HR community, it was incredibly mixed so the focus was about educating the HRBPs to be more insight-led and not instinct-led, and for them to see analytics as a core part of their role, not a nice-to-have.

The positive aspect that drove the change was that the HR leadership team were genuinely committed to developing a function that was driven/led by people-based data analytics. The core business lived and breathed data and had a huge appetite for information and insight, so the key question that was being asked was: why isn't HR using people data and information in a more strategic way? The arrival of Olly as a global leader to head up the analytics team with regional resources reporting to him was a key signal of intent for a global, not a regional, solution.

Starting the journey

There were three strands which drove the journey as it started to embed a more data-based approach across the HR function:

1 **Technology**: Technology was early on the agenda within the global analytics team, as there was a clear need to find a way of freeing up the capacity of the team to do more insightful high impact analytics with an ability for technology to provide to the business and the HRBPs the ability to access data and undertake self-service, core data-based business intelligence. Visier's platform was chosen based on the following criteria:

   o Consolidating multiple data sources. In Experian's case this was up to nine different systems which would have taken them some 12–18 months to complete using Oracle. The ongoing consolidation of data by Visier on a monthly basis has enabled the team to have a "single source of truth", with all the data combined in one place and visualized in an intuitive way that eases understanding.

   o A purpose-built HR system. It was crucial that any system was built for HR people data, rather than some of the other business intelligence-based solutions and visualization tools that are available. An early challenge was the whole definition of what was meant by various terms across the business (eg "resignation"). With their experience in other organizations and settings, clear definitions were outlined so that decisions relating to criteria and various demographics could be clearly defined, moving forward quickly.

   o Quality of outputs. The way in which outputs are collated and packaged is crucial. Visier use a tool called Topic Guidebook which allows people to ask questions, or use prebuilt questions, that the data and analytics process will answer using charts and visualizations. This enabled HRBPs to be prompted with the core 10 questions they should be asking themselves about the business they are operating within.

2 **Strategy alignment**: This was perceived as being a core part of the approach, ensuring that alignment with the people and business strategy was clearly visible. A simple KPI dashboard was built with between 10 and 15 key metrics in it that aligned to the strategy. This again was a signal of change, because whilst management information dashboards were in place, they weren't aligned to the key business imperatives. This approach started to shift the mindset about measurement, and also triggered debate about what was important and what needed to be reported on.

3 **Showing the possible through predictive analytics**: The key was to show the art of the possible to the business, and to reinforce to the HR community what could be done. Due to the nature of Experian's business, it was known that if the business got engaged then it would accelerate everything that needed to be done.

Whilst there is some merit in the maturity curves that are promoted in the people analytics sector, sometime business opportunities occur which mean that getting the basics in place first and then moving through the various types of analytics isn't right for every organization. Experian was one of those instances, as there were already a number of data scientists across the business as a part of Experian's core business offering.

Olly's team engaged with them and looked to build a pilot approach that was based around a key business problem, which at the time was attrition. That partnership has continued to evolve over recent years.

Implementing the change

Having created interest across the business and defined a clear approach that was aligned to the business and people strategies, the next stage of the evolution focused on four key areas.

Education and analytics awareness

From 2015 onwards, there was an increased emphasis around education and awareness within the functions. Training programmes were developed that revolved around e-learning, workshop-based learning and classroom-based learning, all very focused on the commercial world that Experian is operating within. The main focus of the training was the HRBPs, with the priority being on showing them the types of conversations that they needed to have, all based around case studies.

The key driver was to try and show them that if they had these types of data-based dialogues, different debates, business outcomes and "value add" initiatives could be demonstrated by them and the HR function as a whole.

Reporting demands and collaboration

The Visier system had been embedded at this stage, so there was a clear focus on determining what constituted scheduled and ad-hoc reporting. By reducing the dependency on the analytics team, capacity was created to focus on the more complex predictive and project-based demands that were emerging rather than facilitating reports that could be produced by the system.

At this time, increased collaboration with Finance was necessary. This revolved around ensuring that core data could be reported consistently, and that HR and Finance were operating from the same place. For example, some businesses identified that Finance said the headcount was "X" whereas HR said the headcount was "Y" – a common challenge across a lot of organizations! Workshops and sessions with Finance were run to identify the differences, and then to mutually agree on how to educate their own functions in terms of being able to explain those differences to business leaders so there was a common understanding as to why there are differences.

Fast forwarding to today, Finance clearly deal with the Profit and Loss (P&L) numbers whereas the workforce analytics team focus on the people numbers – and Finance rely on them to deliver people insights and data.

Evolution of analytics tools and methods

The predictive attrition tool had continued to be developed, and that was rolled out to the business and piloted in a number of regions. This created real traction and demonstrated what was possible and that different types of insights could be provided by using data in different ways. This of course raised expectations in the business!

The different sources of data that were available to the analytics team were also being explored at this stage. This embraced more qualitative data and insights, such as employee surveys, social media information and Glassdoor and LinkedIn information. This in turn led to a shift within the analytics team in terms of the sort of capabilities required. To that point the team had had a strong technical data orientation, but with increasing predictive work emerging and the different types of conversations that were now developing, there was an increased need for more of a consultative mindset which was fulfilled with training and acquisition of talent into the team.

Ongoing education and learning

The ongoing education programme and support was revised at this time. The focus remained on HRBPs, but was broadened to include the HR centres of excellence and the talent acquisition and reward teams to clarify how they could use data better within their roles.

Whilst operational challenges were raised in response to this initiative, the future demanding growth plans for recruitment and the need to use reward data with other people practices based data meant that business challenges required a higher level of data-based insight from those teams.

Looking to the future

The workforce/people analytics journey of the last five years has been challenging and demanding, but hugely successful. It has meant a complete change in approach in the way data and insights are used to drive problem solving and the way that the HR function operates with its business clients. Looking to the future, there are some core initiatives that will build upon the infrastructure and approach that is now in place:

COMMERCIALIZING PREDICTIVE WORKFORCE ANALYTICS

Having rolled out the predictive attrition tool internally globally, over the past couple of years (attrition reduced to 12 per cent from 15 per cent), a commercial proposition then emerged given that it was perceived to be innovative and unique in the way that it worked. A couple of external clients were approached and following successful pilots with them, the solution was launched as a commercial product that other organizations could buy in 2019.[1]

The success of this and other tools have also been formally showcased in Experian's 2019 Annual Report, alongside the team being shortlisted for awards across the globe. The analytics team is certainly driving the mantra of developing a profit centre-based approach, rather than the function remaining a cost centre.

THE INNOVATION LAB

Having made a lot of progress with the people analytics journey and the launch of the commercial tool externally, there is an expectation for the momentum to be continued. A lab to explore and push the boundaries has been set up to look at the next predictive tool that could be developed internally, with an eye to its use externally.

ROBOTIC PROCESS AUTOMATION (RPA)

There is now a robot in the team via a computer program that is based on RPA, in an effort to drive down the ad-hoc requests that are made of the team. It's working 24/7, largely to collate reports (something like 40 to 50 a day) and email them out to the clients. It's believed to be saving approximately half a full-time employee.

The success of the analytics team, Olly Britnell believes, is down to two key factors:

- a strong business buy-in from senior leaders who value the potential contribution of analytics, combined with strong HR leadership to support the implementation;
- a highly capable analytics team who see their role as being not just to produce models, but also to make sure the benefits are realized in the business.

Key learnings

As Olly Britnell looks back over the journey, he sees the following as being his key learnings:

- Don't be constrained by analytics maturity models and approaches that dictate that there is a defined sequence of events to undertaking analytics. Seek out the opportunities, and build interest in what analytics can bring to form a very different HR proposition.
- Focus on getting the basics right in terms of quality data and technology-based infrastructure.
- It's crucial to get the HR community, and especially the HRBPs, on board with the data-based approach. It's an ongoing education challenge and no one-off event will fulfil the mindset change that is needed.
- Identify the right stakeholders (not necessarily the most senior) who both have an interest in an analytics-based approach and, more importantly, will champion the value of the process once initial activity has been undertaken and challenge their peers.
- Ensure that the analytics team (or an individual undertaking the work) have consultative skills and are provocative in terms of questioning and challenging the business and the HR community.

www.experian.com (archived at https://perma.cc/JYG7-VVT8)

Experian, as outliers in this space, have taken the people analytics agenda to another level by becoming a profit centre through the expertise that they have developed over the past few years. Not all organizations will aspire to this, or even want to adopt that approach, but for us, it shows what can be done.

KEY TAKEAWAYS FROM THIS CHAPTER

1   There tend to be four types of analytics that are undertaken; descriptive, which focuses on what has happened or is currently happening; diagnostic, which reveals the underlying causes behind data; predictive, which focuses on what might happen in the future; and prescriptive, which focuses on recommendations and what to do based on those evidence-based predictions.

2 Each of our case studies reveal their own specific learnings based on their journey, but the key trends revolve around having a strategy, being mindful of the organization's culture, developing an approach that fits with business demands/interests and ensuring that the capability to undertake the analysis process is in place across all your HR practitioners.

3 There is no "one size fits all" approach to implementing analytics into your people function.

4 Whatever analytics maturity model you use to review your journey, it does not have to be a sequential order of activity; it's a framework to consider what is working and what needs to be done to move your journey onwards.

Reference

1 Experian (2019) Workforce Analytics for Staff Retention, *Experian* [Online] www.experian.co.uk/business/analytics-and-decisioning/advanced-analytics/workforce-analytics-for-retention/ (archived at https://perma.cc/32WJ-RQHZ)

8

Delivering people analytics projects

We've outlined some of the external challenges for the HR function, and shared perspectives on what needs to change and how this can be undertaken. We've shared some great organizational stories about their analytical journeys, all of which have reiterated that there is no one clear way of becoming more evidence-based in your approach.

Now we focus on some of the infrastructure parameters that will embed data and more of an analytical approach into your and your organization's way of working.

This chapter will cover:

- **Developing a data/analytics culture:** One of the underlying themes that has emerged from our research is that the culture of the organization can both aid and get in the way of a data-driven approach.

- **How to run people analytics projects successfully:** Although there is no one way of running people analytics-based projects, nevertheless, we outline some of the key elements for success.

- **Avoiding people analytics project failure:** Success is not always guaranteed, and just because you are undertaking a project doesn't mean that your underlying issue will be resolved. Data alone doesn't mean a problem is solved. We share some of our experiences from projects that haven't gone according to plan.

Developing a data/analytics culture

What is organizational culture?

Culture is a complex topic, and yet is somewhat of a vague term. Culture is the set of behaviours, values, artefacts, reward systems and rituals that make up your organization, and therefore shapes the way it operates. Some define it as "what happens when nobody is looking". You can "feel" culture when you visit an organization, because it is often evident through people's behaviour, enthusiasm and the space that they work in.

However you define culture, it is increasingly becoming an important subject that executives and senior leaders are looking at. Ed Houghton, head of research and people analytics at CIPD, states: "Over the last five years, boards are now in particular asking questions around culture and behaviour that only a data rich analytics team can answer". The late management guru Peter Drucker is believed to have made the commonly quoted observation: "Culture eats strategy for breakfast". Drucker certainly believed that an organization's culture normally thwarts any attempt to create or enforce a strategy that is incompatible with that culture.

Today, most business leaders would like to see data being insightfully used throughout their whole organizations, especially as enormous amounts of data are being collected every day. If you look at successful data-savvy organizations such as Google, Facebook, and Amazon, you can see why leaders want to replicate some of the competitive gains and advantages that they have demonstrated. Their ability to establish and cultivate a data-driven culture, one that leverages data whenever and wherever possible, has enhanced their business efficiency and effectiveness.

Culture and leadership

Understanding organizational culture can assist the people function to explain many organizational phenomena, as culture can either aid or hinder organizational effectiveness. It is important to understand that leadership is the fundamental process by which organizational cultures are formed, changed or destroyed.

Culture and leadership are two sides of the same coin, and neither can be really understood by itself. The only thing of real importance that leaders do is to create and manage culture, and it is important for the people function to recognize the centrality of managing culture as one of their strategic initiatives.[1]

Organizational culture is therefore, a social control system in which shared expectations guides people's behaviour.[2] Andy Bayley, an associate lecturer at Loughborough University, informed us of a recent conversation with one of his colleagues who had visited the Tesla car manufacturing plant: "It was very interesting because no one at the plant thought Tesla as being a car company, and what they actually talked about was them being an energy management company".

Rather than being a car manufacturing company, what people thought about at Tesla is that they are making use of energy management in a different way and, therefore, they think innovatively. Rather than improving the car, what they might be thinking about is how to reuse this energy in a different way, all integrated into the culture through leadership and the people function.

Creating a data-driven culture

From our research and findings, there is no simple recipe for creating a data-driven culture other than it requires a significant investment of time, effort, money and focus. What we do know is that replicating 'best practices' is not recommended.[3] Our suggestions for a culture change programme revolve around seven themes to consider as a part of your analytics journey:

1 **What is your starting point?** Measurement and understanding of the current mindsets and the patterns of behaviour within the current culture is crucial. It tells you where you are starting from, and can also help you understand what shifts or changes are required to support a new way of operating.

2 **Future culture vision:** What ideally should your future culture look like from a systems, and behaviour approach? If you've measured the culture at the start, you'll have a framework to prioritize what needs to change and why.

3 **Don't look at culture in isolation:** Culture is a part of your organizational system that includes purpose, values and strategy, and must have a measurable outcome that will sustain the effort. This may be aspects such as improved safety, quicker product cycles, improved workforce wellbeing and so on.

4 **Executives as role models:** Your leadership team must be prepared to immerse themselves in data and exemplify the behaviours that they want to see their organization emulate. Remember that your senior leaders are those most likely to derail, or champion, your desired culture.[4]

5 **Change big:** Create a plan of action and try to identify a significant symbolic culture change initiative, that will resonate with the whole workforce, and then execute it rigorously. From there support the change

with other initiatives, large and small, that start to reinforce what is expected moving forward.

6 **Question and challenge:** Ensure that there are key culture champions who continue to ask the key question, "if our culture is supposed to be X, why do we keep doing Y?"

7 **Values, culture and strategy alignment:** There needs to be a clear and consistent alignment among the values, the norms that express the values (the culture), and specific attitudes and behaviours that are based on these values and that build core capabilities.

The measurement element is vital. That does not mean looking at an employee engagement survey and trying to draw cultural conclusions from it. It was designed to measure engagement, not culture, so don't expect insights from it for which it was never designed.

Dynamic capabilities

Organizations that can demonstrate timely responsiveness and innovation coupled with management capability have a unique competitive advantage over their competitors. Industry experts have observed the disadvantages of implementing digital technologies without understanding and integrating it to their workforce capability, primarily because humans are slow to adapt to technology and have an innate resistance to change.[5]

The people function should be at the forefront of leading organizations toward understanding and enhancing their dynamic capabilities. By dynamic capabilities, we mean "the capacity to sense and shape opportunities and threats, to seize opportunities, and to maintain competitiveness through enhancing, combining, protecting, and, when necessary, reconfiguring the business enterprise's intangible and tangible assets".[6]

Organizations become more agile by enabling people to experiment and encouraging them to try new things, considering that not everything will work. Take Brompton Bikes, a British manufacturer of folding bicycles, which has allocated a special fund of £50,000 that allows every employee to try out something new and experiment. Teams are encouraged to work cross-functionally and prototype an idea that they are passionate about. As the concept is to experiment and learn from failure, this allows Brompton to assess opportunities in the market without fully deploying all their assets and resources towards an area that may or may not bear fruit. If it doesn't work, no questions are asked and if it does work then the team is allocated further resources to mobilize their idea on a grand scale.

This has been a key tactic for Brompton Bikes to launch some of their most successful products. All these aspects are genuinely built into the culture of Brompton, to promote experimentation and agility into their workforce. From a change management perspective, this initiates rapid prototyping and encourages agile decision-making, which are core elements for unleashing dynamic capabilities that create value for the organization.

The opportunity here for the people function is to create an environment and culture where the workforce can nurture their skills, stay engaged and motivated to work towards a shared organizational vision. The Brompton Bikes case study explores the role of data in building and measuring value in their organization.

CASE STUDY
Brompton Bikes: the role of data in business growth

Built in Britain

A quintessential British product, Brompton is the brainchild of ardent cyclist and engineer Andrew Ritchie, who invented the first prototype in 1976 in his flat not long after graduating from Cambridge. Over the years, Brompton has carved out a niche market of enthusiasts for the folding bike, which was produced under a railway arch in Brentford before moving to its current manufacturing plant in Greenford.

In 2008, Will Butler-Adams became chief executive of Brompton. Will has taken turnover from £1.7m to £43m in 2019, with profits of £3.4m. It is on course to hit £50m of sales in 2020. Brompton had just 24 staff producing 7,000 bikes the year Will joined in 2002; it now has over 350 employees and is on course to make 50,000 bikes in 2020. With 16 billion possible permutations of the bike, including different colours, handlebars, gears, lighting and other accessories, each Brompton is fully customizable and is still manufactured in London.

Reinventing the wheel

Today Brompton is a lifestyle product that connects people from different cultures and continents. An enthusiastic brand evangelist believes that what makes the Brompton so special is that it unites people and transcends gender, race and religion. Brompton is among the few successful privately held businesses in Britain, selling to 44 countries around the world with 80 per cent of its bikes (called 'folders') exported.

There is little doubt about Will's success in leading Brompton to new heights, with his philosophy being: "It's all about the collective knowledge of the people". What sets Brompton apart is that their culture encourages the use of analytics across the various functions to optimize business performance.

Quality over quantity

Brompton collects the data on the shop floor on Excel spreadsheets. Although this data is collected daily, it is analysed on a weekly basis, to take an average of the performance and quantity "brazed", brazing being the metal-joining process that merges the bike frames together. Over the years, Brompton have managed to identify the level of productivity and the quality of items that are expected based on the data that they have been collecting.

THE IMPORTANCE OF AVERAGES IN PRODUCTIVITY

In terms of production, the number of parts that need to be produced are outlined by engineering. For example, on average it takes ten minutes to braze the main frame of the bike together. This means that when a brazer is working for an hour, their manager expect that six frames will be completed. However, if one day they complete five frames, and the day after they complete seven in an hour and so on, they remain on target, as the data is analysed on a weekly basis.

The standard of six frames are in essence an average, which is based upon all the information Brompton have looked at over many years. This forms an acceptable level of quality and productivity that is based upon extensive data collection over many years and the establishment of averages to drive activity.

WHY COLLECT DATA?

Because people may push to get the quantity to six frames per hour, Brompton promotes the message of quality over quantity through their culture. It is a complex process to change the culture around collecting data and change how people feel about their data being collected. Nicolas Duhem, head of business process, outlined that when you start to record the number of completed items, the employee will always be scared into reaching that quantity because they are focused on the number rather than the quality.

He believes that it is very important for the operators to understand why Brompton is collecting this data. Understanding the number of completed items along the process is vital, but the main message is always about the quality, not quantity. He believes that by spreading the message among operators that they are allowed to produce 5 per cent fewer frames with a higher quality finish, rather than focusing on just the number of frames to be produced, leads to greater efficiency and reinforces the quality message.

SAFETY FIRST

In 2013, Nicolas observed the installation of a massive dashboard on the shop floor with columns stating 'Cost, Delivery, Quantity and Safety'. He informed the management that this was the wrong order and it will spread the wrong message that cost is the first thing we are looking at and that the right order is Safety, Quality, Delivery and Cost (S, Q, D, C). After a prolonged discussion, the management scrapped the dashboard and replaced it with the changed order.

Today this aspect is driving the culture at Brompton. People unconsciously look at these types of signals and understand more clearly the priorities of the organization. Boards around the factory, provide visual support for their workforce to understand that the most important aspect for Brompton is their staff's safety and their product quality. These elements drive the culture, and as this starts to evolve, employees truly understand the organizational priorities and why things are being conveyed to them in a particular way. This has created a transparency so that employees understand that they are doing the right things, in the right way and to the right standards.

Data informs change

Brompton initially started collecting data using Excel, but this has been improved and enhanced over the past two years. The data is now collected via trade platforms and mobile apps that are then imported collectively into Excel and then use Microsoft Power BI to analyse it. This data has been collected for over two years, and now that it has been linked to Power BI, dashboards have now been built. Brompton are now merging the data from finance and building a clearer dashboard that people can now have access to.

DATA QUALITY

The way that Brompton records data has become more extensive in terms of evidence and information about what is happening on the production line at any given time. They have many small systems, but are now not only collecting but using data to make decisions more than ever before. They collect data on delivery, on-time production, right first-time data and reworked activity on the assembly line. This data enables them to improve the quality of bike production and enables them to make decisions regarding product delivery times, shipping arrangements and more.

SALES ANALYTICS

The way Brompton collects sales data has also changed over the years. Today, they are undertaking global forecasting at a far more sophisticated level, for example, they have realized that by conducting small experiments and pilots they can make better local business decisions. Brompton exports 10 per cent of its production to Japan, and their sales data informed them that all Japanese bike configurations demanded a standard seat position rather than the telescopic seat option.

That small insight enabled the sales department to inform the supply chain team at an earlier stage the number of bikes that were going to be produced for Japan for the next quarter, and therefore ensured that the correct production items were ordered, in this case standard seat posts. The data was therefore informing the link that needed to be made between sales forecasting, production process and supply chain.

The current process is manual, but it works because the whole workforce understands numbers, how to configure them and are comfortable with basic data demands.

DATA SAVVY STAFF

Brompton stresses that much of their workforce should be comfortable with data and basic Excel functionality such as pivot tables that calculate and analyse data so that comparisons, patterns and trends can be identified. If that level of capability doesn't exist, then your workforce will not be able to understand what the system is telling them and won't be able to question or interrogate the data that is available. If employees are not numerate, they will have to spend a lot of time and resource on basic activities that add limited value to the process.

At Brompton, managers are encouraged to guide and challenge their employees to become more data savvy. Operators are allowed to challenge other departments such as sales to request a new forecast from them so that when they have to forecast, they can consider their own planning process, component ordering and so on. This challenge to their teams revolves around collecting more relevant data and ensuring that better data analysis occurs, all revolving around the S, Q, D, C methodology.

Design driven development to people centric design thinking:

There are many more people involved in the new product design (NPD) and new product information (NPI) processes. Previously at Brompton this was much more design driven, from beginning to almost the release date, and along the way Brompton experienced some hiccups in terms of new products.

Today Brompton encourages every department to understand the product, and participate and provide input during the NPD and NPI processes. It's now about pulling together all the knowledge and insights from across the organization; it has moved from being a design-driven development process to more of a human-centred, design thinking-based initiative.

There is now more of a balance between what the designers say is great, and the practical operational implications of design implementation.

Key learnings

- **Role of HR**: Nicolas believes that HR needs to not only understand the data, but also appreciate its importance to the business in terms of what employees will be required to do with data, how to collect it and how to forecast with it in their jobs. He sees recruitment as being crucial today, and if someone is not comfortable with data in Excel, it is a big risk for the business to hire that person – as they won't challenge the data, or try to build something new using it.

- **Change**: The whole data process has been underpinned by change. Brompton has grown significantly over the past five years, and Nicolas believes: "Change will never be easy, because the change needs to come from the people who are doing the job. You can't enforce change, but you need to be sure that people are ready for it." The whole workforce needs to be willing to change and be receptive to new things, and they have to be prepared to bring the changes into the business.

- **The data journey**: Nicolas believes that Brompton wouldn't have done many things differently on their data journey. He sees it as a series of steps, some small and some somewhat larger. To have tried to implement large data-based process changes would have been difficult and created probably more challenges than they were trying to solve. "At Brompton, the data informs us what to do next", says Nicolas.

www.brompton.com (archived at https://perma.cc/H29E-MS5N)

The key learnings for us are that:

- the data-driven culture at Brompton has taken years to be adopted; it has required a sustained series of cultural changes to embed it into their organization;

- in this instance, recruitment practices focused on data-savvy employees to support that shift;

- Brompton's dynamic and high involvement strategies have developed an organization that is creating value through the expertise, feedback and data-based insights.

Our case study below highlights a change of culture requirement – in this instance, a bank needing to be more innovative to remain competitive. It required data and an analytical approach to unlock that potential.

CASE STUDY
Culture and the impact on innovation – is the place "fit for purpose"?

Business problem

This case study stems from a history of failed innovation in a bank when digital banking is growing as a customer need as well as being seen in the market as a key competitive driver. The organization had tried to develop a number of initiatives to promote more effective innovation, but these had not achieved the impact the company had hoped for.

As a consequence, the company's strategic group were tasked with understanding why the company was struggling with innovation and an insight team was created to address the challenge. One of the underlying issues revolved around a lack of clarity around what innovation meant for them as an organization.

Process

The insight team tackled this by exploring CultureScope by iPsychTec's cultural diagnostics and analytics research relating to innovation. They learnt that innovation was reflected by two approaches, a tactical one and a more strategic approach.

Having completed the mapping process in terms of what to assess, the next step was to gather data from the people tasked with innovation to see how they measured up to the definition of strategic innovation. These insights led to the development of a number of other questions related to the workplace, a realization that innovation requires the strategic ability to manage two places, the wider business and the specific work setting for those tasked with innovation. They used these insights to frame discussions with the company's executive committee and the line managers of the company's innovator teams.

Findings

The bank saw tactical innovation as "here and now" firefighting-based problem solving, and as the mode of innovation they had trapped themselves in. Strategic innovation was the mode they needed to move towards to transform the bank's operations and promote the company as innovating in its industry. Table 8.1 summarizes some of the underlying characteristics relating to tactical and strategic innovation

TABLE 8.1   Tactical and strategic innovation characteristics

Tactical innovation	Strategic innovation
Standardized	Flexible
Moderate	Radical
Tactical	Strategic
Conformity	Non-conformity
Sequential	Synchronous
Consolidate	Innovate
Inner focus	Outer focus

With the definition of strategic innovation in place, data was then gathered on 382 employees working in the company's innovation lab, as well as employees working outside that lab who were seen as potential innovators according to manager ratings.

That data showed a distinct profile that:

- Mapped to the definition of strategic innovation.

- Was very distinct from the general employee profile. In other words, those tasked with innovation or seen as offering innovation potential did in fact measure up to the potential required to realize strategic innovation.

- Showed that the problem was clearly with the place of work, and not with the people.

This led to two clear insights:

- How the company's innovators saw the workplace was very consistent with how other employees saw the workplace. The workplace was clearly a potential blocker to the adoption of innovation given substantial differences in the profiles of the people and the workplace for strategic innovation. This raised the question: "How do we help our innovators manage the challenge of the workplace so that they can realize the innovations they develop?"

- Alongside that obstacle was another challenge within the working environment of those tasked with innovation, as their own working context mapped closely to the profile of the wider organization. This then led to the question: "How do we create a more effective environment for our innovators to work in?"

A briefing to the company's executive committee led to the recognition that the working context required for effective innovation was very different to that of the wider business. This led to the sanction by the executive committee that the innovators in the company needed to be provided with a different working context. In other words, how we structure, organize and reward our innovators has to be different from how we operate in the wider company.

The next step was to work through what that meant in practice. To explore that, the values working group brought the company's innovators together for three days, to enable them to discuss what it meant to be an innovator and what the challenges of being an innovator in the company were:

- The participants were asked to plot out how they saw themselves, and the results mirrored exactly the results from the CultureScope survey. This was used to reassure participants that they had a clear and shared understanding of their talents, and that those talents mapped to the company's definition of strategic innovation.

- The participants were then asked to plot how they saw the workplace – and again, the results mirrored almost exactly the results from the survey. This was used to show participants that they were not only consistent in how they, as a group, saw the company, but that they also shared a consistent view of the company as a workplace with other employees. This was used to start discussions about how the company could support them in managing the gap between them, the people, and the wider workplace.

- With the framework established regarding the specific behaviours and challenges to innovation, participants were then encouraged to explore these with other companies through, for example, short placements with FinTech firms. The mandate was for participants to explore how other companies identified, developed and rewarded their innovators, and how those innovators were supported in managing challenges to the adoption of innovation by the wider organization.

- The data gathered from this meeting was then shared with the next tier of managers responsible for managing the company's innovators. One specific action identified from this discussion was that processes used in the wider company, for example approval processes, hampered those working in innovation. This led to work on how to develop and implement fast-track processes within the innovation community in the organization – ie to differentiate the operational process needs of innovation teams and groups from operational processes used in the wider company.

- A final insight or learning from this project was that, as the workplace represented by the wider organization had to change for the adoption of innovation to be effective, there were specific behaviours that should be encouraged across the organization.

Outcomes

Key outcomes from this project, driven specifically by the data and analytical research undertaken, included:

- clarity around the type of innovation the company wanted to promote – strategic, and not tactical;

- clarity around the talents needed among their people to realize the aspiration for strategic innovation;

- clarity around the problem – it's the workplace, and not the people or both;

- clarity around how to manage the tension between the wider working environment, working practices in the organization and working practices required to foster performance within their innovator community – the key differences and why some need to be preserved;

- the platform to create an innovator community – using the data to show people that they share a common set of talents and understanding of the challenges;
- the platform to educate those tasked with managing the company's innovators in how to manage them more effectively – these people have what we need, but share a number of obstacles to realizing the talents they have;
- clarity around how to manage the tension between the wider organization and the place that fosters innovation, how to enable their innovators to manage that tension, and targeted behaviours to be fostered in the wider organization to promote more effective adoption of innovation.

Courtesy of CultureScope by iPsychTec: https://ipsychtec.com/culturescope/ (archived at https://perma.cc/UDV8-ZTJR)

The key learnings from this are that:

- measurement of culture defines the next stages of action and change;
- people analytics can be brought to the fore as a way of changing culture and understanding the perceptions of the workforce about what it is like to work in your organization;
- high levels of involvement across the workforce is vital to any change in approach;
- cultural change is about behavioural change across the whole workplace.

Another people analytics-based case study now follows, where again a change in culture was required, this time driven by external regulatory forces.

CASE STUDY
Creating an accountable culture that delivers sustainable regulated compliance activity

Business problem

A small/medium sized Arab bank in the UK needed to demonstrate to the UK financial services regulator, the Financial Conduct Authority (FCA), that risk assumption processes and risk compliance activity had been comprehensively reviewed and that a clear action plan had been created to urgently address deep-seated cultural issues.

The bank had conducted an engagement survey, but it was felt that the survey was unable to provide clarity around the drivers or reasons for low employee engagement scores, which was perceived to be a potential root cause of inadequate levels of risk compliance and risk mitigation. Additionally, it was proving to be difficult to link the results of this survey to tangible actions as part of the organization's plan for transformation that was so necessary.

Process

CultureScope by iPsychTec, experts in cultural diagnostics and analytics, were used to measure how individuals across the organization were behaving and responding to the organization's culture. They collected behavioural-based survey data, with an 80 per cent completion rate, and this was complemented with insights and data via three focus groups and 12 personal interviews with the Executive Committee.

Findings

Insights were drawn from three different data sets and the following three priorities were identified and shared with the Regulator.

LEADERSHIP TEAM: RISK MANAGEMENT

- An excessive command and control culture was being demonstrated with directives not being supported consistently and led to employee confusion regarding rules.
- Misalignment/working independently was in evidence, with a lack of team work being seen.
- A lack of sufficient decision-making was being seen, which led to increased risk.

VALUES

- The organization as a whole didn't "walk the walk". This led to rules being applied inconsistently.
- Integrity, teamwork and lack of ability to drive change were key areas of concern.
- The need for innovation was not understood.

CHANGE

- Too much change was in evidence and was being seen too often; there was a need for stability.
- There was a lack of consistent communication to employees from the senior team particularly around redundancies.

Outcomes

The Regulator carried out an internal audit and highlighted that the management had taken a proactive approach to measure and understand the culture, and as a result implement change based on the cultural and behavioural analysis. After analysing the data-based findings, the code of conduct was recreated to establish a culture of accountability, focused on driving the right behaviours, managing risk effectively and providing clear leadership.

TABLE 8.2   Code of conduct

Leadership	Behaviours	Competencies	Values
Shapes strategic thinking	Development Mutual respect	Driving results	Client-centric
Achieves results	Accessible and visible collaboration	Leadership and influence	Teamwork
Cultivates productive working relationships	Feedback empowerment	Judgement and accountability	Integrity Innovation Excellence
Exemplifies personal drive and integrity	Managing conflict Participative approach	Knowledge and expertise	
Communicates with influence	Expressing and managing own emotions Taking responsibility	Governance	
Demonstrates professional leadership	Communication Empathy Acting with integrity		

As a result of the implementation of this programme and improved monitoring of activity, the FCA removed a Section 166 notice which enabled the bank to continue trading. Without this work and the analytical-based approach to the culture challenge, the bank would inevitably have ceased trading. Today, its profitability has significantly improved.

Courtesy of CultureScope by iPsychTec: https://ipsychtec.com/culturescope/ (archived at https://perma.cc/UDV8-ZTJR)

The key learnings from this are:

- the measurement of culture defined the rigorous action plan that was required to ensure that behavioural changes were made in the way that the organization operated;

- the power of listening to the employees and the workforce ensured that a clear understanding about the real enterprise issues emerged;
- people analytics can be a game changer when trying to diagnose and change the culture in your organization.

Changing culture is not an easy programme. We know that organizations that outperform their competition are more likely to both have strong leadership and democratized data access and use and, furthermore, data-driven organizations are more likely to outperform their competitors when it comes to profitability.[7] The challenge is how to drive that forward in a sustainable and engaging way while understanding where you are starting from.

Every culture change is different; the desire to adopt a data-based approach is no different and should be planned like any other major organizational initiative. Ed Houghton, head of research and people analytics at CIPD, says: "If we were to move the dial on analytics to make it a core part of how businesses think and how HR professionals act, we have to fully understand analytics cultures."

How to run people analytics projects successfully

In our experience, it's only beginners who start a people analytics project without a plan, thinking that spontaneity equates to being agile! The most successful analytics leaders continually reinforce to us that it is vital to commit to a plan of action before starting any analytics-based project. It enables everyone to understand what is going to be done and ensures that you don't get distracted down particular areas that consume time, resources and focus.

Framework to run people analytics

This doesn't mean that you need to create new levels of extensive paperwork. Let's review what you as an HR, learning and development or people practitioner probably already do in terms of process when interacting with your business leaders and managers, your clients.

CURRENT PRACTITIONER AND LEADERSHIP PROCESS
Figure 8.1 outlines the process that we have observed practitioners undertaking via extensive job shadowing and job analysis.

FIGURE 8.1   HR and people analytics project process

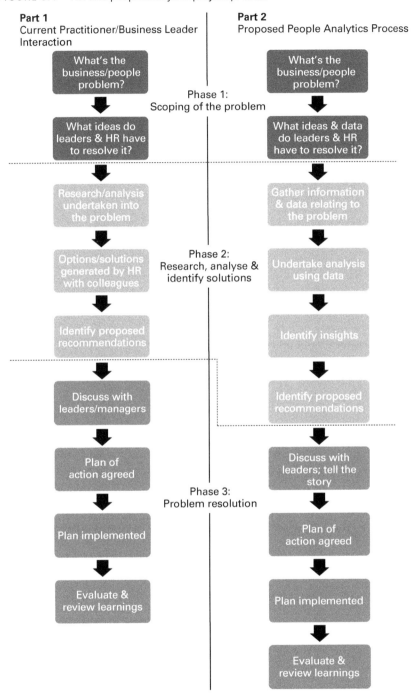

Phase 1: Scoping of the problem:

- What's the business/people problem that needs to be addressed?
- What ideas do the business leaders/managers and the HR practitioner have to resolve it?

Phase 2: Research, analyse and identify solutions:

- Undertake research/analysis into the problem.
- Generate options/solutions, possibly with colleagues' input.
- Identify proposed recommendations that are to be shared with the client.

Phase 3: Problem resolution:

- Discuss the recommendations with the client and obtain their feedback.
- Identify the agreed plan of action.
- Ensure the plan is implemented.
- Evaluate and review the learnings from the process.

This is a common process that outlines three distinct phases, clearly positions the practitioner with the business leaders/managers and enables them to build on their relationship skills with some core consulting capabilities, which are particularly relevant for the HR business partner role and the scenarios that they face on a daily basis.

PROPOSED PEOPLE ANALYTICS FRAMEWORK

The type of data-based analysis process is not that different to the typical interaction process that you are likely to be adopting already.

Phase 1: Scoping of the problem:

- What's the business/people problem that needs to be addressed?
- What ideas and data do the business leaders/managers and HR have to help understand and resolve the problem?

Phase 2: Research, analyse and identify solutions:

- Gather relevant information and data relating to the problem.
- Undertake the necessary qualitative and quantitative analysis using the available relevant quality data.
- Identify insights that have emerged from the analysis.

- Identify the proposed recommendations that will be shared with the business leaders/managers.

Phase 3: Problem resolution:

- Discuss the recommendations with the business leaders/managers; tell the story and obtain their feedback.
- Identify the agreed plan of action.
- Ensure the plan is implemented.
- Evaluate and review the learnings from the process; this provides the opportunity to embed the solution in a more systematic way that can resolve future such issues occurring again.

The three-stage process is anchored in the same business leader/HR relationship that already works; the differences naturally revolve around data accessibility, in terms of what quality data is available or can be obtained to help make sense of the problem that is being investigated. The analysis process is naturally more comprehensive, with the evaluation of the issues driving the insights that can ultimately generate options for consideration. The process is not that different, though.

This has to be underpinned by ongoing stakeholder communication throughout the process, as they may have other perspectives that need to be considered as the project moves forward. It's easy to make assumptions or to quickly think that the data backs up a preconceived idea that you, or the stakeholder, had – but this could mean that you miss something that is particularly relevant to resolving the problem.

Always try to ensure that you have got to the root cause of the problem, as you can never assume that your analysis captures all the issues the first time around. That may mean working with your stakeholders and their managers to truly understand the issues at play, and a consequence of this will be that managers will have different expectations, as you are operating more in their field, data, than perhaps yours. The involvement of and with managers is only going to increase, as Bill Gerrard, professor at Leeds University, outlines below.

THOUGHT LEADERSHIP INSIGHT
Managers and analysts working together

Jeremy Snape, founder and managing director of Sporting Edge, in conversation with Bill Gerrard, professor of business and sports analytics at Leeds University and data analyst at Az Alkmaar Football Club

Bill's principal research focus is sports analytics, and the statistical analysis of performance data within an evidence-based coaching regime in both individual and team sports. Bill has worked with a number of elite sports teams around the world including working with Billy Beane, the general manager of the Oakland Athletics, whose application of sports analytics has been the subject of the Hollywood film and best-selling book, *Moneyball*.

Jeremy Snape, CEO of high-performance consultancy Sporting Edge, interviewed Bill Gerrard about his insights into the world of analytics in sport, and the subject of managers working with analysts emerged. Bill's thoughts were as follows:

"I think the most important thing is that the leaders of the future have a recognition of what analytics can do. They need to have a sense of the types of questions that analytics can help answer or provide guidance on. It's not the case of coaches of managers having to become analysts, that's why you have technicians like myself to do the analysis. This can be most effective when there's a meeting of minds, where the coach and the analyst, or the manager and the analyst, have a shared understanding of the problem so that the analyst can be the translator.

"The analyst has got to take the manager's problem, translate that into an analytical problem and then translate it back into recommendations. I call it the TAR model of analytics:

- Talk with the manager.
- Analyse the data.
- Recommend to the manager.

"So, a lot of what you know is the hard skills, the science or statistical skills, for the analysis. They are important, but it's the soft skills that are even more important – the ability to have a conversation and a meeting of minds between the analyst and the manager. Without those soft skills you end up with a very frustrated analyst who thinks they're doing great work. Technically they may be doing great work, but if they are not able to translate it into practical recommendations, and that presupposes that they've actually understood what it is the coach and the manager is trying to do, without that you can have the best analysis in the world in technical terms, but it's going to make absolutely no difference.

"That's why being able to talk with one another is so important."

Courtesy of Sporting Edge: www.sportingedge.com (archived at https://perma.cc/ML35-6XVT)

Avoiding people analytics project failure

Purposeful analytics are regarded as being the key to successful people analytics processes; that means that the focus must always be on solving problems that are meaningful to the business and cannot be regarded as irrelevant or nice-to-do. If that is taken as a key principle for all analytics projects, we wanted to outline some of the issues that sometimes get in the way.

HR functions today are starting to come under more pressure, as interest in people analytics continues to increase momentum. With increasing interest comes the pressure to just do something in this space, and that means that mistakes can happen. Accordingly, Tables 8.3, 8.4 and 8.5 cover some of the issues that we have seen from being involved with a cross-section of people analytics projects, involving onboarding, recruiting, workforce capability, learning, productivity, engagement and employee experience-based projects:

Phase 1: Scoping of the problem

TABLE 8.3   Scoping of the problem

Challenges and issues have revolved around:	Solutions revolve around:
• Focusing on issues and problems that were not perceived to be a priority for a business, and yet provided access to robust quality data.	• Focus on the business issues that need to be resolved, not the availability of high-quality data.
• Focusing on issues that lacked project sponsorship and stakeholder commitment.	• Obtain that buy-in before proceeding with the project.

TABLE 8.3   *continued*

Challenges and issues have revolved around:	Solutions revolve around:
• Focusing on large complex analytical projects that are resource-intensive and riskier to complete.	• Consider a "quick wins" approach to prove the concept quickly and in an organized way.
• Not creating a defined project plan of action and trying to be too spontaneous in their approach, which inevitably means that "project creep" will occur and inappropriate expectations exist.	• A project plan, whilst frustrating at times, provides the focus and communication that needs to be in place.

Phase 2: Research, analyse and identify solutions

TABLE 8.4   Research, analyse and identify solutions

Challenges and issues have revolved around:	Solutions revolve around:
• Privacy concerns. The misuse of personal data is an important issue to consider in the context of a project. Employees are becoming increasingly aware of how their data should and should not be used.	• Establishing well-defined policies, security safeguards, transparency measures and ongoing communication around the use of people data.
• Data quality. An incomplete, inaccurate or irrelevant data set can create challenges and time pressures.	• Data perfection is hard to achieve, so focus on what data is available and try to create an analysis with that data set.
• Unwillingness to either buy, build or borrow the necessary analytical capability to drive the project successfully.	• The project plan will define what resources and capabilities will be needed. Without the right skills the analysis won't be effective.
• Lack of access to appropriate technology systems that will provide the data and automated analytical insights that can be invaluable to the project.	• A range of technology solutions are available to support the project process. Investigate and seek feedback from external peers, analysts and influencers.

Phase 3: Problem resolution

TABLE 8.5   Problem resolution

Challenges and issues have revolved around:	Solutions revolve around:
• Focusing on a client presentation that is lengthy and full of data.	• Tell the story behind the data and the insights that have emerged. "Less is more" – focus on a maximum six to eight slides to get your messages across.
• Leaving the next steps in the hands of the leaders/managers.	• Ensure that a defined plan of action with joint accountability (HR and management) is in place.
• Lack of perceived actionable insights.	• Focus on the actionability of your data and outcomes so that practical implementable solutions are shared with the stakeholders.
• Moving on from the project to another issue.	• Ensure that a review is completed to critique not just the process, but also the evaluation of the implemented solution. This will provide vital learning moving forward.

Remember that just because you've undertaken an analytics project, that doesn't always mean that you will have tangible data-based insights for the business to take forward. The management of expectations, especially in the early days of your analytics journey is important to the success of any project.

As your capabilities develop, whether you are a practitioner working with the business, or starting to undertake the analysis, you will start to value the implementation of structured projects, which provide you with a safety net to ensure that you execute in line with expectations.[8]

KEY TAKEAWAYS FROM THIS CHAPTER

1   Developing a data-driven culture, one that leverages data whenever and wherever possible, is an important element that is necessary for people analytics to be successfully implemented in an organization.

2   Creating a data-driven culture requires many consistent parts to be in place, such as future vision, the operating model of the organization and the role of leaders in modelling the desired changes.

3   The measurement of culture can be a significant tool in determining how to become more data-orientated in your approach in your organization, as it can help to understand the complexities that need to be understood.

4   Develop a framework to undertake your people analytics projects; trying to run them without a plan or a structure won't work. The process does not need to be that different from your normal client project-based interactions, the only difference is the significant focus upon the data required to inform the research and solution identification process. The framework won't guarantee success, but it will ensure that you have a greater chance of achieving quality project outcomes.

References

1   Schein, E H (2010) *Organizational Culture and Leadership* (2nd ed), John Wiley & Sons, Chichester and New York

2   O'Reilly, C A and Pfeffer, J (2000) *Hidden Value: How great companies achieve extraordinary results with ordinary people*, Harvard Business Press, Brighton, MA

3   Jaw-Madson, K (2018) *Culture Your Culture: Innovating experiences @work*, Emerald Publishing, Bingley

4   Collins, J (2009) *Good to Great: Why some companies make the leap and others don't*, Random House Business Books, New York

5   Teece, D J, Pisano, G and Shuen, A (1997) Dynamic capabilities and strategic management, *Strategic Management Journal*, 18 (7), pp 509–33

6   Teece, D J (2007) Explicating dynamic capabilities: the nature and micro-foundations of (sustainable) enterprise performance, *Strategic Management Journal*, 28 (13), pp 1319–50

7   Economist Intelligence Unit (2014) The virtuous circle of data: engaging employees in data and transforming your business, *Teradata* [Online] http://assets.teradata.com/resourceCenter/downloads/WhitePapers/THE_VIRTUOUS_CIRCLE_OF_DATA_EIU_Teradata_WEB.pdf (archived at https://perma.cc/KME3-E2M7)

8   Kenton, B and Yarnall, J (2005) *HR – The Business Partner Shaping a New Direction*, Elsevier: Butterworth Heinemann, Oxford

PART FOUR

Looking to the future

9

How to be more data-driven and people analytics-focused

The importance of developing a data-driven based approach throughout the HR community, as outlined in previous chapters, is vital to the function's future success. According to Ed Houghton, head of research and people analytics at CIPD: "CIPD research has demonstrated that HR practitioners have real gaps in capability at every level of analytics, particularly at the more advanced level. This is not just in terms of skills, but in terms of confidence too. These gaps present real challenges but also huge opportunities for the profession."

The basis of this chapter is to share how to develop in-house analytics capability, providing development-based tips and ideas that can be of help as you start, continue or reinforce the change in behaviour that is necessary to become more data-orientated in the workplace as a people practitioner.

It's important to reinforce that the expectation is not for every HR, learning and development (L&D) and people practitioner to suddenly analyse every piece of data that comes across your desk, but it is important that a more data-based, scientific approach is adopted. Digitalization may eventually remove the traditional HR knowledge and skill areas as self-service and AI based algorithms take over routine activities in organizations.[1] The resultant impact of this is that new capabilities around analytics will become more crucial than before.

This chapter will cover:

- **Stories from in and around the function**: Understanding how other HR functions have changed and adopted can prove beneficial to show that this type of change can be done. Examples of how other providers see the development challenge are also covered.

- **Developing your capability to be more data-driven**: Development tips are provided based around a four-stage framework, all of which are designed to help you make those changes in mindset that are vital to embrace the possibilities and opportunities that data and more of an analytics approach can bring to your HR role and to the function.

- **Developing HR capability is a business imperative**: To conclude this section, we outline why this development focus is probably going to be some of the most important self-development you have ever undertaken.

The focus will enable you to consider what changes you can – and want to – make in your busy role at work, so that numbers and data become an integral part of the way that you and your colleagues operate. The people function of the future needs to invest in developing its own talent in the same way that it supports the business in identifying and developing talent more generally.[2]

Leena Nair, CHRO of Unilever, strongly believes that personal learning agility is a key capability for the function if it is to rid itself of self-doubt and build its confidence and swagger when dealing with business leaders. She also believes that if you're not investing at least 100 hours a year in your personal learning, you are falling behind.[3]

Stories from in and around the function

The development of a people analytics team for a number of organizations is regarded as the solution to the gap in the capability of the function. Whether an analytics team is created or not, the different focus upon the HR practitioner and in particular the HR business partner (HRBP) role will become a key challenge.

AstraZeneca outline their development journey and the challenge and approaches that they adopted to change the behaviour of their HR community.

CASE STUDY

AstraZeneca: Developing your HR function and your HRBPs to be more data-driven

Charlotte Allen, global head of organization development, HR strategy and analytics

AstraZeneca is a global, science-led biopharmaceutical company with a major UK presence. Their purpose is to push the boundaries of science to deliver life-changing medicines that are used by millions of patients worldwide. They employ approximately 65,000 employees operating in over 100 countries.

Context for change

The story began in 2015 with the implementation of Workday, starting with the core HR and performance management modules, which gave us a global system of record for our employees. This gave us a foundation to be able to do workforce analytics and reporting because we have a consistent way of capturing employee-related data.

We then continued to implement additional Workday modules which extended the workforce-related data we capture and HR process-related information. For example, we use Workday recruiting, which provides us with data on our recruitment process efficiency and effectiveness.

Alongside the Workday implementation, we evolved our HR operating model to ensure that we have the right HR capabilities and organization to support our employees and line managers. An important part of that was the executive vice-president of HR's vision for the HR function to be data-driven, and this has led to a focus on building that capability particularly within the HRBPs. The focus of this has been how to use data and insights to make and influence people- and workforce-related decisions.

Starting the journey

We have separate teams in HR focusing on workforce analytics, reporting and HR data management. After a reorganization, while we maintained these separate teams, we moved the ownership of the reporting global process owner responsibilities to the workforce analytics team.

It's important to have a joined-up strategy from data to reporting through to analytics, because they are part of a continuum and you can't think of these elements in isolation. Our global process owner accountabilities include setting the vision and strategy for the HR process, so this means we have a consistent view across analytics and reporting, and we work very closely with our global HR data lead to ensure we are all aligned.

In terms of starting to build capability within our HR function, we established a series of global HR capability calls. The first call was a basic introduction to using Workday for reporting on employee-related information. These calls were hugely successful – considering the various time zones that we need to cover, we'd normally get around 200 people join each call, which at that time represented almost 50 per cent of the HR function. The calls weren't mandatory, so we were quite surprised that we had so many people attend, which demonstrated that there was an appetite to learn and develop this knowledge.

Continuing the journey

The journey to continue to build the data and analytics capability in HR function has continued via the following key initiatives.

GLOBAL HR CAPABILITY CALLS

These calls have continued to happen, and while they cover a wide range of subjects, a number have been focused on data and analytics, covering subjects such as:

- how to make data-driven decisions, with examples of how some of our HR teams have done this;
- storytelling and bringing data to life through clear and succinct analysis;
- workforce planning and how to use data to make workforce decisions that can meet changing business priorities and objectives;
- an overview of the Workday dashboards we have developed, and how to use them in conversations with line managers.

WORKFORCE ANALYTICS PORTAL

A portal with workforce analytics and reporting information was created in 2017. This was designed to extend the reach of analytics and reporting information available to all of our HR teams based in countries around the world. The portal contains videos, call recordings, information, external insights, tips and tools, all aimed at helping HR to become more comfortable with a data-driven approach; it's become a one-stop shop for analytics and reporting-related information.

One of the key documents available is a glossary of key HR metrics so that we can drive consistency across the globe in how we define and talk about data. It means that when we're talking about turnover, we make sure there is a clear definition and advice on how the measure can be calculated if you want to do it manually, with guidelines for using and interpreting it and how insights can be drawn from those metrics. The portal helped us to establish that foundation of consistency, so whether it's in China, Russia or UK, we are all talking the same language across the function. In the first 11 months of going live, there were 2,200 views from a total HR function of around 850.

ANALYTICS NETWORK

To further extend our reach and build further capability in the more data-savvy members of our HR function, a workforce analytics network was launched globally. This was a development opportunity for HR employees that wanted to learn more and help embed more advanced analytic practices across the global HR function. The aim was to get about 20 champions; we've now got 80 champions across 26 countries representing all parts of our HR function including the HRBP community.

There is a danger you can assume that nobody in HR is data-orientated or wants to work with numbers (outside of those in areas such as payroll or reward), but we have found this isn't the case. We have a number of HRBPs who are now key champions who are data-driven and continue to build this capability. This has really inspired other people in the function because it shows that capability in this area is not restricted to analytics people or "data geeks".

NEW ANALYTICS TOOLS

One of the biggest things that made a difference was the launch of the MicroStrategy analytics tool. MicroStrategy is the tool we use to analyse data from multiple sources of HR, workforce or people-related data which provides us with additional analytics and insights above and beyond the reporting we do from Workday.

Since its launch in 2018, all HR colleagues have been given access. The launch was predominantly focused on the HRBPs, and training sessions were delivered for them. In the nine months following launch, 72 per cent of those with access had used the tool at least once and we'd had more than 3,000 unique visits since going live.

WORKFORCE ANALYTICS PARTNERS

Our workforce analytics team is a global and centralized team. Within the last year, each of the team members were also given an alignment against a specific part of our business. This was done for two primary reasons:

- To help build the business knowledge of our analytics team, so that the work we do is grounded in the business context and supports the business priorities.
- To continue to build the analytics knowledge within the various HRBP leadership teams. The workforce analytics partners sit as part of the extended leadership teams, and this regular interaction, helps the HRBPs understand how data and analytics can be used to support the work they are doing.

HR LEADERSHIP SUPPORT

It's critical when building a capability that there is leadership support. The executive vice-president of HR takes every opportunity to reinforce the importance of being a data-driven HR function by talking about it in global HR calls, local HR meetings and by implementing a series of annual meetings whereby HRBPs present the strategic workforce plans, supported by relevant data and analytics, for their areas.
These collective initiatives have helped to:

- ensure that HR and the HRBPs understand when and how to use data;
- create capacity in the workforce analytics and reporting teams to pilot new systems, approaches and frameworks, and then test them out with HR colleagues;

- ensure that the democratization of data became a reality, as everybody now has access to the data they want in a way that is easy to use and access.

Looking to the future

AstraZeneca is a company based on science and in all areas of our business – R&D, Manufacturing and Sales – data is used every day to make decisions. This should be no different in HR.

It's an ongoing process to promote the way we'd like our HRBPs to use data in their day-to-day work. For example, before as part of the preparation for a meeting with a business leader, they should be considering:

- Business issues: what are the priorities for this leader?
- Supporting data: what workforce and people data is relevant for these priorities and what insights can I bring to the leader that will help them?
- Measuring implementation: when we agree the actions, what data do we have available that will show whether we are successful or not?

The workforce analytics team journey

The analytics team has been on a journey as well, starting with the predominantly reporting-based activity that focused on historic trends and responding to request for data whatever those may be.

The team has changed its name from HR analytics to workforce analytics, reflecting the broad scope and focus of the data and insights provided. HR measurement and metrics remains a key part of what is done in the team, but we need to think more broadly about the workforce as a whole. The team continues to innovate either through the use of technology to automate what we do and/or to improve the insights provided, or new analytical approaches to providing additional insights.

Conclusion

The whole HR function has undoubtedly become more data-driven as a result of the journey that has been undertaken over the past few years. Now we have HR colleagues who are regularly using data and providing the insights themselves. There are always pockets of people who still aren't quite there, but that's where the consistent reinforcement of why it's important to use data is crucial.

There will always be instances where either the wrong analysis has been undertaken or where there is "death by data", with charts being regarded as the solution to every problem – but these instances are few and far between. We now have an infrastructure that can minimize these occurrences.

www.astrazeneca.com (archived at https://perma.cc/P7XE-89UX)

The takeaways from AstraZeneca for us are that it wasn't easy, but a relentless push from practitioners meant that they have made great progress in the HR community, as the organization has moved from Box 1, to Box 2, to Box 3/4 (see Chapter 6).

The development challenge needed constant reinforcement to demonstrate the value and opportunities that a more numerical approach will have on the role and the expectations of the business leaders. The support infrastructure in this instance was created and developed very effectively in-house. There are other support methodologies that can be provided for individual people practitioners and smaller organizations; one such example is Analytics in HR (AIHR).

Their story is outlined below, incorporating their learnings along the way.

THOUGHT LEADERSHIP INSIGHT

The rise in demand for people analytics-based education: the AIHR story

Erik Van Vulpen, founder of AIHR

In June 2016, Nando Steenhuis and I founded AIHR. AIHR is the largest people analytics community in the world, drawing well over a million visitors during 2019. From this perspective, here are some of our learnings and unique insights from the people analytics space.

We were both active in the HR technology space but a theme that was emerging was that of people analytics, the use of data to make better people decisions. In our initial market research, we found that there was a lot of misinformation regarding this topic. Most senior HR managers in large Dutch companies had heard of analytics but didn't really know what it was. Whenever we had a conversation about the topic we always were asked what it is, what they could do with it internally, if there's a business case for it and what tools are required to do it.

We didn't hear these questions once or twice; we heard them all the time.

We analysed Google search behaviour on analytics and metrics-related keywords to find quantitative evidence for the interest in people analytics. HR professionals from all over the world asked Google the same questions, tens of thousands of times a month. Interestingly, the websites that then appeared in the search results didn't really answer these questions. We then decided that the time was right to jump into this knowledge gap, and that's how www.analyticsinhr.com (archived at https://perma.cc/6L9R-K2PW) got started. By writing articles that answered these often-asked questions, we were able to quickly build a community of people analytics practitioners that was sharing experiences and answering each other's questions. The website has well over 100,000 sessions per month in 2019, and is still growing.

When it comes to people analytics, we are trying to teach companies to do it themselves. This means that we give analytics practitioners a platform to share their experiences and we write detailed do-it-yourself guides. Since 2014 it has grown from something peripheral, with a few conferences on the topic, to the 2019 Deloitte's Global Human Capital Trends report, where people analytics wasn't explicitly mentioned but was now integrated in the different technology solutions mentioned in the report.

If it had been measured, the gap between importance and readiness would have been even bigger when we started the website in 2016; people knew that there was something important going on, but at the same time had no clue how to get started. Because of this, we entered a field where everyone was looking for information but where the only good information you could get was either at an expensive conference, or by reading an article written by one of the few brilliant people analytics writers in the space, most of which have never done any analytics in their life.

After starting the website, we received an increasing amount of enquiries looking for more detailed information. People reached out asking if we could recommend workshops or offline training in analytics. Because there were only a few people who really understood analytics, it was hard to point them in the right direction. This is where the idea for e-learning originated and why we started providing online training to help people develop their people analytics capabilities. We started with one course and we now offer over a dozen courses on the different aspects of people analytics and digital HR, ranging from basic data acumen to learning how to set up and lead a people analytics team. We can now safely call ourselves the largest online educator in people analytics in the world.

What people are interested in

Our position as a media platform provides us with unique insights into what HR professionals are looking for when it comes to content related to people analytics. Over 75 per cent of our visitors come to our website via Google, so our visitor data is a treasure trove of information which tells us what the market in general is looking for, what to produce content on, and which new courses to launch.

We publish articles on people or HR analytics, which we have defined as a data-driven approach to managing people at work (in line with Gal, Jensen and Stein[4]). This means we publish not only articles on advanced, predictive analytics but also articles that relate to simpler metrics and data-driven HR culture. We have written a lot of articles and this is where we get most of our visitors from. These visitors are:

- mostly HR professionals working at larger organizations;
- between 25 and 44 years old (70 per cent falls in this age bracket);
- largely female from the US (57 per cent), which is far below the 73 per cent of HR practitioners at the manager level who are female as reported by the US Bureau of Labor Statistics.

This indicates that people analytics is, relatively speaking, a bit of a man's world when it comes to the HR demographics. One could make a convincing argument that people analytics is one of the STEM fields of HR. Men have been historically overrepresented in these fields compared to women.

The main areas of educational interest are:

1 **Metrics and key performance indicators (KPIs)**: 25 per cent of website visitors look for information about measurements in HR. The most popular article on this topic, which is also the most-read article on the website, is a list of employee performance metrics. Measuring employee performance is still a key challenge for HR professionals today. Other articles of interest are about general HR metrics, recruiting metrics and how to formulate and structure HR KPIs.

2 **Reporting and dashboarding**: Once you know about metrics and have made them strategic, you want to report on them in an HR report or dashboard. These enable you to easily communicate basic data to relevant stakeholders, including managers and HRBPs.

3 **Advanced analytics**: We also see a lot of interest about analytics that include an introductory article titled 'What is HR Analytics?', a number of guides on how to do analytics, different published case studies and business cases, and more technical content.

If we reviewed this information in a simple pyramid shape, you would easily recognize a model that looks similar to a people analytics maturity model with simple metrics and KPIs at the bottom (operational reporting), HR reports and dashboards in the middle (advanced reporting), and analytics at the top (predictive analytics). Most interest is focused on the bottom of the pyramid.

We see the same in the e-learnings we produce with greater interest in more introductory courses rather than the more technically advanced courses.

This also reflects that HR are still working with data exports in Excel, and so a big win is to understand more advanced Excel functionalities such as pivot tables, aggregation and visualization tools that help to create basic insights from data that does not require advanced data analytics capabilities.

The future

As a media platform, you have to balance between providing relevant content that is interesting to people today and also future-orientated. The latter category is usually less popular, but will help in shaping what people think. An example is employee experience, a topic that no one was writing about in 2016 but that everyone is talking about today, with new articles published every month on this topic.

AIHR has grown by acquiring Digital HR Tech, a leading online platform for HR professionals with high-quality articles and video content about the latest developments in HR technology, best practices, and the future of work written by experts from all over the world. This is driven by our desire to integrate analytics, or rather evidence-based practices, into everything HR does, and help to futureproof HR by equipping its practitioners with the necessary tools, knowledge and skills to grow.

www.aihr.com (archived at https://perma.cc/3QW9-3AG3),
www.analyticsinhr.com (archived at https://perma.cc/6L9R-K2PW),
www.digitalhrtech.com (archived at https://perma.cc/C9Y2-YZ9H)

The level of interest in this topic continues to increase and as Eric Van Vulpen has outlined, the number of people focusing on this subject continues to grow; this whole topic area is here to stay.

Developing your capability to be more data-driven

Whatever your people analytics approach might be, a formal analytics team or using the in-house capabilities of HR or other teams, the success of your people analytics programme is likely to depend upon your HRBPs or frontline HR practitioners. The core analytics team can never handle all the questions that get sent their way, so you'll need to upskill and train your HRBPs in some way.

The usual riposte is that HR and HRBPs are not numbers people, and are not inclined to want to learn statistics or a more numerical approach. Teaching statistics to HRBPs is difficult, but the majority of analytics problems don't need anything more sophisticated than mathematics, as we have said already. The value of an analytics mindset comes from taking HRBPs to a world where numbers can help drive better informed decision-making with their clients. This is where the data and analytics translator role emerges, as outlined in Chapter 4 (see Figure 9.1 for the summary).

FIGURE 9.1   Data and analytics translator future role

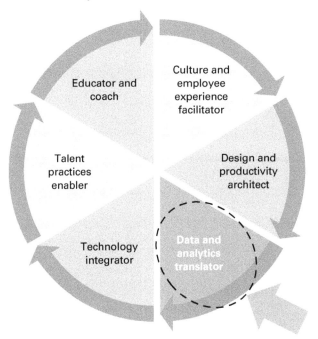

To help provide ideas and thoughts about how to move into that data and analytics translator role, John Pensom, co-founder and CEO of PeopleInsight.com, has shared their playbook, *HR business partners: a practical guide to becoming data-driven.*[5] It incorporates their development framework and associated ideas for capability improvement, which we have adapted with additional input from our own HRBP behavioural research. See Figure 9.2.

FIGURE 9.2   Data and analytics translator development framework

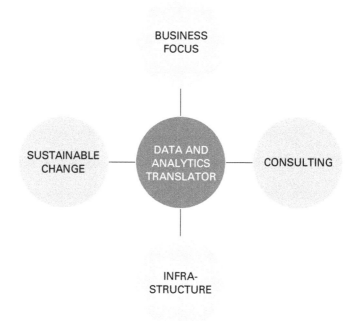

The framework focuses on four key areas:

1 **Business focus**: When it comes to workforce planning, different business functions and areas will have different objectives, drivers and issues but there will also be common ground. HRBPs need a solid understanding of both the enterprise-wide people objectives, and the specific objectives of the business units they serve.

2 **Consulting**: Some HRBPs are more naturally analytical, business-savvy, data-driven and strategic than others. It's therefore becoming more commonplace that HRBPs build upon their transactional HR skills and experience, becoming change enablers and help drive the people side of business outcomes. This means articulating the opportunity and understanding of issues, consulting, driving decisions, planning and implementing change, and optimizing business results with the aid of data.

3 **Infrastructure**: Smart technological tools can sometimes flounder if they don't operate within a culture that supports their purpose. For an HRBP to be successful in a data-driven world, there must be a framework,

strategic focus and processes in place to ensure the relevant trusted data is captured.

4 **Sustainable change**: "Becoming data-driven" implies that change will occur, and this change must be sustainable and not just a one-off project. These four areas of focus must work together to ensure clarity of purpose, adoption and motivation for the future state, leadership support, a concrete plan for implementation, in addition to clearly defined, yet achievable success.

Business focus

The business focus needs to be driven by the "big picture"; this is driven by the Do, Help, Fix model which helps you invest in data-driven activities across three areas. See Figure 9.3.

OPERATIONAL REPORTING AND ANALYTICS (ORA) – DO THINGS
These are the basic areas that an HRBP should already be doing – Box 1 in the people analytics capability model, Figure 6.1. ORA should help you improve the efficiency and effectiveness of standard people programme activities for the business. This should include hiring, headcount management, turnover, L&D and performance management. This will help focus on the core HR day-to-day activity and gain the trust of the business area by using HR data to help deliver both efficient and effective HR processes and programmes.

ORA is all about taking a data-driven approach to doing core activities better.

STRATEGIC REPORTING AND ANALYTICS (SRA) – HELP THINGS
These are activities that are focused on helping the business area achieve its strategic objectives – Box 2 or Box 3 from Figure 6.1. SRA will help focus on the crucial business issues that need to be addressed. These are driven directly by what is important to the organization and the business area and will be aligned with the one-year, three-year or five-year business strategy or the strategic business plan milestones.

An example would be using a data-driven approach to prepare and mobilize a new customer support team for a new product launch in six months' time. SRA is about you helping the business to execute on issues that they need help with, specifically from the people side, and adopting a data-driven approach to shape the results.

FIGURE 9.3   Business focus – Do, Help, Fix model

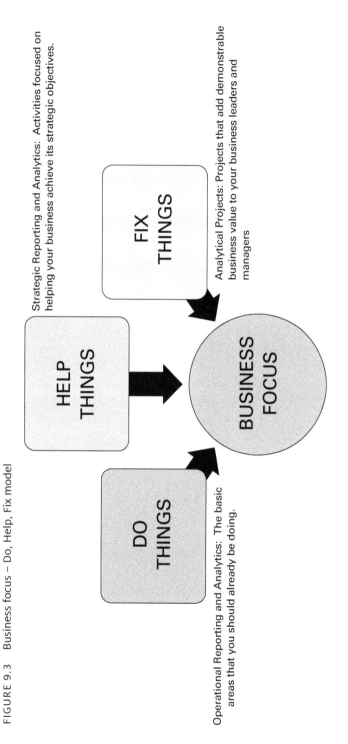

Strategic Reporting and Analytics: Activities focused on helping your business achieve its strategic objectives.

FIX THINGS

Analytical Projects: Projects that add demonstrable business value to your business leaders and managers

HELP THINGS

DO THINGS

BUSINESS FOCUS

Operational Reporting and Analytics: The basic areas that you should already be doing.

ANALYTICAL PROJECTS (AP) – FIX THINGS

These will be projects that need to be addressed within the HRBP's scope – Box 3 or Box 4 in Figure 6.1. APs are focused on identifying and understanding outliers, both the good and bad, and for implementing projects and change based on the data-driven insights. These projects might be focused on improving an abnormally high turnover rate of experienced hires in their first two years, or improving retention rates of key performers in their first year. APs are all about fixing things using a data and evidence-based approach.

ACTION

Review the current range of activities and projects in your role. Identify which of these three areas you currently report on and that your data-based analytics activities relate to. There may be some crossover or grey areas, but identify the "best fit". Ideally there should be three ORAs, two SRAs and one AP that could be focused on.

The quantity is up to you; the most important aspect is that you are focused on making some changes in approach as identified by these three themes.

THE FIRST ANALYTICAL PROJECT OPPORTUNITY

In Chapter 8 we scoped out a three-stage framework that outlined a method by which to undertake an analytics-based project. This process is designed to build on that and enable work on a project that could be considered "low-hanging fruit", that is, a small data project that is easy, affordable and yet impactful. See Figure 9.4.

Stage 1:

1 Review the corporate business and workforce plan.

2 Review the business area plan.

3 Discuss and "play back" key observations to the leadership team to ensure there is a mutual understanding of the challenges and opportunities.

4 Articulate how an analytics project could support the key areas of focus for the business area.

FIGURE 9.4   The first analytical project opportunity

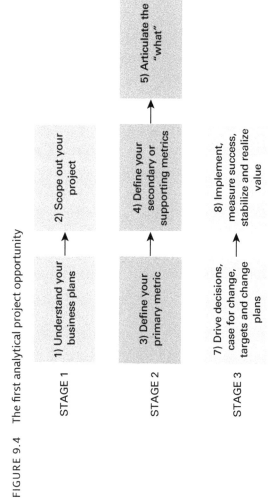

STAGE 1   1) Understand your business plans → 2) Scope out your project

STAGE 2   3) Define your primary metric → 4) Define your secondary or supporting metrics → 5) Articulate the "what" → 6) Articulate the "why" behind the "what"

STAGE 3   7) Drive decisions, case for change, targets and change plans → 8) Implement, measure success, stabilize and realize value

5 Research, brainstorm and document the following:

- o the specific project objectives, outcomes and metrics;
- o the people and organizational requirements and capabilities for delivering this;
- o the gaps when it comes to HR and people programmes;
- o the risk, implications and business impacts of not closing that gap.

6 Brief the leadership team on the findings from Step 5, gain a deeper understanding, alignment and support for the project through that dialogue.

7 Reinforce the demand for the project by continuing to seek support and momentum at all levels by those leaders and managers who could be impacted by this project.

Now define the project in more detail and then execute. There are several steps to this.

Stage 2:

1 **Define your primary metric:** This captures the essence of what the project is focused on achieving. It needs to be as specific, and detailed as possible as this is the foundation of all subsequent steps. An example would look like this: "Decrease turnover of our top performers (rated outstanding and exceptional) in their first year of tenure in the sales department".

- o Keep this directional in nature (ie decrease or increase), and don't get into specific targets. Targets can be established in a subsequent stage when access to hard data is available.
- o Define the scope of the project: eg who constitutes "top performers"?
- o Quantify (state the current facts regarding) the primary metric: the extent of the issue, in terms of numbers (rate, magnitude).

2 **Data analysis:** To achieve a comprehensive understanding, the primary metric needs to be looked at through many lenses. This means reviewing and segmenting the data that is available. If powerful workforce analytics or business intelligence tools are available, this will be simpler. If calculating in a spreadsheet, see if the analytics team, finance team or numerically-adept colleagues can help.

3 **Define your secondary or supporting metrics:** This is about the additional data and segmentation that may be important to the analysis. The extent

of this segmentation is about where the most insightful observations and storylines can come from, in terms of any anomalies based on demographics such as location, manager, learning log completion, recruitment channel, engagement and so on.

4 **Make quantitative observations – articulate the "what":** Continue segmenting and analysing the data, making observations focused on anomalies (outliers in the data, hotspots where acceptable thresholds are exceeded, or where the sheer mass or magnitude of an issue can represent an opportunity or lack thereof).

5 **Articulate the "why" behind the "what":** By now a collection of facts will have been compiled, for example, top performer turnover in sales for employees in their first year of tenure. With this analysis, dig deeper into the storylines, understand the context in which they occurred, and ask "why" to those who are best positioned to share logical reasons and hypotheses.

This can be accomplished through a variety of techniques, but tends to be qualitative in nature. For example, run some focus groups with top performers in their second year of tenure who can shed some light on their experience, review onboarding data, one-to-one interviews with leaders, managers, key employees and/or stakeholders of the project. The objective is to obtain insights and views so the data can be balanced with context, and enable you to tell the story in a more compelling way.

Stage 3:

1 **Drive decisions, case for change, targets and change plans:** Sense-check; if the project won't drive decisions and change, then seriously consider stopping now and focusing on something that the business, or people function, would value. Decision-making must be in consultation with the support of the client. It's critical that the client has been informed throughout the prior steps and has access to the facts, context and opinion. Decision-making is about return on investment (ROI), which requires the HRBP to lead the development of a case for change. The case for change is a maximum ten-slide summary and recommendation as follows:

   o executive summary;

   o background, context and current environment/issue identification (facts and context);

   o opportunity;

- o proposed solution(s) and targeted outcomes;
- o costs and benefits (ROI);
- o implementation approach and resources required;
- o recommendation and next steps.

2 **Implement change plans, stabilize, measure success and realize value:** A plan for change translates the key outcomes into a timeline that shows when key activities need to begin and be completed by. Transition is different, as it is an internal psychological process that moves through three phases:

a endings: understanding how to leave the old situation behind;

b a neutral zone: the time between the old and the new being implemented;

c new beginnings: signalling a readiness to make new commitments and to do things in different ways with new attitudes and approaches.

Many change programmes are undermined and falter, or are sometimes sabotaged, because leaders fail to think through how they can support transition when change occurs.

Consulting

Regardless of specific focus, becoming a great practitioner/HRBP is all about delivering business value. A genuine partner relationship occurs when goals are aligned, wins are mutual and each party brings something unique to the table which is valued and appreciated.

There are three key development themes to consider when considering your consulting and consultative capabilities; your environment, your behavioural analytical capabilities and your commercial orientation capabilities.

YOUR ENVIRONMENT
This must embrace four elements:

1 **Business value:** HRBPs must focus their efforts on delivering value and ensuring that everything is focused on tangible business outcomes. That's why the people analytics agenda is both vital to the function, but also to the credibility of the people function. If true value isn't delivered, then the

simple reality is that they will, over time, look for alternatives, just like we all do with our "suppliers".

2 **Embed yourself into the business**: HRBPs must strategically position themselves to become a critical component of how the business delivers value to the organization at large. The HRBP needs to understand the business, their processes, their desired outcomes, and the competitive environment that they work in.

3 **Have complete clarity in who your customer is and what they do**: There are some very simple elements here that need to be done well:

   o If the customer and what business they are in (ie who they serve) is not well known, then ask.

   o If customer expectations are not really clear or known, then, again, ask.

4 **Do the right things, right**: This means four things:

   a Execute the people programmes which are stated in the business areas plan.

   b Engage with the business leaders to identify, prioritize, design and implement the people programmes with the best ROI and impact, that will ensure the business achieves its strategic plan.

   c Proactively assess, manage and mitigate people and organizational risk and/or facilitate those aspects that could become future risks if not addressed.

   d Focus on where the value of what is delivered comes from. For example, does the HRBP become easily immersed in detail, or should they move to an 80/20 model; ie 80 per cent of the value comes from 20 per cent of their effort.

YOUR BEHAVIOURAL ANALYTICAL CAPABILITIES

In Chapter 4, we outlined data that we had collected regarding the capability of the HR community. One of the key behavioural aspects of the research was breakthrough thinking, the ability to make sense about problems, issues and opportunities and provide different ways of looking at an issue before making a decision. This underpins the data and analytics translator role in terms of making sense of data, information and insights that emerge from any analytical process or investigation.

Based on our research and job analysis over many years, below are some behavioural ideas and tips about how to embrace more of a breakthrough thinking mindset. See Table 9.1.

TABLE 9.1 Breakthrough thinking behavioural development ideas

Foundation level	Developing level	Complex level	Systems level
• Apply logic and common sense when analysing problems.	• Understand the possible implications that an existing or potential problem may have on the future (cause/effect).	• Identify business scenarios requiring detailed analysis and interpretation.	• Develop people analytics strategies to resolve issues through the involvement and problem-solving capabilities of others.
• Link information together so that a problem or issue is fully understood.	• Assess an issue from different angles to ensure all the relevant issues are considered.	• Step back from situations to consider the "bigger picture" when assessing issues.	• Build on the ideas of others to provide a more thorough understanding of issues affecting the organization through the instigation of sustainable data channels.
• Investigate a situation and find out what is going on.	• Identify inconsistencies in business results, processes or systems.	• When considering a problem, identify a number of individuals with relevant viewpoints and explore these fully to improve your own understanding.	
• Identify the most critical parts of a problem or situation.	• Define HR and people reporting and data requirements and develop appropriate reporting tools.	• Implement a range of statistical and financial modelling tools and methodologies.	• Get other people to develop options and ideas that solve issues that cut across the organization based upon the data and analytics insights.
• Demonstrate ability to manipulate data to maximize the use of standard reporting tools.	• Look at a problem from a variety of different viewpoints to ensure that you understand it in more depth; think about issues relating to this problem that potentially may arise in the future.	• Can flex between the micro and macro issues when dealing with problems.	• Consider combining aspects of different solutions to provide a preferred solution to an issue.
• Work with an individual who is considered to be strong in analysis on a problem-solving or analytics-based project or task; learn through observation and experience.			
• Consider the "what-if" implications of a problem; ie what will happen if something else was to occur.			

TABLE 9.1 *continued*

Foundation level	Developing level	Complex level	Systems level
• Uncover causes of problems by asking "why" until you have enough.	• When faced with a problem, try not to let a single aspect dominate your analysis; consider all the different aspects/issues (eg customers' needs, staff needs, operational requirements, training needs, premises constraints). If it helps, write them down and explore each aspect independently.	• Provide breakthrough thinking that brings a new perspective to familiar situations.	• Ensure that other people's options are explored, understood and valued when considering a way forward in relation to an underlying issue that is being investigated through quantitative research.
• Identify patterns and links that are not obviously related to the issue in hand, and understand the implications of them.		• Demonstrate the ability to separate issues in a complex data set and identify/propose options for action.	
• Draw relevant conclusions from straightforward data and information.	• Look at an assessment of a previous analytics project or task that was not totally successful to identify what could be done differently next time.	• Prior to deciding on a solution, conduct a risk assessment to help you identify the costs and benefits associated with a particular course of action as well as the implications of taking forward those ideas.	• Anticipate potential issues and/or opportunities and incorporate these into long-term HR business plans and people analytics strategies.
• Develop feasible, practical solutions to problems.			
• Generate other ideas/options before deciding on a particular course of action – don't always decide on the first solution that comes to mind.	• Evaluate the appropriateness of each solution generated by your analytical process by focusing on the pros and cons of implementing them in a given situation.	• Create innovative approaches and ideas to resolve problems.	
		• Provide high-quality solutions by incorporating elements of different ideas into one.	
• Identify the knock-on effect of implementing different solutions.	• Apply sound judgement to the interpretation of data.	• Develop robust strategies and implementation plans.	
• Consider other people's input when considering solutions.			
• Use business-related data to good effect in supporting the diagnosis of an issue.	• Develop a range of feasible and practical people solutions to problems that resolve root causes rather than symptoms.		
	• Think through the consequences of implementing different options and solutions.		

Infrastructure

This section is about focusing on those aspects that will develop an ongoing capability in the world of data and people analytics for the business. Success tends to be achieved when people, processes and technology work together to achieve strategic goals. This is about putting in place the plans and the infrastructure that will ensure that a more data-driven focus can occur. There are four elements to this – see Figure 9.5.

FIGURE 9.5   Infrastructure framework

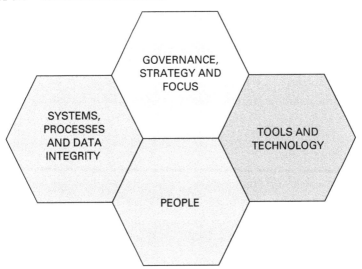

GOVERNANCE

The adoption of a robust governance framework is essential, but people can get bogged down in trying to design and implement a strict governance methodology far too early. It means that any early framework will probably change and countless hours can be spent focusing on elements that may not be business relevant. We know of organizations where they have spent so much time creating a framework that they were unable to undertake any analytical projects, and the opportunity to demonstrate the value of the approach was lost – although there was a great governance framework in place!

An interim step is to consider a simple, practical and easily applied approach that is built around the key ingredients of good governance:

1 Identify and ask the organizational champion for people analytics – this could be the CHRO/CPO, the head of HR, head of HR operations or head of talent management – to sit on a steering committee for people analytics.

2 Ask a senior leader from the business area that is most interested in this initiative to attend.

3 Establish a monthly rhythm of one-hour meetings that focus on monthly accomplishments and updates from your user cases, a cumulative list of business impacts delivered through people analytics to date, planned activities for next month, help and resources needed from the steering committee, open discussion, action items and learnings to date.

After six months, once the format has been established, formalize the governance requirements that the learnings from the first six months of project work have outlined. In the meantime, this meeting should suffice as the important issues, such as management of individuals' data, should flow from this format.

STRATEGY AND FOCUS

Step 1 – Understand your primary user of HR information and define customer needs
Who are your customers, and what's important to them? There will be several key people, each with different roles, who will act as the stakeholder that will be delivered to. Create a planning sheet that:

1 identifies each of the customers;

2 describes them in terms of their purpose and role;

3 explains what's important to them; their priorities;

4 explains how these priorities translate into possible data streams and areas of opportunity based on your insight into them as a customer.

Step 2 – Identify your HR reporting and analytics use cases
If you recall, the Do, Help, Fix model (see earlier in this chapter) helps focus on where best to use the people data that is available within the business area. The next part of the planning process is about helping identify which of those priorities could help focus on which projects could be best served by the Do, Help, Fix model. This will help in regular meetings with clients, to discuss, rationalize, prioritize and translate these requirements into the most relevant projects.

Step 3: Understand availability, quality and cost of data collection
The next step helps to define the possible/actual projects in more detail. For each of the projects identified, ask:

- What's the data availability?
- What's the quality of that data?
- What cost constraints are there?
- Where is the data?
- Which systems does the data reside in?
- Who owns the system? Who owns the data?
- Is the data available and accessible for use?
- What is the cleanliness, trust and accuracy of the data?

Step 4: Estimate and articulate value of each project
For each of the projects, there are some key questions to consider:

- How important is accessing and using robust and clean data?
- What's the overall value of this project to the business area you operate with?
- What is the risk or business impact if we do nothing? This could be in terms of revenue impact (increase or missed), cost impact, talent efficiency and effectiveness, customer, operational and other business impacts.
- If the data is known to have errors, what is the margin of error that everyone is willing to accept? Consider the following before deciding:
  - value of the HR data at its current level of cleanliness;
  - value of HR data after improving its quality;
  - value of HR data after perfecting its quality.

"Perfect data" is a misnomer. There are pockets of "perfect" data, but it is quite hard to come by especially if the data is generated through transactional processing. The key question is, where is it we absolutely need "perfect" data such as payroll, salary grades or headcount at year end, and where will we accept some margin of error? The key thing to realize when it comes to reporting and analytics is that iterative data cleansing means focusing on data quality efforts, not only in the areas that matter, but when it matters.

"Areas that matter" translates to data categories with large impact, such as employee satisfaction (payroll data accuracy), business plan execution (headcount growth data), and financial results (sales team attrition/recruit-ment pipeline). Decisions must be made regarding those ones that are of greatest importance. For instance, calculating the cost of turnover can elicit many different cost scenarios:

- Should we use the industry standard of 1.5x salary? What does that include?
- Should we include recruitment expenses?
- Should we include the missed productivity of an unfilled position?
- Should we include the anticipated lower productivity of the new employee, etc.?

Start with the data that's available and get to an educated estimate on the magnitude of the issue and the value of the opportunity you are considering, using the available data, and qualify it if data inaccuracies are believed to exist. For example, this will enable HRBPs to say something like: "We have a c£1.5m per year issue (low estimate £1m, high estimate £2m) with sales executive turnover and unfilled positions. Whether it be the low end or high end of that estimate, this is still a significant issue and one which could deliver a significant impact to future sales results and enable us to achieve our corporate business plan."

It will enable a focus on value, business results and issues that matter. If the issue is important, iterative data cleansing and increased accuracy will happen naturally because the leader's attention about the data has been flagged. This can accelerate a specific data cleansing activity, but there will be more focus and purpose than a broad-based HR data cleansing exercise, which can take significant time and resource to achieve, and in the meantime opportunities to make an impact on the business have not been realized.

Step 5: Assess and map use cases to a decision-making framework to help you prioritize

At this point, there are some possible/actual projects identified across the Do, Help, Fix model, and some high-level thinking and documentation has been completed about each. Perform a top-down self-assessment rating on the projects, which once they are mapped to the decision-making matrix (see Figure 9.6) will help prioritization, and also provide a reality check on their feasibility.

The self-assessment rating includes six questions:

- three questions focused on effort and cost of implementation (question 1, 5 and 6 following);

FIGURE 9.6   Decision-making framework to drive prioritization

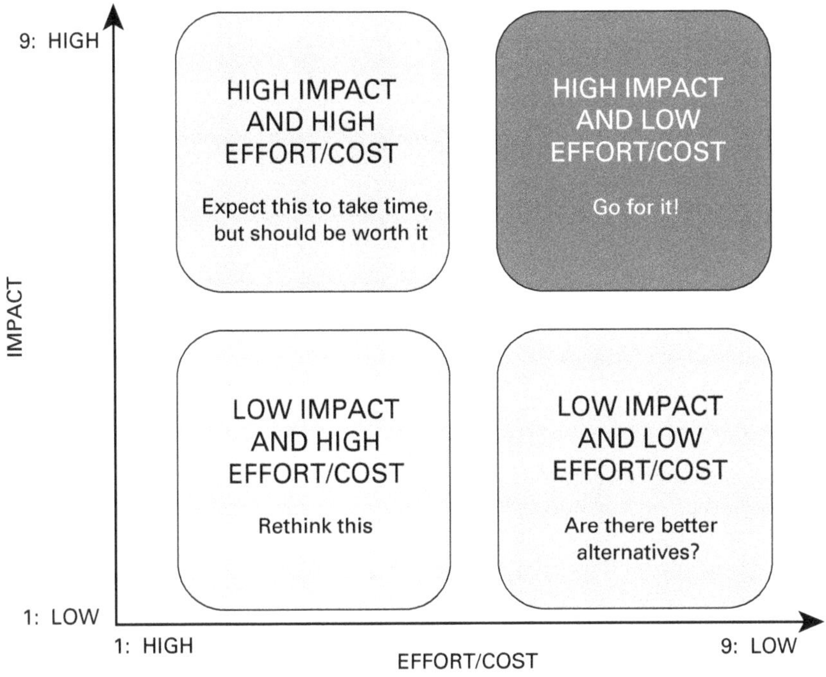

three questions focused on value or business impact (questions 2, 3 and 4 below).

Use a three-point Likert scale: 1 = not really, 2 = somewhat, 3 = very much so.

1 Is the project critical and important to the business area?

2 Is the data available?

3 Is the data easy, inexpensive and not resource intensive to access?

4 Is the data clean and trusted?

5 Are there significant business risks if ignored?

6 Is the project valuable (in terms of bottom line or business outcomes)?

For each project, perform a reality check, which will help make the final prioritization decisions (see Figure 9.6 for the framework).

Now a plan exists; what's next? Revisit the Business focus section earlier in this chapter, and focus on the three stages contained within that section. The best-laid plans may not always come off. Explore the feasibility of the project, the access to the clean and reliable data needed, and the overall business impact of doing nothing; your project or initiative may fall short of the previous expectations that were held.

This whole process is iterative, so remember to formally revisit the scope, approach and plans for all the business areas. Remember there is always data being collected, every minute of every day!

SYSTEMS, PROCESSES AND DATA INTEGRITY

Accessing data from source systems

Once possible/actual project(s) have been identified, then clarify the overall data needs, where this data resides and who owns it. The data will come from a number of source systems, and that means that consolidation of this data into a single data source will be required. While there are many different approaches and tools to help with data consolidation, the simplest way is through a spreadsheet.

There are pros and cons to the spreadsheet approach (see Table 9.2), as with all of the other approaches.

TABLE 9.2   Spreadsheet approach pros and cons

Pros	Cons
• Spreadsheet programs will already be on your computer, laptop and/or tablet.	• Upgrading your spreadsheet skills might be more difficult than it sounds.
• Ease of use for basic number collation and analysis.	• You will need to focus on things like moving and manipulating data, cleaning and formatting data, pivot tables, developing formulas, developing charts and presenting dynamic data.
• Most spreadsheets are relatively intuitive, but you will need some further advanced training/learning.	
• Spreadsheets can be fed with .csv data dumps/extracts/flat files from most systems.	• There are data security and privacy risks of spreadsheet-based reporting.
	• Data and formula integrity in the reporting spreadsheet is always at risk.
	• Each spreadsheet tends to be at a point in time, and can require a lot of manual manipulation every time you need a new version of a report.
	• You can spend a lot of time in spreadsheet maintenance mode, as opposed to actually using your data to drive decisions and build value for your business.

Process control and data integrity

Perfect data is incredibly rare, but deep understanding into a crucial issue can still be gained with far from perfect data. Known inaccuracies of your reporting, and a margin of error (for instance, +/–25 per cent) for your estimate will need to be shared with stakeholders. A £2m turnover issue is still material with or without a +/–25 per cent margin of error.

Secondly, data is often incomplete, invalid or inaccurate because HR processes and systems have been typically set up to execute transactions, as opposed to enhancing decision-making purposes. When starting to use HR data more frequently to support decisions, its quality and process controls will inevitably improve as HR processes will become tighter and more focused on upfront data quality and accuracy.

There isn't an overnight fix and improving data quality takes time and focus; it's a journey in itself.

TOOLS AND TECHNOLOGY

The fundamentals behind any analytical project is that there are:

1 multiple sources of people and business data;

2 unification of these disparate sources of data into one single repository designed for storage and manipulation of the people data, with both a technical and functional focus on data discovery and analysis, not transactional processing;

3 algorithms using mathematics and statistics calculating people metrics and relevant analytical user cases;

4 presentation, reporting, outputs and/or visualization of the data, based on the analysis and discovery criteria which a user defines.

These components must work together and if the Human Resource Information System isn't employing a data warehouse for your reporting and data analysis, then it isn't a people analytics solution, even though they might market the solution as "people analytics".

There is an array of options to consider to help the analytical based efforts, summarized in Table 9.3.

TABLE 9.3   People analytics tool options

Tool/approach and description	Pros	Cons
• **Making use of native reporting in your transactional HR tools:** While capabilities can vary greatly, you will likely have some reporting capability within your transactional HR technology. This might be in the form of fixed reports or reports which you can configure yourself.	• Already enabled as part of your HR technology. • Configurable.	• Usually limited in terms of scope. • Normally difficult to connect to other relevant sources of data. • Data modelling and technical processing of the reports is inefficient and not optimized for business intelligence. • Frequently difficult and expensive to configure. • Usually impossible to configure exactly how you'd like them, or to process metrics and analytics in the way you need.
• **Spreadsheets:** Desktop data processing tools which can manage data, calculate formulas and display results. Typically used for basic calculations and small data sets. Usually part of a desktop office suite. Examples: Google Sheets, Microsoft Excel.	• Already on your desktop, probably at no extra cost. • Many people have already used and have basic skills with spreadsheets. • Flexible and very useful for basic calculations and business needs.	• Data security and access management is typically wide open. • Hard to integrate multiple data sets, specifically HR data which is complex. • Does not scale effectively. • Difficult to support ongoing reporting and analytics. • Algorithms have to be developed and customized – many of which are very complex. • Many points of failure once you move beyond basic requirements.

TABLE 9.3   *continued*

Tool/approach and description	Pros	Cons
Do-it-yourself business intelligence tools: More advanced data management and processing tools with embedded ability to calculate and process large amounts of data, and visualize the output in more advanced ways. These tools require minimal technical infrastructure (often on a desktop/laptop) and there is no need for highly technical skills. They are generic tools as opposed to being built with a specific business function in mind. Examples: Qlik, Tableau, Microsoft Power BI	• Powerful data management and processing tools. • Powerful data visualization tools. • Powerful and highly configurable for metrics creation and statistical analysis. • Sometimes come with limited fixed metrics/analytic algorithms which are relevant for HR. • Much more affordable than previous business intelligence (BI) tools. • Great for one-off/one-time analytical projects.	• Require strong skills to build out the data model (integrations with source systems), algorithms, visualizations and user access. • Careful design and consideration needed when using this approach for ongoing operations and "production" reporting and analytics. • Can expose you to data security, as they tend to be loaded on a single desktop/laptop. • Can be risky to sustain and expose you to a solution which is deemed unsupportable if the developer leaves the organization.
In-house, enterprise class BI platform: Large-scale, on-premises enterprise class BI platforms which require numerous levels of technical infrastructure, data integration and management, and configuration for both implementation and ongoing maintenance. Examples: SAP, IBM Cognos	• Enterprise grade. • Implemented within an organization's technical architecture. • Advanced reporting and analytical capabilities. • Can scale to deliver exactly what the business needs with ongoing customization.	• Expensive to licence, configure and support. • Many layers to the technical architecture. • Highly technical skillsets required for development. • Complex to implement, with a history of failed implementations. • While there are many skilled resources out there to assist with configuration and maintenance, there are relatively few who have deep HR data model experience.

TABLE 9.3   *continued*

Tool/approach and description	Pros	Cons
• **People analytics pure-play:** A business intelligence platform which has been built specifically for the nuances, complexities and volume of effective-dated HR data. Examples: PeopleInsight, Visier, Crunchr, Concentra UK/ OrgVue, Perceptyx, MHR Analytics	• Exclusively focused on people analytics use cases and using data to support/drive decision making. • An HR specific data model and data warehouse technical infrastructure which has BI as a sole purpose and is more powerful for data discovery. • Enables multidimensional data discovery from a single source of unified HR and people data. • Powerful segmentation abilities enabling you to analyse trends, look at things from new perspectives, aggregate and drill down into individual records and criteria-based lists, and present your data in a visually appealing way. • Ongoing (continually fed), multi-system HR data management and integration, transformation of that data into a single, unified and effective-dated corporate record for employee data, algorithms to drive calculations related HR metrics and people analytics, powerful visualization and data discovery, role based user access, all within a GDPR-compliant environment. • Cloud-based and cloud-first with lower total cost of ownership and much faster deployment. • Proven solution which is deployed across many companies using industry best practice metrics. • Minimized risk of implementation failure.	• Requires your HR data to be processed in the cloud by a third party. • Requires you to partner, versus build or buy. • May not be a fit for your organization if you have sophisticated BI capabilities in-house that can be dedicated to HR and people analytics.

PEOPLE

Ultimately, it takes smart people to glean insight from data and information, and it also takes smart and influential people to use those insights in an actionable and valuable way. There are, therefore, a number of roles which are critical for developing your data-driven capability:

- **People analytics leader:** This tends to be an executive-level leader who believes in fact-based decision-making and its criticalness to the success of the people function. They will support the capability of a data-driven based people function, model the right behaviour, and actively market this capability to the organization as a business imperative that will also futureproof the function.

- **People analytics evangelist:** These are executives and managers who genuinely believe that employees have a critical role to play in delivering business outcomes. They are driven to continually deliver improved performance and understand that not all employees are equal; in fact, some are in roles which are designed to deliver differentiated value, such as sales.

- **Functional leads within HR:** These people are likely to own specific sources of HR data. If taken on the analytics journey, they will be in a position to understand, over time, how their data can contribute to making smarter hiring decisions, understanding which employees create greater business value, how to retain key talent and understand the ROI of people programmes. They will see a difference between the transactional side of their business, the processes and technology in support of workflow, and the strategic decision-making value of the data which is generated.

The key element is that every people practitioner across the people function will be a champion for the shift to a more data-based approach to the practices that they operate. That means influencing others, communicating an authentic belief in the data-driven approach, demonstrating visible leadership so that any resistance to change and issues that arise will be facilitated positively, and ensuring that appropriate communication, training and support is available for everyone across the function.

Over to you now! Helpful templates relating to the process that has been outlined can be found at http://www.peopleinsight.com/DDHRBP (archived at https://perma.cc/CQM9-JMQZ)

Sustainable change

Becoming data-driven is not a one-off project, it's about building a new way of approaching HR, one which is sustainable and that builds and improves over time.

FIGURE 9.7   Sustainable change

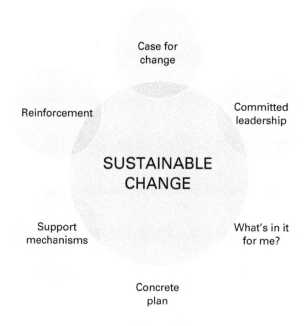

That means that change needs to be a clear part of the whole adoption process; six key elements are outlined (see Figure 9.7).

CASE FOR CHANGE
This is about communicating the urgency of your data-driven projects and how they link to delivering improved results for the business clients. This will involve meeting with key people, briefing them and seeking their input. It's vital that the clients see these projects as being key to them achieving their strategic and operational goals and improved results.

COMMITTED LEADERSHIP
This is about leveraging and soliciting the direct support of any leader within the business who has articulated the need for evidence-based or

data-driven decision-making, whether this be an executive or the head of a business unit. The goal is to convince the business area that the projects identified are important and need to happen, and that they fully support them. They then need to help sell these initiatives, whilst the HRBPs remain accountable for project execution. Many leaders think it is good enough to "support" an initiative, but this needs to be very specific and they need to be involved, outlining the behaviour required from them and the messages they need to share.

WHAT'S IN IT FOR ME?

The concept of "what's in it for me" really translates into motivation. What naturally motivates people, and how will data-driven projects help them? Building upon the autonomy, mastery and purpose model from Daniel Pink's book *Drive*:[6]

- Autonomy: How can data-driven HR help the clients accomplish their goals? How can this initiative help them be more self-sufficient and independent?
- Mastery: How can data-driven HR give the clients the ability to be better at what they do and become more successful?
- Purpose: What is the link between smarter hiring decisions, retaining key talent and better people programmes, and the overall purpose as an organization/business area? How will this project help accomplish this purpose?

Answer all enquires, so that every individual can see how they will see a benefit for them by this approach.

CONCRETE PLAN

Our focus throughout this chapter has been to ensure that there is a plan. Randomness won't work. When there is a concrete and credible plan of action in getting more of a data-driven approach implemented, it becomes part of "the way things are done around here".

The plan should clearly lay out the steps and tasks which need to be accomplished over the next six-month period, with the understanding that as this phase is completed, another plan for the next phase will be developed. The plan will have clear objectives, goals, outputs and the steps required to get the phase completed. As with all good plans, ensure that the resources needed to invest in the project are defined. Ensure the stakeholders support the detailed plan and that the governance meeting, outlined earlier, has captured the support of the people analytics champion and key leaders.

SUPPORT MECHANISMS

Part of developing the plan will be to understand and define the requirements for the tools, resources and support mechanisms which need to be in place for implementation to be a success. This may include communications and training plans, briefings, reporting metrics, checklists, processes or standard approaches to driving a decision, implementing change and tracking benefits.

REINFORCEMENT

Reinforcement should be extended to include defining success criteria, measuring results, capturing benefits and celebrating success. There are five fundamentals to this:

1 Success criteria should be defined with stakeholders, to jointly agree a picture of success.

2 At the individual and team level, remember that recognition for help, support and results is important.

3 Reinforcement is about managing performance and ensuring that the goals that were set out initially are accomplished.

4 Business case realization is easy to ignore as the next project or operational issue takes priority. Time must be spent quantifying accomplishments and successes, sharing these with the people that matter.

5 Determine the ROI of the initiative:

   o On one side of the ROI equation, articulate the new value created through this initiative.

   o On the other side of the equation, articulate the cost of the initiative (days effort in working this project can be converted to a daily cost rate). Use this as your denominator.

   o Subtract the cost from the new value and call the result "net new value" – use this as the numerator.

   o Divide the net new value by the cost, and multiply by 100 to determine the ROI for this data-driven project.

LEARNING SCENARIO

John Pensom, CEO of PeopleInsight

Here is a simple example that a technology client of PeopleInsight completed to assess the value of the data-driven activity that had been undertaken with them.

Following the analytics-based intervention that had been made, the turnover of one specific key technical role had decreased by 25 per cent in the first year after implementing analytical tools that enabled their managers greater visibility into their behaviour and outcomes. Data segmentation had been enabled, and the vice president of HR directly attributed the impact of lower turnover due to this increased visibility. This resulted in a cost avoidance of $750k for the first year.

The cost of the investment was less than $25k.

The net new value was $750k − $25k = ¢725k.

The ROI of this investment in analytical tools was therefore: ($725k/$25K) × 100 = **2,900 per cent**.

The goal is to implement a sustainable, iterative capability that is valuable to the business, and valued by the stakeholders. It's about starting small, thinking big, and then scale fast when ROI can be proven.

The development of analytics-based capability is not an easy journey; but if it was easy, everyone in HR would already be undertaking people analytics in their role. It's the future of the profession – so grab the opportunity and seek the support of line management to support your L&D activity and make the change!

Developing HR capability as a business imperative

Today's business leaders have increasingly high expectations of HR. The focus has to be about remedying some of the perceived operational deficiencies that stem from the function having capabilities and mindsets that have hindered its growth and ability to make more of a tangible evidence-based impact.

Lexy Martin has been investigating the world of HR through research-based data for over 20 years, and her views on the HRBP are well-documented. Here she shares her thoughts about the next post-analytics challenge, namely analytics evangelism.

THOUGHT LEADERSHIP INSIGHT

The HRBP as people analytics evangelists: Are they ready – no!
Can they be – yes!

Lexy Martin, principal of research and customer value at Visier

In early January 2019, a headline on the McKinsey Leadership and Organization blog caught my eye: *The critical importance of the HR business partner (HRBP).*[7] The article outlined how HR continues to struggle to deliver effective talent strategy. The disconnect centres on the lack of capability of the HRBP, those who counsel managers on talent issues. The article remarks that the value of great HRBPs remains unquestioned, but a great HRBP is hard to find, and the structure of the HRBP role requires re-engineering.

From my research, not only must these senior partners deliver strategic advice to business leaders on talent issues, they must also support these leaders in getting optimal performance from their talent. They must be able to measure talent performance – but to do this, HRBPs must develop data and analytical skills.

Research says HRBPs are not data-savvy and can be an obstacle to people
*   analytics*

In my research, HRBPs are not yet succeeding with the challenge to be comfortable using data. Indeed, they may not even be the right evangelists! In 2018, I embarked on research to determine critical practices to succeed with people analytics. I also looked into key roles that contribute to the success of analytics.

A vice president responsible for HR operations at a top US bank told me that their HRBPs weren't up to the task of evangelizing people analytics and despite the transformation work the bank had done to enhance the strategic capabilities of its HRBPs, they were not even yet truly strategists. Additionally, only 10 per cent were comfortable and competent with data! It was a refrain I heard often as I continued to do interviews looking at great people analytics practices. We also confirmed this with survey data.

In Visier's 2018 Age of People Analytics Survey, it was discovered that a key obstacle to the success of people analytics was "we do not have a 'data-driven' skillset within HR and/or our HRBPs".[8] This was particularly prevalent in organizations just getting started with people analytics! When I present these findings at conferences and in workshops and ask audiences if they have similar issues, the audience laughs! "Of course! It's our primary challenge too!"

Why is people analytics important?

Let's look at some long-running research based on the Sierra-Cedar HR Systems Survey, which I managed for its first 16 years. It speaks to why people analytics is important. This survey stated back in 2000 that organizations with some form of workforce analytics outperform organizations without.

The characteristics of these organizations include:

- a high level of people analytics process maturity, including the use of a people analytics solution;

- a higher than average number of data sources integrated;

- a higher than average number of analytics topics (metrics) available for analysis;

- higher than average use by managers, as opposed to just the HR community.

Organizations typically start to enable people analytics usage primarily among the HR community, but the above shows a correlation between managers as people analytics users and improved financial performance. Thus, when beginning to enable people analytics, the question that is important is: "Do you enable usage directly by business leaders and managers or through HRBPs?"

If it's going to be the latter, we need to better prepare them. Keep in mind that not only does the HRBP role require re-engineering, which means expansion of their role definition to include these data and analytical skills, but individual HRBPs also can benefit from having HRBP managers that manifest these skills as well.

Preparing HRBPS to be more data-savvy

Here are a few ways to prepare HRBPs to be data-savvy so they can evangelize people analytics.

DEFINE THEIR ROLES AND RESPONSIBILITIES RELATED TO DATA AND ANALYTICS

First, ask what you want them to do. In talking with numerous executives at organizations, and drawing on previous research, they suggested the data-savvy HRBP of the future must be able to do the following:

- Link the business strategy with talent strategy and back this up with data on how the workforce is doing in meeting the key business outcomes of the strategy.

- Be open to using, and also becoming, a champion of people analytics.

- Learn to use people analytics solutions and champion them among business leaders.

- Use analytics to become a "data-driven" strategic HRBP. Come prepared to any discussion with your business leaders to show how the workforce is meeting business goals.

- Apply analytics to improve talent processes. Across the employee lifecycle, show measures of the process in how the organization is doing with acquiring, developing, and retaining the best talent.

- Stimulate other HRBPs to work collaboratively to use and promote people analytics. Learning together breeds comfort with people analytics. Take on a project as an HRBP team to address a key challenge of the business, such as how to be a more agile organization.

- Learn to tell a story with data. Don't just report metrics, tell the story about how the data relates to a business challenge. For example, don't just report trending turnover of 15 per cent, but talk about how that translates into increased costs of hire and decreased revenue.

- Put the right HRBP manager in charge of the team. In addition to having responsibilities for the HR aspects of the job, this person should enable people analytics within the organization.

ASSESS HRBP SKILLS

Start by assessing your HRBPs' capabilities, and then work to help them develop the necessary skills, whether that be how to use a people analytics solution, how to use data and analytics or how to tell stories with data. We suggest using gap analysis to determine which HRBPs have the skills, who they need to develop and who they need to replace to get the skills needed.

In Table 9.4 we show the key capabilities that HRBPs need to be effective as promoters of people analytics usage. We use this model to assess the capabilities of HRBPs and identify which capabilities to enhance.

TABLE 9.4 Visier HRBP capability model

DATA CAPABILITY DIMENSIONS			ANALYTICS CAPABILITY DIMENSIONS			
Data and sources	Data definitions	Navigation	Linking business and workforce issues	Interpreting analytics and building hypothesis	Storytelling and influencing	Intervention selection
Knows the different data sources, system of record approach flow between the systems	Knows the method for defining and calculating the most frequently used data elements	Can navigate and share slideshows, adjust parameters, use metric explore and talent adviser	Can list critical business issues and workforce implication for their portfolio	Can interpret a visualization or data element and explain it to others, identify root cause and direct deeper inquiry	Can tell how to use data to bust a myth and walk through the explanation of a data trend	Can identify the type and strength of a solution based on the data presented

UNDERSTAND HOW THE HRBP DELIVERS WORKFORCE INSIGHTS IN A TRANSFORMED HR SERVICE DELIVERY MODEL

When it comes to using HRBPs as your evangelizers of people analytics, it's important to understand how HR service delivery is changing. Until recently, the transformation of the HR service delivery model focused on leveraging automation for record-keeping and transaction management, while moving the HRBP into a strategic consultative role. The emerging strategic services model elevates the ability of HRBPs to deliver workforce insights within and beyond HR so they are able to consistently use data to advise leaders and people managers on strategy.

For example, a not-for-profit healthcare organization with over 50,000 employees developed a programme to enable its HRBPs to deliver quantifiable business impact. Its evidence-based partner consulting model consists of a three-pronged approach to ensure this impact:

1 it has a toolkit that HR uses to bring data, analysis, and insights to the forefront of problem-solving;

2 it is building a skillset in the appropriate use of the toolkit, along with developing consultative HR competencies applied to problem-solving;

3 it is also impacting mindset, a business-focused approach to problem-solving, one that uses the toolkit and skillset in partnering with leaders to drive outcomes and success in meeting the organization's goals and objectives.

DEVELOP HRBPS

Changing the mindset and skillset of HRBPs to have a business- and data-focused approach to problem-solving requires development and training. This will vary by organization. If just getting started, develop and train pilot users or superusers. Then take a train-the-trainer approach for others. If the organization is further along, the focus of development may need to be to help HRBPs develop a hypothesis and tell stories with data.

While HRBPs are learning and developing enhanced capabilities, it's important to give them time to learn and excel. They need to be freed from other work. In the previously mentioned survey, we saw that advanced organizations much more frequently free their HRBPs from other activities while they are helping them become effective agents of change.

COMMUNICATE AT A REGULAR CADENCE

Once organizations start on the journey to change the mindset and skillset of their HRBPs, it's important to create a communication plan, and then to maintain a regular cadence to build momentum as you move your organization to a data-driven culture. We see organizations providing newsletters, "learn at lunch" sessions, and wikis to build capability so that HRBPs can engage with their business leaders and manager clients.

PROVIDE HRBPS WITH SUPPORT THROUGH A PEOPLE ANALYTICS CENTRE OF EXCELLENCE

Beyond training and communications, the organization needs to set up a way to support HRBPs and other users. Among advanced organizations, we see them establishing a centre of excellence focused on people analytics support. With this, they can apply a "fit for purpose" approach to both get data, education, and support to the broad set of stakeholders within the organization, including their HRBPs.

This kind of support structure also ends up freeing the people with deep analytics skills to focus on the more sophisticated analytics needed within organizations.

TRACK HRBP PROGRESS AND RESULTS AND REWARD WITH RECOGNITION

We've all heard the saying: "What gets measured gets done". Not only that, but what gets measured gets improved upon! HRBPs should be challenged to set goals they wish to accomplish with people analytics, and then periodically review them and assess their success. Both individuals and organizations can benefit from a continuous process improvement approach.

More importantly, recognize your HRBPs for their progress and results. Give your HRBPs badges for completing tasks on their action plans and goals. That public recognition reminds not only the individual, but their colleagues, and their business leaders just how important it is to the organization to become data-driven.

Conclusion

We have to re-engineer what HRBPs need to be doing going forward by defining their new roles and responsibilities related to data and analytics. We need to honestly assess the skills of what we do have, and may need to hire a new HRBP manager to jumpstart creating more appropriate HRBPs.

As we go through HR transformation, whether of the HR organization itself or through HR digitization, we need to reassess the role of service delivery in a future with new people analytics tools and capabilities. We need to develop HRBP skills with sensitivity to the level of maturity of the organization with people analytics. Once we start on our people analytics journey, we need a regular cadence of communications to our HRBPs as well as to the organization.

> We need to evolve to a support structure through a people analytics centre of excellence, and we need to track HRBP goals and performance against goals and recognize them for their achievements.
>
> Courtesy of Visier: http://www.visier.com (archived at https://perma.cc/9GJ4-ZPAF)

The data side of HR, whether it is the traditional HR reporting function or a modern advanced analytics function, is often far removed from the HRBPs. If you want to have a people function that makes decisions based on data and evidence, then move HRBPs into the centre of the analytics equation so that they collectively operate in a different way and ultimately evangelize the benefits that drive such an approach.

This requires a mindset change that embraces data as an approach, and a commitment to improve and change behaviour through a learning log with your manager to achieve:

- **A comfort zone shift**: If there are areas of a role that you are not attracted to, or are not good at, those are the improvement areas that a personal action plan can help develop.

- **Strength development**: You might be comfortable with a data-based approach already, so any development activity can reinforce those areas that you regard as a strength. You can reach your potential and achieve growth by developing the capabilities that you are already good at.

- **A confidence boost**: Committing to improve your data and analytics capabilities takes you a step closer to feeling more confident. Most of the issues associated with data and analytics approaches are anchored in a reluctance to embrace new approaches that you think you won't be good at. Small steps along the analytics journey can only help make you feel more engaged with the subject.

- **Improved self-awareness**: Personal development is closely linked to self-awareness. It gives you the chance to honestly look at the areas of your professional life that need improvement and which will ultimately improve your fulfilment at work; your employee experience!

As Nigel Diaz, managing director of 3nStrategy and chair of the HR Analytics ThinkTank, outlines, the key to your development is to learn and understand from others' experiences as they can help you shape your own approach and also learn from their mistakes.

The HR Analytics ThinkTank, founded in 2015, has been researching the use of HR data and analytics in people decision-making. Analysing and tracking the journeys of over 100 HR analytics functions, the research part of ThinkTank explores what value different functions create, how those functions have grown – and how others can develop (and speed up) their own journeys. This is complemented with members receiving access to the research and also connecting with like-minded peers via webinars and regular meetups in the UK and across the globe, to learn about their challenges, learnings and ideas to drive change and embed a culture of evidence-based people decision-making.

Every year the ThinkTank identifies dozens of trends (www.hranalytics-thinktank.com (archived at https://perma.cc/59F6-LZ8B)), but there are two consistent findings:

- That HR analytics functions tend to be sponsored by very senior HR leadership, but those sponsors do not usually have an appropriate understanding about what they are sponsoring. This undermines functions from the beginning, when they do not have clear goals or ideas for success, even though they might have some budget.

- There is a lack of consistency when organizations make investments into technology and capabilities. Subsequently, functions struggle to build business cases for the tools and skill sets they need. Based on research and experience, functions that invest more time in concretely defining the value they will create over time ultimately enjoy the most success.

He goes on to say that there is no one-size-fits-all solution to building people analytics capability in an organization, but the ability to learn and understand from others is vital, and that opportunities to do that do exist. The HR Analytics ThinkTank is one of those options.

As we have outlined, the opportunity to learn and develop your analytics expertise is extensive and there is no excuse not to do it, especially as the future of the function is transforming towards data and analytics.

KEY TAKEAWAYS FROM THIS CHAPTER

1 The development of the wider HR community is vital to support any analytics-based activity that is undertaken in your organization; your research, data and analysis is only as good as the people who will make the actual change happen.

2 The development journey to build a people analytics capability is a relentless one, and is likely to require a multiple-based approach that will connect with the wide range of mindsets that exist across both the HR, L&D and management populations.

3 Develop a plan that structures your development and the way in which you approach your people analytics opportunities.

4 There are multiple sources of help, advice and support channels available – you are not alone on this journey.

References

1 Scott-Jackson, W and Mayo, A (2016) *HR with Purpose: Future Models of HR* (technical report), Henley Business School, University of Reading, Reading

2 Pillans, G (2017) *High Impact HR – How Do We Create a More Business-Relevant Function?*, Corporate Research Forum report, London

3 Harrington, S (2019) HR needs more swagger, says Unilever CHRO Leena Nair, *The PeopleSpace* [Online] http://www.thepeoplespace.com/ideas/articles/hr-needs-more-swagger-says-unilever-chro-leena-nair-i-couldnt-agree-more (archived at https://perma.cc/2CTQ-YDQT)

4 Gal, U, Jensen, T and Stein, M-K (2017) *People Analytics in the Age of Big Data: An Agenda for IS Research*, Copenhagen Business School, Copenhagen

5 Pensom, J (2019) HR business partners: a practical guide to becoming data-driven, *PeopleInsight* [Online] http://www.peopleinsight.com/blog/5-minute-friday-data-driven-hrbp-playbook (archived at https://perma.cc/R9M2-V46F)

6 Pink, D (2010) *Drive: The surprising truth about what motivates us*, Canongate Books, Edinburgh

7 Gandhi, N (2018) The critical importance of the HR business partner (HRBP), *McKinsey* [Online] http://www.mckinsey.com/business-functions/organization/our-insights/the-organization-blog/the-critical-importance-of-the-hr-business-partner (archived at https://perma.cc/NKF4-DQPA)

8 Visier (2018) The Age of People Analytics Research Report, *Visier* [Online] https://hello.visier.com/age-of-people-analytics-research-report.html (archived at https://perma.cc/4G3Y-FJAQ)

10

The road ahead

Turning intent into tomorrow's people function through people analytics

This chapter provides the future-based themes and trends that we are observing from a diverse range of organizations who are taking the leap towards and analysing the industry trends towards the establishment of a people function. It brings us full circle from some of the initial challenges and issues that were identified in Chapter 1 *Redefining HR: the context for change*, and looks at the people function of the future.

Establishing the people function is an iterative process of constant loops where testing and developing solutions to key issues such as establishing organizational agility, building networks, creating trust across the organization, gathering insights through data and developing a growth culture that is focused on futureproofing the organization are all crucial. The people function is more than just an HR function operating in a vacuum; it should transcend all organizational boundaries as it provides insights relevant to the whole workforce and business.

This chapter will cover:

- **Defining a people analytics strategy**: This looks at some of the key elements that need to be considered when formulating your people analytics strategy; irrespective whether you are operating as an individual HR business partner (HRBP) or as a part of an analytics team. We also consider the role and positioning of Strategic Workforce Planning (SWP) and data-based approaches.

- **The future of people analytics**: This considers some of the major trends that we are seeing – what's next for the world of people analytics, once you are on your journey and have developed some core capability in this area?

- **The future people function**: We finish off by looking at the features of a people-centred organization, which the future people function should aim to incorporate within its strategic goals.

Defining a people analytics strategy

The business strategy

When businesses talk about strategy, they mean a process that involves longer-term planning and thinking to establish a direction or a goal for an organization. The concept of strategy is changing as it becomes a more dynamic process. In the old days, executives went into a boardroom and came out with a plan, and then, irrespective of what was happening around them, the workforce executed that plan.

Andy Bayley of Loughborough University says: "The world has changed; now companies have a strategy and look to get employee buy-in so that its people understand the direction the organization is going in and hopefully have the right behaviours and actions to achieve that." Most of this has occurred through the development of digital technologies. He further adds: "The internal communication systems are now so well-developed, but the old hierarchy that used to exist are disappearing and what we are seeing are agile organizational structures. Strategically, what that does is let you still move in a long-term direction but make adjustments when the world changes." Consequently, the up-to-date view of strategy is that it's about thinking longer-term but not being constrained by that, so that as opportunities emerge organizations are able to react and respond quickly. After all, the ideas for strategic interventions can and do emerge from anywhere within the organization.

So how do you produce strategy in a changing world? We suggest the use of the three horizons of growth model by McKinsey:[1]

- Horizon 1: provides continuous innovation to an organization's existing business model and core capabilities in the short term.

- Horizon 2: extends an organization's existing business model and core capabilities to new customers, markets, or targets.

- Horizon 3: creates new capabilities and business to take advantage of or respond to disruptive opportunities or to counter disruption.

We need to ensure we have the most capable people working in the future-focused third horizon, and that we have competent people managing today's horizon. Then we only need to worry about the second horizon, and that's how you shift from where you are today to where you want to be tomorrow. But you only worry about that once you have described what tomorrow looks like.

Some experts have lamented the use of this model in such turbulent times.[2] We suggest that the three horizons model is used as a roadmap, so that when setting out on a journey we can reroute to other points along the way.

CAPABILITIES

Leadership and people capabilities plays a significant role in strategy development and implementation. You can have two very similar companies with two very similar strategies and yet only one is a success, the difference being down to the leadership and significant players who are actually able to deliver and guide people through turbulent times.

Paul Sparrow of Lancaster University sheds light on the important role of strategic HR to align the business strategy with the people strategy, saying: "It's not just about your internal cadre of strategists or high potential people, or more importantly how to manage them, but also about the broader skills capability of the organization in today's environment." It is important to understand the new areas of knowledge and hybrid professions being created, which we know are going to be very important for the future of the business.

The people analytics strategy

Against this backdrop you will need to formulate a long-term plan or strategy in terms of how to take people analytics forward. The business strategy is a crucial element behind the formation of that plan. From our experience, some HR functions are still struggling with out-of-date HR technology, disparate sets of questionable data across their organization and a lack of data analytics capability. To make any changes there needs to be a strategy and a plan to shift the needle, so we therefore need to move to not only support the people strategy, but refine it.

When we look from a long-term view and move to a high maturity model, people analytics helps us to refine, define and execute the people strategy.

FIGURE 10.1   People analytics strategy

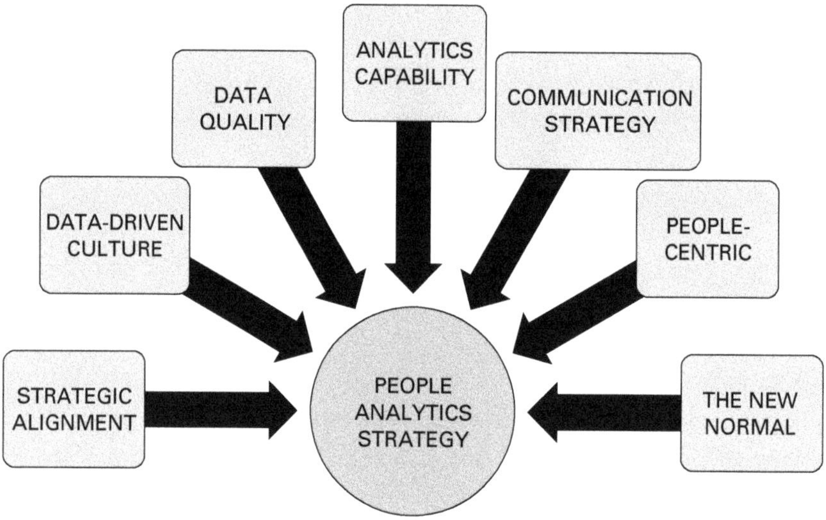

Here are our suggestions (see Figure 10.1) for shaping a people analytics strategy:

- **Align your people analytics strategy with your business and people strategies:** It's vital your people analytics strategy is aligned and regarded as an integral part of achieving your organization's business objectives. Remember people analytics provides your organization with a comprehensive evidence-based insight into what is and what isn't working regarding your workforce. That means you can manage people risk, match employees to jobs, reward people appropriately, improve productivity and efficiency across your people practices.

- **Data and analytics culture:** We talked about this in Chapter 8, and this underpins the shift from an intuitive approach to decision-making to more of an evidence-based approach where decisions are informed by data-based insights.

- **Data quality:** Without data, you have nothing. It is critical that you have enough historical data, that it is located in one place, or at least can be drawn together easily and that it is clean. There is little point in having old or useless data which will slow you down. You need to ask your data the right questions to help you answer the business problems that you have been set. This may well demand a better technological solution to be able to respond to this in the future.

- **Data analytics capability**: One of the biggest challenges for HR practitioners is the lack of analytics expertise to interpret the data. Expertise in people analytics is the most in-demand skill today, so we need to ensure that constant learning in this area is available for all practitioners.[3] As outlined in Chapter 9, the whole HR and learning and development community needs to up-skill their capabilities so that they can apply their domain knowledge and expertise in this data world. Making pragmatic sense of what the data is saying is something that robots and algorithms can't do, yet.

- **Communication strategy**: To maximize the impact on the organization, HR must be able to communicate its results clearly and with confidence. This isn't just about storytelling with the clients and business leaders, but about sharing the findings across the organization and creating a momentum and interest in the analytics approach.

- **Put people at the centre of people analytics**: Although strategy, process, and technology are used to drive business objectives, it is the people that drive your business. People analytics can help employees have a positive impact on your business. For example, by using data, the people function can proactively support employee wellbeing, thereby creating happier, healthier and more engaged employees, which will in turn boost their performances and their longevity with the organization.[4]

- **Make people analytics the new normal**: People functions need to promote people analytics as the new normal, not as an add-on or a "nice-to-have", but an integral part of the future way to operate and support the organization's business strategies with better, faster workforce decisions informed by data. This will raise expectations, particularly when it comes to other processes such as SWP. There will be a perception that data exists for all the key business practices, and as outlined below SWP has levels of complexity that need to be facilitated.

STRATEGIC WORKFORCE PLANNING (SWP)

SWP is a process to ensure organizations have the resources needed to meet their business goals by proactively mapping, aligning and forecasting current and future workforce capabilities. SWP is becoming increasingly important as greater sophistication is now being sought given the shift to a more data-based approach to issues.

An Rycek, who manages workforce planning and analytics for global virtual sales and engineering at Cisco, describes how she aligns the business strategy to the workforce strategy. She believes: "Workforce planning should be an integral part of business planning. It should not be an HR process. When we have the yearly business and headcount planning, we should make sure to integrate them over time so that people can also plan for future skills."

Workforce planning is all about getting the right people, in the right roles, with the right skills, at the right place, at the right cost, at the right time to deliver the right results. For organizations, it's about making sure that the business strategy is completely aligned to the workforce strategy. An further adds: "SWP makes sure our workforce is almost completely aligned to our evolving business strategy." At Cisco, they have a great process that is making sure SWP is really business-orientated, instead of an HR focused process only. An's role is one of the examples of how this is executed, as she is part of business strategy and planning partnering with HR.

Nick Kemsley, an experienced SWP practitioner, outlines his thoughts about the issues and changes that need to be made to the SWP approach.

THOUGHT LEADERSHIP INSIGHT
SWP: The five mistakes to avoid

Nick Kemsley, founder of N Kemsley Consulting and associate at the Corporate Research Forum

SWP remains a largely under-exploited opportunity for both the enabling and de-risking of business strategy execution and the establishment of HR as a key strategic partner. Organizations are encountering the same broad set of issues in implementing SWP, many of which are self-inflicted and could be avoided.

Organizations waste a lot of effort positioning SWP in entirely the wrong way, often as an HR or a one-off process that the business must be persuaded to undertake. The term "SWP" doesn't help; my own experience is that it is mainly HR who use this term, whilst the leaders of businesses talk of organizational capability, risks to execution and confidence that the organization can deliver. Isn't SWP simply the people and organizational dimension of strategic planning? Why position the people and organizational element separately?

Here are five key pitfalls to avoid to maximize the chances of adding real business value through SWP.

FIGURE 10.2 Integrated SWP process

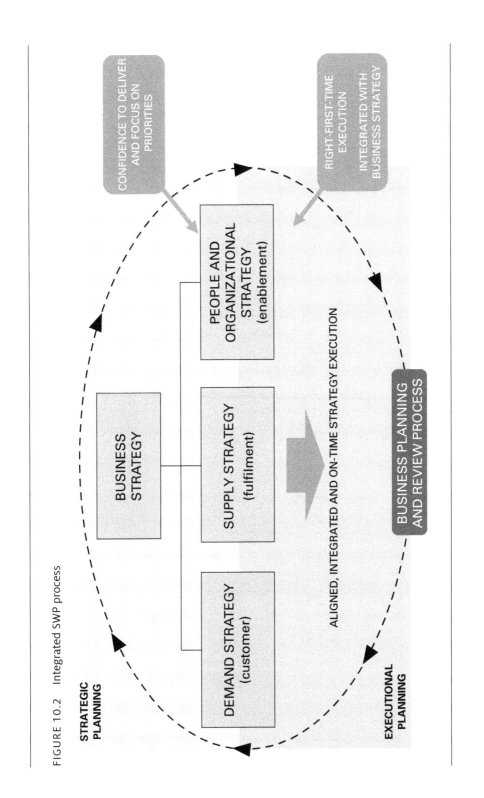

Avoid positioning SWP as a separate or HR process

Position SWP as the "third leg" of a business' strategic planning process, and seek to integrate it with existing business planning processes from the start. Many of the challenges that we have regarding the wider business and SWP stem from this fundamental mispositioning and confusion. The starting point for SWP is not the filling in of a spreadsheet asking for predicted full time employees' data across different job families over the next few years, but it is the inclusion of thinking that is all too often missing at a strategy level. See Figure 10.2.

If not rectified, strategy can progress to the execution phase without important risks and opportunities having being identified, such as new skill requirements, retention, leadership and so on. Take the increasing number of organizations with a digital strategy who have discovered during recruitment efforts that they did not have the employer value proposition to attract the talent they needed. This could easily have been identified as a predictable risk, and a strategy to mitigate it developed.

Positive examples include the large-scale infrastructure project which used SWP thinking and subsequent modelling to identify the risk that other concurrent national infrastructure projects were likely to attract a large proportion of the resource they had previously assumed could be recruited. They took steps to invest in developing their own in-house supply of talent over the next few years.

Don't be afraid to use the word 'risk'.

Business talks about risk every day; HR sometimes don't talk about it nearly often enough. Sometimes risk is considered unduly negative, yet it is a subject that has the power to unite the worlds of commercial business, people and organizations. It is at the very heart of how business operates.

Look at what an organization is trying to achieve over time, and translate this into potential implications in the people and organizational space, identifying:

- where potential gaps exist;
- where these gaps may represent risks requiring mitigation;
- which strategies and activities would address them.

If we want our leaders to be engaged in forward thinking about people and organization, we need to position it in language they understand. By positioning SWP as a way of managing risks to strategy execution, why would our leaders not want to be involved? The benefit of a risk-based approach is that it enables the organization to align limited resources to focus on agreed priorities. It allows us to align people processes to deliver what is needed, both effectively and economically.

There is a clear confusion and lack of consistent definition around the way that we describe SWP. Sometimes it's headcount-orientated, sometimes it's based around critical roles, sometimes around workforce mix and profile over time. More often than not, there is confusion between what is badged as SWP and "resource forecasting". Is it any wonder that we struggle to engage our businesses in the concept if HR are not clear on it ourselves?

None of these interpretations are necessarily incorrect, but they are simply sub-elements of SWP and none of them properly represents its entirety. They are simply snapshots of different stages in an end-to-end SWP journey. SWP does not replace operational planning. It simply gives it the necessary context to focus it on the right things and ensures that we have covered all the bases. See Figure 10.3.

Don't position SWP too narrowly or as a discrete, one-off activity

The reality is that we need to talk about SWP as a journey with different stages with different characteristics at various stages in this journey.

- **Strategic translation or dialogue**: Here, SWP is facilitative and consultative, helping to provide a framework to translate from what is known about the strategy to what it might mean in terms of people and organizational implications. There will be no numbers, no precision, no certainty, but the opportunity is to get a top-level sense and shape of the challenges and opportunities which, with some further work, can be further refined into potential gaps and risks to explore.

- **Risk identification**: Taking these top-level inputs and conducting further work to understand whether or not these should be treated as priorities, look at the data and other sources of insight as to current capability, external trends, talent availability, the ease or difficulty of closing gaps and exploring the likelihood and potential impact of different scenarios. Identify the organizational big-ticket areas where simply letting them run their course with business-as-usual processes represents too great a risk. These will represent the key questions that must be answered and will guide the next level of activities.

FIGURE 10.3   Influences on SWP

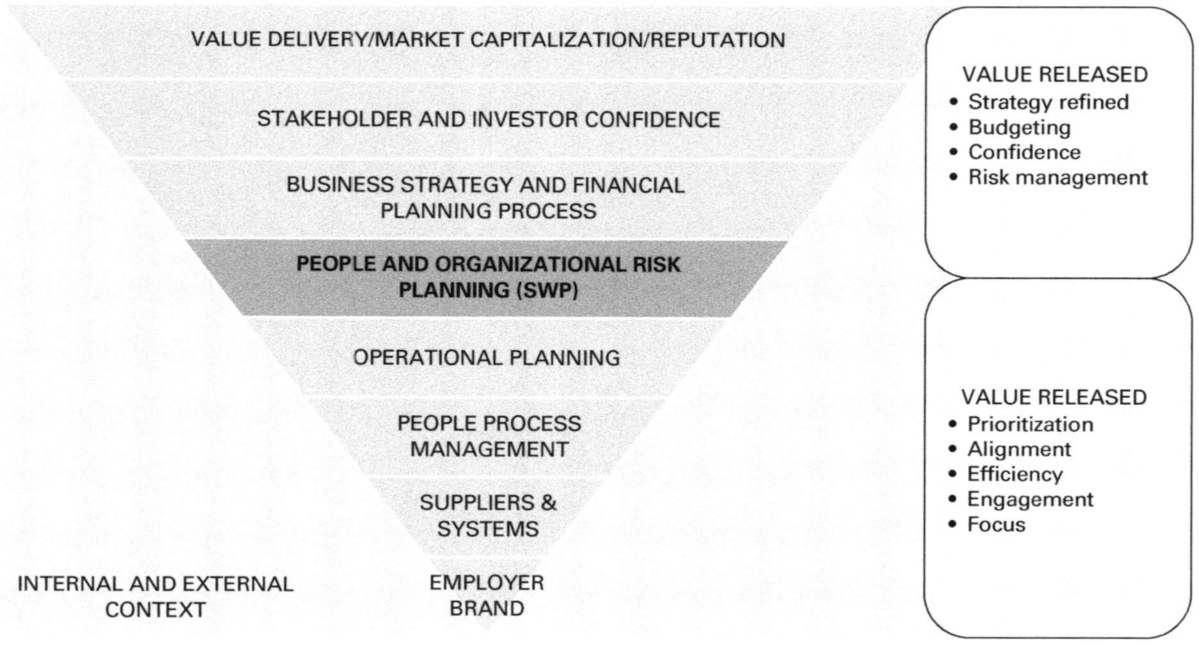

VALUE DELIVERY/MARKET CAPITALIZATION/REPUTATION

STAKEHOLDER AND INVESTOR CONFIDENCE

BUSINESS STRATEGY AND FINANCIAL PLANNING PROCESS

PEOPLE AND ORGANIZATIONAL RISK PLANNING (SWP)

OPERATIONAL PLANNING

PEOPLE PROCESS MANAGEMENT

SUPPLIERS & SYSTEMS

EMPLOYER BRAND

INTERNAL AND EXTERNAL CONTEXT

VALUE RELEASED
- Strategy refined
- Budgeting
- Confidence
- Risk management

VALUE RELEASED
- Prioritization
- Alignment
- Efficiency
- Engagement
- Focus

- **Modelling/analysis**: Using data and analytical tools from spreadsheets through to HR Information Systems (HRIS) through to proprietary SWP modelling software, different organizational and workforce scenarios can be explored. This allows us to size any potential risks or opportunities, and also to experiment with different approaches to addressing them. This helps us understand the impact on changes in workforce mix over time, on age demographics, on changes in the size of talent pools and of potential workforce cost.

- **Strategy development**: The identification of the most appropriate strategies to meet these needs or risks is about the world of build, buy, retain, rent and redeploy; we are now focused on addressing the right questions. Emerging strategies must be compared with existing organizational plans and people strategies to ensure congruence and relevance, and any necessary reprioritizations made. We have now bridged the gap between SWP and assessing whether our people processes are fit for delivering against these needs, or whether they require modification.

- **Operational planning and implementation**: Informed by SWP methodologies, our operational plans are now configured around doing the right things at the right time and in the right way. We must now follow them through and execute strongly upon these plans. We have passed through the threshold beyond which we are able to engage with numbers and specificity, and are using our operational planning tools to load the right information into the organization at the right time.

- **Measurement and review**: Having articulated our view of key risks means that we have a basis for reviewing the degree to which they are being mitigated. SWP, if done right, tells us what we need to measure. It is the difference between measuring attrition across the whole population, and measuring attrition in strategically-important talent segments in specific locations. It allows us to move from information to insight in terms of the data we interrogate and present. Being able to review and update your SWP, and connect this back to the wider business planning processes described earlier, provides focus and sustainable relevance as well as a sense of progress and clear accountability.

Resist trying to force SWP to numbers too early or confusing it with resource forecasting

Many approaches try to move quickly to critical roles, job families or simple headcount. There is benefit in our start point encompassing the organization fully and exploring the interdependencies between its different dimensions. This means a starting definition that spans, for example:

- operating models and organizational structure, physical locations, overall workforce size, roles and responsibilities;

- systems and processes directly or indirectly influencing what is needed both at business process and people process levels;

- skills and knowledge required to maintain or develop competitive advantage;

- behavioural needs to achieve cultural goals and to enact change;

- leadership and engagement requirements in terms of what our leaders may need to change, as well as how to motivate, recognize and protect the wellbeing of our employees.

As we explore, refine and develop the SWP conversation, we can focus the implications on specific elements such as roles and headcount, but we risk missing key needs if these are our start point. This is the reason that the use of an organizational system framework is helpful. It matters less which one is used, and more that the right questions are asked. It is frequently through doing this, and contemplating how different elements interact, for example culture and leadership, that we gain our most powerful insights.

We cannot force SWP into a numerical form before it is ready, yet equally, we cannot wait for this to happen before we act. This dilemma is "bigger spreadsheet syndrome", and it frequently results in an unhealthy stand-off between HR and the wider business. It is this dilemma that means SWP fails to get off the ground.

There is a common misconception that engaging with SWP means stopping the strategy evolution. SWP thinking can be applied at any point, often effectively positioned as an in-motion health-check or validation to ensure that we have thought about the right things. What is true is that the nearer the point of strategy creation that it occurs, the better. In today's world it is highly unlikely that these luxuries of clarity and due process will be available when we need them, so we must be able to engage at a higher level and work with uninformed and moving needs.

Don't involve the wrong people or make a single individual accountable for SWP outcomes

This has two dimensions: the capability of the individuals involved and the breadth of the knowledge available. If you like certainty and a neat process, then the upper reaches of SWP will not play to your preferences. If you like to act on clear instructions from above, rather than take the lead in guiding business leaders to new insights, then again, you may be more effective joining the SWP journey in its later stages when certainty is more of a feature.

SWP demands people that are comfortable with ambiguity and pragmatism, and highly skilled in consulting and facilitation approaches. Using the wrong people in the wrong place is a sure-fire way to scupper your SWP efforts. SWP success should not rest on the shoulders of just one individual, even if they possess these attributes.

Successful SWP is characterized by cross-functional groups – HR, Finance, Business Planning, Supply, Marketing and so on, all working together to co-create SWP insights and priorities. It makes sense for it to be led from HR, but remember that it is a business activity, not just an HR one.

Summary

We need to break through a threshold on SWP. Our businesses badly need it, and there are enormous and multi-faceted benefits in many areas, not just "right people, right time". But we are too frequently shooting ourselves in the foot with the way in which we position it, and SWP fatigue is a real risk.

The five traps, if avoided, will be most helpful to correcting this before the opportunity is lost. If we can make it work, then we can leverage not just a key plank in business performance, but a major milestone for HR's credibility. Data and the analytical process that supports the information gathered is vital, but as you can see, there are many other elements to the SWP process that need to be in place to truly make it a valued and credible process that aligns HR to strategic and operational business needs on an ongoing basis.

www.crforum.co.uk (archived at https://perma.cc/DPL8-RVPQ)

Our learning from this is that:

- SWP will become an even more critical business process. We already know that a lot of analytics teams are being challenged to make the SWP process more robust and data-based.

- SWP is an important aspect of people analytics, but there is so much more to it than just data and numbers.[5]

- The evolution of a data-based approach to people practices will place further challenges on the people function to merge qualitative and quantitative approaches and ensure that a more sustainable ongoing database of capabilities, etc will be readily available in the future.

- SWP must be incorporated into your people analytics strategy, as SWP acts as a critical bridge between the business and people strategies.

The future of people analytics

Will Butler-Adams, CEO of Brompton Bikes, is very clear about the importance of analytics in his role. A CEO's role is to direct the organization and to oversee the implementation of their ambition and strategy. As the organization gets larger you need to be able to see what the organization is doing more clearly.

The analogy of an aeroplane is a good example. When an aeroplane is flying in a cloud we are flying at three hundred and fifty miles an hour, on a particular altitude and we cannot see anything and there may be mountains or other objects in our surroundings, and yet the pilot can fly the aeroplane from one side of the world to another within a minute of the planned journey. It's possible because the captain has instruments giving him information that allows him to steer the plane in the right direction, and to do so with confidence and accuracy.

Leading the business is akin to flying an aeroplane, as Will describes. "I don't know everything that is going on as the business is just too big. I used to be able to but not anymore. I now have to rely on data from different parts of the organization that is communicated to me in a very clear and effective way that allows me to steer the business and to investigate if there is a problem and we are moving off track. It allows me to plan because, depending on data, I might then decide to change my strategy. There might suddenly be a storm blowing up, which wasn't there when I set off, but it appeared half way through the journey. If I didn't have the data to tell me that, I might have flown right into the storm, and so to me, data is everything."

We are observing a number of key trends that are evolving and emerging in the people analytics space – see Figure 10.4. People analytics will emerge as a strategic tool enabling organizations to grow, but we would like you to remain cautious of the challenges, disciplines and structures that we've described earlier in the book. Also, it is important to be mindful of and learn from those organizations that are already on their journey, and the imminent opportunities for the business.

FIGURE 10.4   Future of people analytics

Attitudes and
automation:
remain cautious

Organizational
development and
change

Systems-level
disruption and
evolution

**FUTURE OF
PEOPLE
ANALYTICS**

Communities of
practice

Agile work and
organizational
design

Organizational
Network Analysis
(ONA)

Attitudes and automation: remain cautious

Not having data creates problems as we are all now aware; for example, making intuitive decisions rather than decisions that focus on evidence and facts means that you may solve the wrong problems or solve the problem incorrectly.[6] But just having data is not enough – it's also about the quality of data and the assumptions that have been made on top of that data.

Will Butler-Adams shared an example where one of his senior executives had made too many assumptions about an issue. That meant the data was wrong and that proved to be fatal. About the importance of the integrity of the data collected, he went on to say: "That's when you crash into a mountain. You think you are flying at 8,000 feet well above the mountain, but actually you are just flying at 1,500 feet and you smack right in the side of a mountain. That is why the integrity of your data is so important, to help you steer your company."

With increasing automation, such as artificial intelligence (AI) and machine learning-based applications, coming our way it is easy to accept that the data and the algorithms that they provide are correct. Mark

Abraham, chartered psychologist at Launchpad Recruits Ltd, suggests some key questions that need to be asked with such applications:

- What is the algorithm actually measuring?
- What population samples were used to build the algorithm?
- What evidence exists to suggest that it is a good algorithm?
- What are the variables used by the algorithm?
- How is the algorithm assessing or scoring employees?
- What steps have been taken to remove adverse impact? This is about what steps have been taken to ensure that data is both processed fairly and that it represents the target population.
- What feedback or outcomes can candidates expect to receive from the process?

Paul Sparrow of Lancaster University also warns: "With analytics, you are trying to capture and model a system, and systems continually change and evolve. With all your metrics and algorithms, even though they may be flexible, you will find that your analytics makes assumptions about the key variables and inputs and outputs. Those assumptions are themselves subject to change and flexibility, so you are always going to have to revisit your models."

As the use of automation and algorithms increases, we are advocating that caution and investigation should be a very important aspect for the people function to consider.

Systems-level disruption and evolution

Systems thinking is a conceptual framework that has been developed over the past five decades, which introduces tools and techniques that enable us to interpret and make clearer the full patterns and assist us in bringing about change effectively.[7] Systems thinking focuses on how the issue and challenge being investigated interacts with the other processes and systems in the organization, all of which interact and drive certain behaviour.

People analytics paves the way for leadership to gain insights through a systems approach. Today technology, Big Data and analytics has allowed us to gather and harness all the insights from within and outside the business, so much quicker than ever before; hence the opportunity for the people function to be at the forefront of creating insightful business intelligence. From one point of view, what's happened with the use of analytics is that organizations are now able to join up much more disparate sorts of data, both internal and external, so that a lot more can be done. But the argument has always been whether the people dimension of this would be best embedded in a general intelligence function, or should the HR function develop its own capability.

Our research clearly reflects the current dilemma HR is in, and the opportunities that await the people function. Experts have argued the need for people practitioners to collect both internal (structured and unstructured data) and external (structured and unstructured data) to obtain insights for the business.[8]

Using analytics, leaders can not only articulate a strong vision for five to 10 years in the future, while being open to iterations on the strategy as they encounter new technology, global events, social changes and economic shifts; but also, be ready for system level disruption and evolution that can help predict how the industry will evolve.[9] See Figure 10.5.

FIGURE 10.5   Responses to disruption

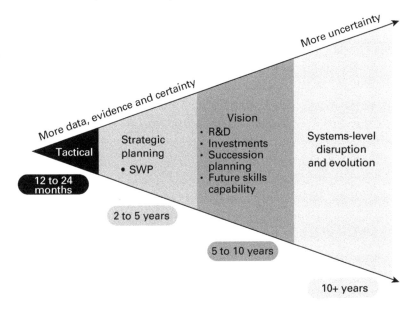

Adapted from Webb, 2019

Agile work and organizational design

Agile-based methodologies were initiated from an IT functional perspective, but these methods have been adopted by other functions, from product development to manufacturing to marketing – and now they are transforming how organizations hire, develop and manage people.[10] For over two decades, agile methods have revolutionized information technology and greatly increased success rates in technology quality, application and speed, and also boosted the motivation and productivity of IT teams. Increasingly, agile methodologies are spreading across a broad range of industries and functions. So how does agile really work?

Some may associate agility with anarchy, everybody does what they want, whereas others take it to mean "doing what I say, only faster". But agile is neither. Agile has several forms that are similar in nature but highlight slightly different things. They include:

- scrum, which focuses on creativity and adaptive teamwork in solving complex problems;
- lean development, which focuses on the continual elimination of waste;
- kanban, which concentrates on reducing lead times and the amount of work in process.

Scrum and its derivatives are employed at least five times as often as the other techniques, and therefore are more appropriate to our premise of improving management practices.[11]

This is where organizational design and dynamic capabilities re-emerge as some of the most strategic interventions we can undertake, namely helping to design the organization of the future. It has no definitive right or wrong answers, but with people being at the centre of organizational success and with it significantly affecting the ability of the organization to compete, this is the strategic activity that the people function of the future should be undertaking – especially as digital transformation and a shift to an agile way of working is becoming a key business driver in a lot of organizations.[12]

Business environments are increasingly unpredictable and need to have a responsive workforce. Therefore, SWP will need to be adaptable by supporting everyday operational planning and being able to carry out rapid scenario planning in key situations. Even with the best laid plans, things can change, such as failed assumptions, skill misalignment, incorrect resource forecasting, significant productivity changes or even organizational structures change. Agile organizations will be using SWP to counter change with contingency planning that reinforces the evolving business goals and strategies.

SWP will enable organizations to plan for disruption and continuous change. Changing, adapting and replacing work will lead to new structures, roles and capabilities; for this to play out, organizations will need to take an analytical approach to understand the impact of the future of work.

Giles Slinger of Concentra Analytics believes there are five key challenges when it comes to designing a future organization:[13]

1 **Imperfect information:** You don't know what you've got.

2 **Complexity:** The future organization is a complex system.

3 **Bundling:** People are a bundle of skills and roles are a bundle of activities and behaviours.

4 **Immeasurability:** Costs are known, but the potential benefits are hard to estimate.

5 **Change:** Even the right answers are only temporary, as change is a constant.

The analytics we need for great organizational design are data-led, multi-dimensional and adaptive. You will need analytics that demonstrate what is already understood and definable, and analytics that can calculate some investments in time and space for the unplanned to emerge, whilst collecting continuous feedback data that indicates what is working and what isn't. So, people analytics will have a strategic role to play in determining what is currently happening in an organization, data-wise, as well as try to predict what could happen if certain scenarios are designed and implemented.

Organizational Network Analysis

With the fast-paced digital world of work, it has become obvious that the traditional hierarchies and protocols have done more harm than good for organizational growth, as they hinder communication and decision-making. The huge rise in the technology industry was due to the application of agile methodologies. Nevertheless, there is a need to understand that the paradigm shift required to become agile is more than just understanding agility.

To implement this concept, the people function will have to not only adopt and submerge itself into agile methodologies, but also break the traditional hierarchies and move to a more robust network system, whether that be teams, communities or clusters of knowledge experts. Andy Bayley of Loughborough University outlined that the changes taking place within organizations are where hierarchies are breaking down and becoming networks that facilitate communication flow. The merger of digital technologies with organizational-based thinking has led us toward the application of network analysis.

Organizational Network Analysis (ONA) is a structured way to visualize how communications, information and decisions flow through an organization, and has received a lot of attention in terms of being the "next big thing" in people analytics. It looks beyond the organizational structure charts, and helps you to understand how your business really operates. Some applications of ONA have been:

- Understanding the challenges associated with effective collaboration in an organization.[14] Who are the informal influencers who resonate with people? How can silos be broken down?
- Strategically managing and levering the alternative workforce to ensure business growth.[15]
- Change and how that can be implemented more successfully based on the networks that exist in an organization.[16]
- Leadership behaviour and the impact of their networks on success.[17]
- Digital transformation and how to implement it more successfully.[18]
- Creating an innovation culture though employee networks and high involvement strategies.[19]

With organizations looking for ways to improve performance, whether that is through individuals or high-involvement teams, the traditional hierarchies are being broken down to networks where people come together to solve problems and then move onto new challenges. The top-down approaches to management has given way to quicker, user-driven methods that are better suited for adapting in the near term, such as rapid prototyping, iterative feedback, team-based decisions, and tasked-centred "sprints".

The opportunity exists for the people function to create and facilitate a network that enables co-operation and flow that can help break down silos within organizations and encourage cross-functional integration of teams and sharing of knowledge within the organization. ONA and the use of data-based insights relating to email flow, connections, etc can help to influence the way that organizations are designed for success.

Cisco's special team intelligence unit provides this kind of support by using proprietary technology called Team Space. They identify the organization's best-performing teams, analyse how they operate, and helps other teams learn how to become more efficient. Team Space tracks data on team projects, needs and achievements to both measure and improve what teams are doing within units and across the company. Cisco envisions the whole organization as a network, rather than a hierarchy.

ONA visualizes complex relationships and provides some powerful insights. Figure 10.6 shows a series of departments shown in different shades. The ONA analysis shows that the people within the department are deeply connected, but only one or two people connect with people in other departments. This can then instigate conversation and further insight into why.

FIGURE 10.6   Organizational network analysis visualization

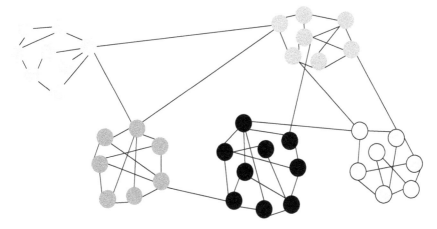

It is important to remember that however powerful the visualizations are, the fundamental issue remains the priority business problem that you are trying to solve. Sometimes the solution can overtake the importance of the issue.

Communities of practice

Building on ONA, a community of practice is a group of people informally bound together by shared expertise and passion for a joint enterprise. This is about people sharing their experiences and knowledge in free-flowing, creative ways that foster new approaches to problems ultimately improving organizational performance in companies as diverse as international banks, car manufacturers and government agencies. Communities of practice can help drive strategy, generate new lines of business, help solve problems, promote and spread best practices, and develop people's professional skills.[20]

They are not easy to build, sustain or to integrate with the rest of the business, and the spontaneous and informal nature of them makes them resistant to supervision and interference. However, Dame Jackie Daniel, CEO of the National Health Service (NHS) in Newcastle, highlights how networks within her organization enable people to work in agile project teams and accomplish tasks that transcend traditional hierarchies, thus creating a culture of trust where people can flourish.

THOUGHT LEADERSHIP INSIGHT

View from the boardroom – the role of the CPO in healthcare

Dame Jackie Daniel, CEO of the NHS in Newcastle upon Tyne

Dame Jackie Daniel's career with the NHS spans over 38 years; she is one of the longest serving CEOs, with a track record of over 17 years. Currently, she is the CEO of NHS Newcastle upon Tyne Hospitals, where she is responsible for over 16,000 staff and £1 billion turnover offering a whole range of services. NHS Newcastle is responsible for the treatment of more than a million patients every year.

Under the leadership of Dame Jackie, NHS Newcastle has recently received an outstanding rating by the Care Quality Commission (CQC) inspection.

Chief People Officer: The curator of culture

As a CEO, my job is to create the environment for all our people to flourish. That's what I talk about all the time with my leadership team; how can we make those conditions to enable our people to flourish. In the NHS, it is becoming more common to now talk about the Chief People Officer (CPO). There are a range of functions that the CPO handles, primarily being the curator of the culture right beside the CEO.

We are both there to understand what type of climate will best support the staff in the working environment. It's about understanding the organization, its strategic objectives, but also equally understanding the workforce. In healthcare, this is quite complex because we have different groups of staff all requiring different types of support.

Data and beyond

When it comes to data, it is about capturing what it means to flourish at work and for that you really need to be collecting data that goes beyond the usual statistics such as attendance, sickness or other surveys that we conduct here

---

in the NHS. So, for example we try to capture how happy people feel at work in the way that you might have observed in the airports today with different sorts of checkpoints that collect data from visitors such as a frowny face to a smiley face.

This all may sound simplistic, but in the overall picture it's important for us to know how our people feel. These indictors are important to us and are collected at much more frequent intervals. It is also about encouraging the collection and use of data on the diversity of the workforce. In healthcare, this is not routinely collected. Although we collect data on disability, we don't routinely collect information around our LGBT (lesbian, gay, bisexual, and transgender) demographics or how staff want to be identified.

Even the BME (black and minority ethnicity) data is patchy and is not as robust as it should be. We have some blank spaces around our understanding of the kind of things that are important to our workforce.

People are living longer

We are living in an economy where people are aging, hopefully living well and living longer. So, we are being challenged to collect all sorts of data. For example, what the older employee is looking for in terms of employment, what works for them; not in terms of hours, but conditions as well. In the NHS, we have consultant medics who are looking for a new career when they reach sixty years old, they are not thinking about retiring. So we need to be collecting much intelligent data regarding such issues, and using this to discuss the options available to the older people in our workforce.

Our employees are part of the population of patients that we are treating. So, we are getting to a point where we would be collecting all sorts of data about their health. Some of the technology wearables now can constantly monitor our heart rhythm and being in healthcare, we have a responsibility to be able to use some of this data to predict the health of our citizens by trying to do a lot of predictive analytics with the data that we have.

Although we have the biggest data warehouse, there is a global discussion of who owns that data and clearly (in my view) – it is the patient. But the key question to ask is how it could be used to predict and plan for the right kind of interventions and healthcare support.

Role of the healthcare CEO

Although some might think the role of a CEO is simply to run the organization effectively, it's now quite clear that we have a bigger responsibility to work with the system around the organization, particularly local government, private sector providers and voluntary sector providers, to think about how we are balancing this equation between health, wealth and wellbeing. So, as a healthcare provider, we are playing our part to do a whole range of things to provide the right interventions and the right care when it is needed.

But really, we would also like to be thinking about predictive health and trying to get ahead of the curve, doing far more prevention and health management. An important part is also driving up the local economy and helping to create jobs by making sure people can have the opportunity to get into properly-paid employment. All of this leads to the inexplicable link between health, wealth and wellbeing that has now become very much part of the role of a healthcare CEO.

Creating the environment for people to flourish

It is becoming increasingly important for us to look at the bigger picture of measurements. General practitioners (GPs) today are giving out tracking devices that can monitor heart rates and rhythm. The key here is to have well connected systems that talk to one another because the only way we are going to be able to track the health of the population is by having digitally compatible platforms. So, another important responsibility of the people function at hospitals is to play the role of integrator.

Hospitals work at scale, we treat millions of patients every year, but those patients also interface with their GPs, with other providers. They might go to the gym, but they obviously do their own retail shopping, and it's therefore about us joining up this intelligence to enable us to see what patterns are emerging, not just of the diseases, or chronic illness, but in terms of people's lifestyles. We can now find out what is happening in people's lives to either contribute, improve or worsen their health conditions. Hence, the performance dials are broadening out.

We are now looking at health trends, societal trends, about income, jobs, about social trends and activity trying to look at a much bigger picture. One of the ways we do that in the NHS is by using a framework that creates an environment and climate that enables people to flourish. Essentially there are three domains to consider:

1 **Leadership: developing the "best you"**: The first domain is focused around leadership behaviour, being able to bring the "best you" to work. Our team does a lot of work to ensure we create the right climate so that people can feel they are in "discovery mode", rather than being defensive because in the world of health it is dangerous if people start to feel defensive. If people hide things and do not report incidents when they

happen, it can become a hazard. Therefore, we spend a lot of time on the development of these sorts of behaviours and we champion the concept of compassionate leadership. Encouraging behaviours that create respect for one another, thinking about the values that drive us, reassuring the ability to speak out when things are not right and all sorts of inclusive behaviours. It's all about communicating these values very widely and providing people with the tools on social media to be visible and to talk about what they are doing and what's important.

2 **Operating framework: aligning the priorities**: Most CEOs usually spend time in this domain, making sure there is a compelling strategy. Organizational values are co-created and should be well understood across the board. Here we look at the robustness of the organizational structure, the performance management system, the communication framework. In health terms, there needs to be a clear line of sight between the board of directors and the ward, or the theatre, or the outpatient department and how all the hospital is functioning together. This may sound very easy to do, but we spend quite a lot of time reviewing governance structure in organizations and that pays real dividends.

3 **Network of activities: developing the conditions to flourish**: The third domain is where we can accelerate pace. This is how you encourage leaders who you probably wouldn't observe in that middle structure. You might not identify them as leaders in a formal structure, but they will come together in communities of interest. As these individuals are passionate about an issue, they will do a piece of work and it might be sort of short-lived like a small project; however, it becomes a piece of work that they complete. Often their work does become part of the formal operating framework, but it's co-created in networks of activities which are much more agile, much faster and not bogged down with bureaucratic procedures and process. A lot of senior leadership teams underplay the value of these networks as they are not part of the formal structure. Many people don't consider these networks as legitimate and that is a big mistake. Today there are more and more organizations in healthcare that are using this and it's certainly catching up.

The reality is that this is a combined effort. As the CEO, I brought this framework through several jobs now, and the first thing that I did when I came to Newcastle is advocate it. Using infographics, I put it up on the walls. I talked to different groups of staff and asked whether they feel this will be a good operating model, whether they felt like the framework will be helpful, whether it belongs here and how would we make it work around here? How could we tailor it to our requirements? And now it's owned by everyone from the top leadership to the bottom.

The CPO needs to not only understand this framework but truly believe in it, and that this is the right way to operate. We must work together to flourish all the three domains that are complementary to one another. The CPO should look at each of these domains, and they must be working effectively, to provide the best environment to operate within. What I think this model does is liberate people's potential and ensure that the CPO has a framework to operate by in the rapidly changing world of work that we now find ourselves in.

www.newcastle-hospitals.org.uk (archived at https://perma.cc/EZ7E-X9BR)

The desire for more flexible and agile ways of operating in organizations based on both the business needs and individuals' interests and experiences at work will be a key feature of future workplaces. The role of people analytics, similar to the evolution of ONA, will make this an area where data and insights can not only prove the concept, but provide the evidence to support it from a knowledge-sharing and employee engagement perspective.

Organizational development and change

Organizational development and change (OD) is a business-critical activity that focuses on successful organizational change and performance-based challenges and issues and tends to revolve around:

- maximizing value from the organization's resources;
- the strategy, values and core purpose of what the organization wants to achieve;
- maximizing the competitive advantage of an organization's people through behavioural science, knowledge, and practices;
- institutionalizing systemic change and improvement across the organization.

A lot of this activity revolves around research, diagnosis/analysis and formulation of solutions for implementation across the organization or parts of it, all of it at a scale and speed never encountered before.[21] This replicates the core principles and frameworks behind people analytics (see Chapter 8).

It's no surprise, therefore, that the positioning of people analytics teams seems to be evolving into the OD function for those organizations with a mature analytics practice.[22]

Merck KGaA are on that journey, and their story is outlined below.

CASE STUDY
Merck KGaA: Organizational development leads the charge to achieve value through analytics

Background

Merck KGaA, Darmstadt, Germany is a leading science and technology company in healthcare, life science, and performance materials. More than 50,000 employees work to further develop technologies that improve and enhance life, from biopharmaceutical therapies to treat cancer or multiple sclerosis, cutting edge systems for scientific research and production, to liquid crystals for smartphones and LCD televisions.

Digitalization helps drive the transformation of the world of work outside laboratories and factory floors. Digital HR and people analytics are key terms in this transition where data is used to glean insights into all aspects of HR work, which can then be applied to tasks such as SWP, talent management and even the gradual optimization of day-to-day operations.

Business challenges

DIGITAL HR TRANSFORMATION STARTED WITH GLOBAL STANDARDIZATION
Until 2011, all talent processes, including recruiting, performance management, compensation, and succession planning were designed and driven by local countries or divisions. The lack of global processes meant that data and associated analytics often varied based on the region from which they were drawn, providing no linkages across processes and regions.

Work began to standardize and integrate its processes and related data to enable a global data view. All the talent processes were moved to a standardized global approach with the aim to have integrated processes. This standardization and process integration set up Merck KGaA for subsequent people analytics, allowing them to see correlations across processes. This aspect of the HR transformation redesign involved parties also reviewing technology they could use to support analysis across the talent processes.

DATA UNIFICATION

The standardization initiative uncovered data from various processes – but what should be done with it? Merck KGaA looked to people analytics technology for three driving reasons:

1 The team was struck by how many people were building reports from process data. Rather than counting heads to monitor reduction in headcount, they wanted to see an increase in the number of employees working on reporting and analytics, with an improvement in the overall quality of the data. Instead of less reporting, they wanted increased use of data and analytics to drive workforce decisions.

2 The team wanted a single source of truth. They had myriad regional systems and managers who were picking and choosing the data they wanted. By moving to global processes, everyone could leverage the same data and definitions. For example, the definition of talent should not vary between China and Germany.

3 The team recognized that certain assumptions about talent trends were not based on data but rather on "gut feelings". For example, many managers believed that talent was not being rewarded, performance was not impacting turnover, and that the wrong people were leaving. The team used analytics as a driver to change mindsets and to encourage leaders to make data-based decisions.

Approach

Using Visier's system, more than 45 million single data points were consolidated. The sources and data included SAP, SuccessFactors HRSuite and employee engagement survey results from an external vendor. Managers and HR colleagues can access information based on user-friendly and non-technical questions that focus on organization and people management: for example: "How are demographic developments impacting our organization?" Then they can slice, dice, and compare the data based upon the results of the entire company, yielding a new standard of transparency.

Coupled with the experience and knowledge of management, the results provide firm footing for making decisions on a wide variety of issues. For example, managers can track how staff turnover is impacted by targeted feedback from the performance assessment process.

Implementation approach

USING ANALYTICS TO CAPITALIZE ON ORGANIZATIONAL DEVELOPMENT

The approach is unusual in that it combines OD and people analytics to deliver practical and differentiated support to the business. As a result, a fundamental shift has occurred. Today the team is no longer asked to provide data, but is asked to provide input on what the data means as well as recommendations for interventions.

The global team is small, operating from within Europe, the US, and Asia Pacific. They combine different expertise from typical implementation teams (OD, mergers and acquisitions, change management and so on) and work closely with HR and business leaders to deliver business-specific insights and consulting that leverage analytics insights. They focus on partnering with internal teams as well as external partners such as universities and research firms. This allows them to constantly combine internal and external trends so they can deliver additional value. The team focuses on telling stories using data, and being close to the business supported by their common knowledge of OD.

ENABLING THE BUSINESS

Leaders attend OD and people analytics enablement sessions to practise how analytics can support organizational and people decisions. The context involves "unleashing the power of we", and delivers on goals by focusing on performance, collaboration, and seizing opportunities through technology. They enable leaders to learn through case study work. Teams are encouraged to start with a business topic or question and not the data. They are asked to break down their topic or question into subquestions, then use analytics to provide insights for discussion, and finally to prioritize findings and actions.

For example, the team wanted to determine whether Merck KGaA was an agile organization. They began by discussing the components that define an agile organization, such as:

- What is our ability to renew/adapt based on internal and external trends? Do we have a healthy employee renewal balance? Is our turnover aligned with our changing needs?
- Are we quick to decide and to mobilize? Are we set up for efficient decision-making?
- Are we encouraging enough movements?

At the end of the enablement sessions, attendees are encouraged to continue working with Visier and participate in ongoing e-learnings.

Interaction via social media and digital collaboration is promoted, and, as a result, attendees can follow OD and people analytics on the internal community platform so they can stay connected and share their experiences in support of organizational learning. Beyond the enablement sessions, the team created a specific HR Analytics Navigator, which serves as a source for internal assets, best practices, tips, and research about people analytics.

Work council collaboration

Many European organizations, especially in Germany, must work closely with their work council to ensure compliance with data privacy and other regulatory requirements.

Kai Beckman of the executive board at Merck KGaA reports: "Introducing and applying HR analytics systems like these obviously has to comply with all data privacy requirements and the appropriate bodies and committees need to be involved in advance. Close collaboration with our works council, for instance, has been crucial."

They took a proactive approach, reaching out to the appropriate bodies and committees in advance and taking appropriate measures to secure the data and the processes. For example, managers cannot drill down into an organization with less than three people, and diversity (age, nationality, and so on) is only shown at the aggregate level.

The issue of data privacy is also addressed within the enablement sessions. Legal pitfalls, especially in the United States, are discussed. Attendees are taught about the sensitivity of the employee information on the system, and are provided with the following guidance to ensure the company can avoid claims and successfully defend against them:

1   Do not share data, analyses or reports internally unless the recipient has Visier privileges and a legitimate business need to know the information.

2   When sharing data, analyses or reports internally, always share it within the system. Do not download, save or print the information.

3   Never disclose data, analyses or reports externally, unless pre-approved by Legal.

4   Never consider or make decisions based on the age, sex or national origin/ citizenship (or any other protected class status) of the applicant or employee in the hiring, promotion, discipline or termination context.

5   Understand how to lawfully execute diversity initiatives before addressing diversity concerns within your group. In the US, targets and quotas are not permitted.

6   Document your reasons for taking any adverse employment action (eg discipline, termination, etc) to demonstrate it wasn't taken on the basis of or in consideration of any protected class status.

Results

Today almost 3,000 managers and hundreds of HR employees can access and use real-time data for decision-making using Visier. They can access robust data on headcount, diversity, turnover, performance results, and compensation, so they can make decisions on a wide variety of issues to improve performance and optimize organizational structure.

HRBPs are transforming from information providers and report generators into data-supported consultants who are now strategic advisers to business managers. With this shift from administration to strategy, Merck KGaA received the 2016 HR Excellence Award from *Human Resources Manager*.

Merck KGaA emphasizes that the value of investment is not monetary, but strategic; people analytics is not for HR, it's a tool for line managers. As a result, HR has become a strategic consultant to line managers. People no longer have to go with a gut feeling on decisions, but instead can rely on data. They believe it has increased the quality of decisions with human capital, while professionalizing HR as a function.

Courtesy of Visier: www.visier.com (archived at https://perma.cc/K93D-YKXU)

Additionally, issues such as privacy and trust relating to data will fall into this practice. Paul Sparrow of Lancaster University believes that: "Analytics will move into an area where it will have even better predictive power, because we will be able to cut through a lot of the background noise in the data and get to important relationships. But it will also encroach on areas around regulations, privacy, ethicality, and so the future is going to become more regulated because there has been a bit of a free-for-all. We need to be clearer about protocols for how people use that data."

As technology enables the tracking of employees at work, it will mean that personal data will become even more accessible, and that in turn will mean that the trust relationship between an organization and its workforce will become increasingly challenging.

The future of people analytics is in the hands of you, the practitioners who control it, use it and apply it to your everyday activities. Its applications are endless and can truly bring value to all organizations, large and small, and build the credibility of the people function that we have been striving for over many years. Remember, if analytics is just a report full of numbers, no one will care; it has to answer real business problems.[23]

It's over to you now to make it part of the way you operate!

The future people function

Businesses are facing an acceleration in ubiquitous technologies and automation, leading to a host of economic, social and political issues that are challenging business strategies. Deloitte's 2019 *Global Human Capital Trends* survey highlighted that 84 per cent of respondents felt the need to rethink their workforce experience to improve productivity, and that to become more agile, 80 per cent believe they need to develop their leaders differently. Although these issues might seem timeless, today they are emerging against a whole new workplace context: focusing organizations to move beyond mission statements and reinventing themselves around a human focus.

Global research on leadership in the Fourth Industrial Revolution informs us of the importance of the connectedness of our people (ie employee and customer satisfaction), profit (ie revenue, profit) and planet (ie diversity, inequality, environment) on measuring success when evaluating annual business performance.[24, 25] See Figure 10.7.

FIGURE 10.7   The Three Ps of the people function

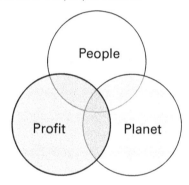

Adapted from Elkington, 1998

We envision the people function acting as a Power Station in the future to not only comprehend the business strategy, but also align and enable the people aspect of the business by calibrating the ethos and culture towards the long-term profitability and sustainability.

Organizations such as FIS, are already on that journey. FIS, with its large global workforce, set out to transform its HR function, instilling elements of self-service, engagement and analytics. Their people function is now undergoing transformation that includes the introduction of agile scrum teams focused on strategic priorities and key business unit initiates. Their case study is below.

CASE STUDY
The people transformation journey

FIS™ is the world's largest global provider dedicated to financial technology solutions. FIS empowers the financial world with software, services, consulting and outsourcing solutions focused on retail and institutional banking, payments, asset and wealth management, risk and compliance, trade enablement, transaction processing and record-keeping. FIS has more than 47,000 employees worldwide who are passionate about moving our clients' business forward.

Starting the transition

FIS embarked on an overall people transformation journey starting in 2016 when it hired its new Chief People Officer, Denise Williams. For FIS, the case for a robust people strategy is critical:

- Talent is the single biggest differentiator for FIS as a company: the organization is only successful if there is strong leadership and committed employees.

- Effective people management can impact the bottom line, not just through the management of its own budgets, but through retention and engagement, as well as supporting FIS's growth agenda with the right people in the right roles with the right skills at the right time.

- The regulatory and geo-political environment is becoming increasingly more complex and requires a robust approach to ensure companies are capitalizing on change and preparing FIS to mitigate any risk.

- Having a robust people strategy ensures that there is alignment around the direction taken with people leadership, and provides a framework to focus efforts consistently across the organization to drive change.

The FIS people office used three key areas to develop its strategy:

1 market trends (what is the future of work) and market data around best practice at top organizations;

2 business strategy;

3 employee voice: leadership interviews as well as employee feedback from focus groups and surveying.

To build out the strategy and embed digital as a core component, the team were focused on replicating the ease with which people interact with technology in the real world. They did this in three ways.

SELF-SERVICE

As part of laying the foundations and driving self-service, FIS implemented one global HRIS system, Workday. It was the starting point to driving self-service. They are also rolling out a chatbot so employees can ask anything. When the team went out to the HR function and asked them what requests they heard most they collected about seven hundred Frequently Asked Questions (FAQs) in the first couple of weeks alone.

Isabel Naidoo, global head of people strategy and analytics, states: "There is a serious gap when it comes to engaging our workforce. When I think about the way that people engage online or in the real world, they are doing it themselves. But when it comes to HR, my experience has been that people are asking us to do their work for them."

DIALOGUE

The move towards digitization was around mimicking the real-time dialogue and action that happens outside the workplace.

Two years ago, FIS partnered with Glint, a survey vendor, to launch a real-time engagement approach at scale across the organization. Glint gives feedback instantly so that there is no time lag in accessing results. This means that managers can now instantly take action and engage in dialogue with their teams, with suggested actions for managers and their teams to implement being made based on their results. This is where FIS want the dialogue to happen, and this has enabled FIS not only to be able to measure and track engagement results, which have shown an increase year on year, but also pinpoint the drivers of engagement that will enhance the employee experience.

The other lever for dialogue was performance management. FIS recently launched a revamped approach with an emphasis on dialogue and frequent connections. They had 250 champions across the company to help drive the initiative, and used creative ideas to launch the change in ways that resonated with the local culture. That's how FIS ended up with a radio show in Milwaukee, donuts in Minnesota, bingo in Sydney and feedback stickers in India!

It's quick and easy from a technology point of view with no long form filling, and the focus is on the quality of dialogue and frequency of feedback. The team knew from their data analysis that employees who receive regular feedback are 35 per cent more likely to stay with the organization.

DATA AND ANALYTICS

The third step in FIS's digitization was looking at how data and analytics are used to inform decisions and pre-empt what's going to happen.

FIS partnered with Visier, a people analytics vendor, to build a cloud-based analytics capability. It brought together data from a whole range of systems that enables FIS to take a close look at where it is making progress against its strategy. They track and measure metrics like headcount and attrition, and can also make correlations between different data sets. Visier is a self-service driven system and is therefore scalable.

New HR core capabilities

To transform the HR function to the people office, FIS focused on developing three core skills.

1 **Coaching**: FIS launched a coaching course for HR practitioners, as well as making it part of their core curriculum for all managers. This isn't just career coaching, but is about advising the business on challenges they are facing, such as how to plan for skills and to think ahead.

2 **Change**: FIS understood the challenge of navigating the VUCA world and the fact that everyone reacts to change in a different way. Since there are so many changes happening in the industry and across the workplace, the people office embedded change management as a core competency across the organization.

3 **Data and analytics**: The third skill was that of a data analyst. The challenge was to understand and use data appropriately. FIS is not just championing data, but also encouraging managers to first identify the business challenge and then think how the available data can help them resolve it.

These three capabilities have become a building block for the wider HR transformation agenda.

The people office

The HR team at FIS, after crowdsourcing across their employees, decided to call themselves the "people office" because, simply stated, they look after their people. One of the principles of the function is co-creation, which encompasses using business data and engaging business leaders on specific challenges that FIS is trying to solve which impact the bottom line.

The mission of the people strategy and analytics team at FIS is to inform decision-making through data. Everything that they do is driven by data. Isabel Naidoo tells us: "It's not enough to put data analytics in the hands of HR, you also need to put data analytics in the hands of the business."

FIS is now planning to launch leadership effectiveness dashboards with clear and transparent data in the hands of all their managers making people data accessible in a way that is truly differentiated.

Throughout the change, the people office learned five key lessons:

1   Not all data is created equal when starting out; you need to make sure that data integrity is a key focus.

2   Executive support can make or break your data efforts. Identify meaningful insights to them and they will want more of it; the challenge is now our capacity to manage the level of interest. You know that when Finance are asking you for data that you have a successful model in place.

3   Make Finance your new "best friend", as you don't want to be presenting numbers that your CFO doesn't think is accurate.

4   Upskill your own HR organization so that they can have the conversations they need to with Finance and the rest of the business around data.

5   Lots of choice exists, so choose wisely. Find a business challenge to solve and go after it or you will be in danger of paralysis by analysis. Platforms like Glint are amazing, but they can also bring with them a risk of data overload, so think business challenge first and that will help you hone your efforts.

The people office structure

The people office at FIS is structured around an Ulrich model with business partners, centres of excellence and people services. The team is focused on continuous improvement and are currently evolving their model to include agile project teams. These teams will be made up of specialists who work in a variety of agile scrum teams, self-organizing, cross functional teams, that are focused on FIS strategic priorities and key business unit initiatives. Running like a quasi-internal consulting function, these teams within the people office will be able to respond in a timely way to the ever-changing needs of the business, with the right capacity to meet demand, as well as grow their own capabilities and specialisms.

The journey has only just begun, but they are making significant changes that are significantly impacting the perception and focus of the people function.

www.fisglobal.com (archived at https://perma.cc/D8GE-EUTT)

The learnings from FIS revolve around the multiple-faceted approach that they have adopted focusing on data, HR capability and collaborative relationships. The change is not an easy one, but the focus on the employee and their experience is clearly there for all to see.

Human-centred organizations will create value through their intangible resources, the main one being their people, but to do that they need to be able to measure value generated through their people, profits and planet (the three Ps) to create long-term sustainability and profitability. As most organizations struggle to quantify this value, they are currently left in a state of perplexity.[26] We see this as a future trend and ongoing research will be needed to quantify this holistic value and trust that the people function will be at the epicentre of this agenda.

Research from leading experts reveals nine key characteristics of people-centric companies that enable them to unleash their people potential:[27]

1 **Putting value and culture first**: Believing in what is important for the organization.

2 **Making the values real**: alignment and consistency: There must be alignment between the organizational values and the practices that express those values. Leadership must believe in them and role-model them consistently.

3 **Strong culture**: There needs to be a clear and consistent alignment between the values and the norms that express these values (the culture).

4 **Hiring for fit**: Screening processes that help organizations to identify people who fit in and possess the abilities that the organization requires.

5 **Investing in people**: Signalling clearly to your workforce how important they are by continued investment in them, providing opportunities for development and career growth.

6 **Widespread information sharing**: Extensive sharing of information throughout the organization for the workforce to be able to understand in detail how the organization is performing and what it is trying to do strategically.

7 **Team-based systems**: Instead of relying on formal control systems, teams rely on the social control of others to ensure that people get the work done. Supervisors aren't in control, teams are.

8 **Rewards and recognition**: The careful alignment of the total rewards systems with values is a crucial lever. Instead of emphasizing money as a primary motivator, they provide intrinsic rewards of fun, growth, teamwork, challenge and accomplishment.

9 **Leading, not managing**: Senior managers view their roles not as managing daily operations or even developing strategy, but as setting and reinforcing the vision, values, and culture of the organization.

Using these insights, the people function can create a culture for the workforce to actively participate in an invaluable learning process, building high performance, agile and people centred organizations.

As always, the focus on the people function will be immense, with significant expectations emerging as digital shifts, automation, skill gaps and so on become business-critical, and the need to act with authenticity becomes greater. The role of data and analytics allied to a change in emphasis is the way for the HR function of old to evolve into the people function of the future. We cannot fail to make that shift this time!

KEY TAKEAWAYS FROM THIS CHAPTER

1   Alignment between the business strategy and the people strategy is vital to ensure that the people function is prioritizing its activities to create the greatest impact. That in turn means that the people analytics strategic approach needs to embrace an impact-based approach, with a clearly defined focus on data, techniques and methodologies that drive improved business outcomes.

2   The future of people analytics has a number of critical elements that focus on the development of organizations, the adoption of increasingly complex systems-level disruption, embracing agility and improving organizational practices that will enable the business to be certain about and be ready for the future of work.

3   The people function is emerging across a number of organizations as they seek to become both more strategic and impactful when addressing the challenges of today and tomorrow. That is underpinned by the application of data and people analytics in terms of demonstrating business value.

4   The future is everything that hasn't happened yet, and the future of the people function is in the hands of its practitioners and their ability to develop and improve their capability.

References

1   (2009) Enduring Ideas: The three horizons of growth, *McKinsey Quarterly* [Online] www.mckinsey.com/business-functions/strategy-and-corporate-finance/our-insights/enduring-ideas-the-three-horizons-of-growth (archived at https://perma.cc/9K7J-NUBK)

2   Blank, S (2019) McKinsey's Three Horizons Model Defined Innovation for Years: Here's Why It No Longer Applies Here, *Harvard Business Review*

[Online] https://hbr.org/2019/02/mckinseys-three-horizons-model-defined-innovation-for-years-heres-why-it-no-longer-applies (archived at https://perma.cc/E6XZ-8CRZ)

3 Ferrar, J (2019) What are the HR Skills of the Future? *myHRfuture* [Online] www.myhrfuture.com/blog/2019/3/14/what-are-the-hr-skills-of-the-future (archived at https://perma.cc/NY43-PUN8)

4 Hancock, C (2018) The Case for Linking Employee Wellbeing and Productivity, *Personnel Today* [Online] www.personneltoday.com/hr/case-linking-employee-wellbeing-productivity/ (archived at https://perma.cc/B297-9RGK)

5 Sparkman, R (2018) *Strategic Workforce Planning: Developing optimized talent strategies for future growth*, Kogan Page, London

6 Dearborn, J and Swanson, D (2017) *The Data-Driven Leader: A powerful approach to delivering measurable business impact through people analytics*, John Wiley & Sons

7 Senge, P M (2006) *The Fifth Discipline: The art and practice of the learning organization*, Broadway Business, New York

8 Michie, J et al (2016) *Do we need HR?: Repositioning people management for success*, Springer, New York

9 Webb, A (2019) How to Do Strategic Planning Like a Futurist, *Harvard Business Review* [Online] https://hbr.org/2019/07/how-to-do-strategic-planning-like-a-futurist (archived at https://perma.cc/T4SM-S868)

10 Cappelli, P and Tavis, A (2018) HR Goes Agile, *Harvard Business Review* [Online] https://hbr.org/2018/03/the-new-rules-of-talent-management#hr-goes-agile (archived at https://perma.cc/RDH3-8K66)

11 Rigby, D, Sutherland, J and Takeuchi, H (2016) Embracing Agile, *Harvard Business Review* [Online] https://hbr.org/2016/05/embracing-agile (archived at https://perma.cc/898N-NHZ2)

12 Veldsman, T H (2019) *Designing Fit for Purpose Organizations: A comprehensive, integrated route map*, KR Publishing, RSA

13 Slinger, G (2018) Advanced Analytics for Agile Organization Design: 5 Principles, *Analytics in HR* [Online] www.analyticsinhr.com/blog/advanced-analytics-for-agile-organization-design-5-principles (archived at https://perma.cc/Z7WJ-S9CX)

14 Cross, R, Rebele, R and Grant, A (2016) Collaborative Overload, *Harvard Business Review* [Online] https://hbr.org/2016/01/collaborative-overload (archived at https://perma.cc/LKR6-BLH8)

15 Deloitte (2019) Leading the social enterprise: Reinvent with a human focus, *Deloitte Global Human Capital Trends* [Online] www2.deloitte.com/content/dam/insights/us/articles/5136_HC-Trends-2019/DI_HC-Trends-2019.pdf (archived at https://perma.cc/H3DV-R6P3)

16 Cross, R, Ernst, C and Pasmore, B (2013) A Bridge Too Far? How Boundary Spanning Networks Drive Organizational Change and Effectiveness, *Organizational Dynamics* [Online] www.robcross.org/wp-content/uploads/2017/02/org_dynamics_boundary_spanning_networks_and_change.pdf (archived at https://perma.cc/626A-YB5D)

17 Cross, R and Thomas, R (2011) Managing Yourself: A Smarter Way to Network, *Harvard Business Review* [Online] https://hbr.org/2011/07/managing-yourself-a-smarter-way-to-network (archived at https://perma.cc/UA68-4NFN)

18 Bulat, H (2018) Organizational Network Analysis: The Missing Piece of Digital Transformation, *Digital HR Tech* [Online] www.digitalhrtech.com/organizational-network-analysis-the-missing-piece-of-digital-transformation/ (archived at https://perma.cc/2ZEZ-P857)

19 Arena, M *et al* (2017) How to Catalyze Innovation in Your Organization, *MIT Sloan Management Review* [Online] https://sloanreview.mit.edu/article/how-to-catalyze-innovation-in-your-organization/ (archived at https://perma.cc/W6N8-M75H)

20 Wenger, E C and Snyder, W M (2000) Communities of practice: the organizational frontier, *Harvard Business Review*, 78 (1), pp 139–46

21 Parry, W (2015) *Big Change, Best Path: Successfully managing organizational change with wisdom, analytics and insight*, Kogan Page, London

22 Morrison, R (2016) Human Resources Analytics: How to Turn Organizational Data into Corporate Strength and Success, *Analytics Magazine* [Online] http://analytics-magazine.org/human-resources-analytics-how-to-turn-organizational-data-into-corporate-strength-and-success/ (archived at https://perma.cc/NP6Z-KDFY)

23 Navin, P and Creelman, D (2018) *The CMO of People: Manage employees like customers with an immersive predictable experience that drives productivity and performance*, Walter de Gruyter Inc, New York

24 Deloitte and Forbes Insights (2019) *Success personified in the Fourth Industrial Revolution: Four leadership personas for an era of change and uncertainty*, Deloitte Insights, New York

25 Elkington, J (1998) Partnerships from cannibals with forks: The triple bottom line of 21st-century business, *Environmental Quality Management*, 8 (1), pp 37–51

26 Slaper, T F and Hall, T J (2011) The triple bottom line: what is it and how does it work? *Indiana Business Review*, **86** (1), pp 4–8

27 O'Reilly, C A and Pfeffer, J (2000) *Hidden Value: How great companies achieve extraordinary results with ordinary people*, Harvard Business Press, Brighton, MA

INDEX

Note: Numbers in headings are filed as spelt out, with the exception of entries for Industry 1.0 etc, which are filed in numerical order. Acronyms are filed as presented. Numbers in *italics* denote Figures/Tables.

Lightning Source UK Ltd.
Milton Keynes UK
UKHW020209151120
373351UK00002B/26